NEW YORK DAYS, NEW YORK NIGHTS

By the same Author

THE OXFORD BOOK OF DREAMS (Editor)

NEW YORK DAYS,
NEW YORK NIGHTS

STEPHEN BROOK

HAMISH HAMILTON
LONDON

First published in Great Britain 1984
by Hamish Hamilton Ltd
Garden House 57-59 Long Acre London WC2E 9JZ

The author and publishers are grateful
to quote: 'Too Much of Nothing', Bob Dylan,
'Rednecks', Randy Newman, both by kind
permission of Warner Bros Music Limited;
'I've Got To Get A Message To You' written
and composed by Robin, Barry and Maurice Gibb,
copyright 1968 Abigail Music

British Library Cataloguing in Publication Data

Brook, Stephen
    New York days, New York nights.
    1. New York (N.Y.)—Description—1951-
    I. Title
    917.47'10443   F128.52
    ISBN 0-241-11114-5

Filmset by Pioneer
Printed and bound in Great Britain
by Billing & Sons Ltd, Worcester

To Elizabeth Neustadt Rosenthal

CONTENTS

ACKNOWLEDGMENTS

Some of those who opened up New York City to me are named in the book that follows, while others must sadly remain anonymous for reasons of confidentiality. I greatly appreciate their help and generosity, whether they are named or unnamed, and also wish to thank Albert Ackel; James and Anna Atlas; Carol Bellamy; Nana Bennett; Peter Conrad; Howard David Deutsch; Tess Donohue; David Z. Plavin and Hugh A. Dunne of the MTA; Lisa Feder and Joe Spitzer; Mark Fleischer; Jonathan Galassi; Peter Goldmark; William Goodman; Victor Gotbaum; Gail Heimann; Bob Henn; Edward Hershey; Jonathan and Sarah Hill; Katy Homans; Nelida Hughes; Timothy Husband; Sachiyo Ito; Juris Jurjevics; Joe Kanon; Donald Katz; Dana Kelly; Jill Kerr; Mayor Edward I. Koch; Elene Margot Kolb; Irving Kristol; Carol Lazare; Robert Lekachman; Samuel Lipman; John D. Mitchell; Ann Morfolgen, Howard Stringer, and Bob Lawlor, all of CBS; Charles Morris; Horace Morris; Louise Nicholson; Doris and Alfred Palca; Lansing and Jane Palmer; Frederic Papert; Rina Pianko; Alice Quinn; A. H. Raskin; Richard Rosan; Phyllis Rose; Lewis Rudin and ABNY; Michelle Shenfeld; Harvey Simmons; Neil Smith; Fred Smoler; Ben Sonnenberg; Anthony R. Smith; Roger Starr; Roger W. Straus; Diana Trilling; Kenneth Waissman; and Margot Wellington. And especially warm thanks to Maria Poythress Epes, artist, space freak, animal trainer, and friend; to Steven and Barbara Isenberg, for their hospitality and invaluable help; to Julie Lewit, indefatigable guide and true friend; to Stephen Silverman; and to LuAnn Walther. Finally, I must thank the staff of Hamish Hamilton for their thoughtfulness and professionalism, especially Clare Alexander and Penelope Hoare, who helped to truss, season, and baste this book until it was finally done.

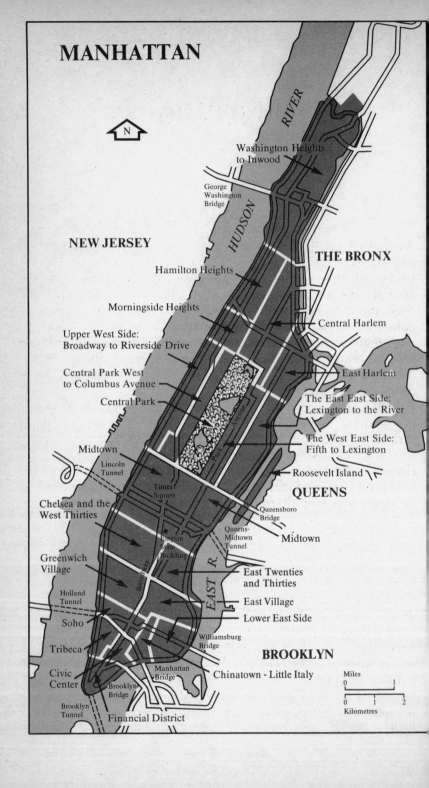

LANDING

As tons of tubular metal drop noisily through cloudbanks any traveller's expectations will be heightened — if only because death momentarily perches on your shoulder — but after a safe landing the airport, any airport, deadens that excitement as, laden with coats, bulging hand luggage, and compulsory duty-free, you run the gauntlet of immigration, customs, baggage handlers and limo touts, while all around you messages are electronically amplified into garblings of distorted sound. Airports everywhere punch holes in the pleasures of travel.

New York, exceptional in so many ways, is no different in this respect. Sailing into New York harbour is the only serious way to arrive, but that great romance is now reserved exclusively for QE2 passengers, who are either very rich or very nervous.

Out on the pavement in the 'fresh' air, the temperature is 30 degrees higher than in the air-conditioned chill of the airport, and sweat burst from all pores as, now additionally leadened with a pair of marmorean suitcases, I lugged these necessaries through the automatic doors. There's a subway that whisks the jet-lagged from Kennedy Airport into the heart of Manhattan — only first you have to take a bus to the subway station. Or there's the bus, if you can find it, that drops you off at the East Side Terminal near the river, far from any likely destination. To hell with them both. These nerve-fraying excuses for public transportation are doubtless sponsored by the city's cab drivers.

I teamed up with an equally weary man who'd sat near me on the plane. We threw our luggage into the yellow maw of the nearest cab and sprawled inelegantly over the ill-sprung back seat.

1

Our driver turned out to be a classic specimen. Central Casting couldn't have done better. He was an Armenian, a fairly recent immigrant, a man in his mid-30s, energetic, opinionated. We spent a considerable part of the journey sitting in a traffic jam waiting to cross the Triboro Bridge. The windows were rolled down to air out the sweltering cab. It was 80 degrees, the city's joke on November, and the heat bounced off the concrete and mingled lushly with the exhaust fumes.

My companion opened the conversation skilfully. 'Have they settled the football strike yet?'

'Maybe today. There's been a meeting. We don't know yet. Guess it'll be on the news tonight. You two from England? So how are things in England? You got lots of strikes there too?'

'Not too bad this year.'

'Here everybody strikes. Strike strike strike all the time.' Oh perfect cabbie, model of your kind! Megaphone for every mean-spirited cliché in the book! 'That's all they do. Strike strike strike. These football players, they make a lotta money.'

He had a point. 'Indeed they do.'

'Yeh, a lotta money. But still they strike. More money, more money. You know something?' Classic cabspeak — opinion disguised as question. 'We just hadda strike of the funeral directors. That's right. Three, four days they been on strike. Nurses doctors football players everybody. I don't go along with it. No strikes in Russia, let me tell you. Open the door 24 hours and there wouldn't be any people left in Russia. Here you can say what you like, even about the President, and nobody does a thing. In Russia they shoot you.'

Curious how a deeply felt appreciation of the genuine liberties that America offers, and of the receptivity of New York in particular to new faces, new groups, curious how that just valuation turns into a belligerence that draws breath from the very oppression it so fiercely resists. As he rabbited on, I gazed out of the window, past the crawling traffic, those battered ungainly cars, past the cemeteries that cover hillside after hillside of suburban Queens, and looked idly at the Manhattan skyline just becoming visible through the late afternoon haze. After a while I tuned back in.

'. . . That's one good thing you gotta say for Reagan. He's tryin' to stop all these people collectin' welfare. Look at me.'

I did. He was unshaven, as raw in appearance as in speech, lightly built, good-looking.

'I been in this country six years, and never had a day without work. I don't drive a taxi usually. I'm an electrician. Not much work around for electricians, so I'm drivin' a taxi.'

There was a germ of truth in what he was saying. In New York, if you're young, able, adaptable, don't have small children to look after, and are possessed of some skills, you can probably find work of some kind for some time. But the city's economic base is changing, and whether he likes it or not, or believes it or not, those changes will not work to the advantage of those already unemployed. As if in confirmation, we drove past large factories that were empty and likely to stay that way.

New York is not the same as Manhattan, which is simply one of the city's five boroughs. The boroughs occupy 319 square miles, while the island of Manhattan alone is a mere 22. Queens is by far the largest borough, with an area of 114 square miles, but adjoining Brooklyn is the most populous, with over two million inhabitants. Brooklyn and Queens fill the western tip of Long Island, and only the Bronx is on the mainland. Beyond the Bronx stretches suburban Westchester County and Connecticut. Staten Island is the smallest and most remote of the boroughs, reached from the tip of Manhattan by the still cheap Staten Island Ferry, or from Brooklyn over the lovely Verrazano Narrows Bridge.

Manhattan is separated from Brooklyn and Queens by the murky East River, from the Bronx by the slender Harlem River, and from New Jersey by the Hudson River to the west. New Jersey, of course, is a separate state administratively independent of New York. Nevertheless the economies of the two states are closely linked, and large numbers of the commuters who work in Manhattan live in one of the conurbations of New Jersey.

The glamour and excitement of New York are concentrated in Manhattan. Although the Bronx and Brooklyn had their decades of glory earlier in this century, when upwardly mobile immigrants moved there from the crowded tenements of Manhattan, those days are long past, and once affluent neighbourhoods have been devastated by urban blight. At the same time there has been a revival in the fashion ratings of, at any rate, parts of Brooklyn. Prompted by rapidly rising property costs and rents, middle-class Manhattan dwellers, especially those with children, have traded their cramped and expensive apartments for roomy brownstone houses, which in Brooklyn cost a fraction of their Manhattan counterparts. Thus they can enjoy spacious and gracious living in an urban environment instead of having to settle for the blandness of the suburbs. This rediscovery of the boroughs is, however, very selective. Gentrification has clearly defined limits.

Despite this partial migration of well-to-do families to the boroughs and the suburbs of Long Island and Westchester, there is still a tremendous snob value attached to being a Manhattan resident. This is confirmed, economically, by the steady rise in the cost of property. For all its drawbacks — the noise, the dirt, the expense, the constant crowds — the island of Manhattan is still the mecca which more and more people want to inhabit — if they can afford it.

Its spell can be potent beyond belief. Glumly, I was staring out onto the cemeteries, the fenced-in playgrounds, the dingy suburban houses, the empty warehouses, the sprawling used-car lots — the familiar townscape of Queens — and a few minutes later, on the other side of the Triboro Bridge we were skimming down the edge of Harlem into the fashionable East Side of Manhattan. On this unseasonably warm evening, the whole city seemed to be on the streets. In Harlem lanky youths in T-shirts ambled past uniform public housing blocks swinging monstrous transistor radios that blared rock and reggae into the air as palpably as the exhaust from the groaning buses. Further south, office workers were darting into delicatessens to pick up groceries or prepared foods for their suppers before returning to the tall characterless white-brick apartment buildings where they occupy a room or two. We passed close by the United Nations, with its complex of secretariat, assembly hall, hotels and missions, before arriving at Tudor City, a neo-Elizabethan conglomeration of flats and shops. As dusk fell the cab carried me across town to the Chelsea Hotel.

Queens had been moribund and torpid, Manhattan was effervescent. The lights had come on in the midtown skyscrapers, the pavements were crowded, the yellow cabs bumped their way over the potholes of the great avenues, and the peddlers displayed their wares and yelled their street cry: 'Check it out!'

I couldn't claim to be home, but I was back.

The Chelsea Hotel, thanks to Andy Warhol, is better known as a freak show than as a hotel. It's had a notorious rather than a glorious past. The days when famous writers and international drunks would dwell at the Chelsea have faded, though it still has its devotees and long-term residents. The lobby preserves the image of the hotel as a haunt of artists. Paintings, mostly derivative avant-garde pastiche, spatter the walls; I recall an especially dull painting of a load of bricks. A green neon coil was suspended from the ceiling. A few guests shuffled in and out; one or two men had long hair, as if they'd stepped in from a defunct decade.

The receptionist crouched in a large booth at the end of the lobby; he combined charm and ineptitude to a remarkable degree. Did they have the room I'd reserved six weeks before? Yes, but not quite the room I'd asked for — a slightly more expensive one, however, was available. He scratched his head, probably deracinating some lice. He'd have to let me in to the room with the master key, since they'd mislaid the guests' key and would have to go out and get a copy made. A retainer took me up in the lift and we shuffled down a long corridor that had all the charm of a Victorian reformatory: the walls were coated with rough beige plaster and the doors were painted a brown as pretty as creosote. Behind which grim door did Bob Dylan write *Sad-Eyed Lady of the Lowlands*?

My room had been untouched since the 1950s, that decade of exquisite taste. The curtains, which matched the bedspread, were dingy orange and covered only half the window, as if shrinking from the shame of their own unappetizing existence. The sink was deep and cracked, with one high tap of great antiquity, and the other a more recent model presumably from the 1950s restoration. After the long flight, and with a clammy heat still in the air, it was good to be able to wash. With my torso dripping I reached out for the towel — there wasn't one. I improvised, and then descended to the lobby, both to inform the concierge, who was still scratching his head in a combined operation that signified puzzlement as well as lice removal, that a towel would be a useful amenity, and to take a stroll down 23rd Street to count the crazies drawn onto the street by the unseasonable weather.

I returned after an hour with some chilled white wine and orange juice. The cheap furniture in the lobby was occupied by the persons and belongings of a hippie couple who seemed to have been frozen in time. Tumbling about the lobby were their three free-range kids. I tried to step on the grubbiest specimen but missed. The ancient retainer was still out getting the key made, and that meant he also had the master, which in turn meant that I was locked out. Fortunately he soon returned and I was able to retreat to the privacy — or semi-privacy given the state of the curtains — of my room.

A huge old refrigerator stood in the room. I wrenched open the door and there they were, the little darlings. It was an entire cockroach convention. I'd seen one roach earlier, gazing thoughtfully down the plughole, but I knew his pals had to be concealed elsewhere, doubtless rehearsing a surprise party for me. Cockroaches, those hard-shelled little beasties about three-quarters of an inch long with twitching antennae, are usually shy retiring creatures, not partial to light and attention. But the little gathering in front of me was clearly used to crowds — some of them had probably been extras in Andy Warhol's movie — and didn't bat a tentacle when I surprised them at play. They just continued to frolic about and some of them enjoyed a diverting little scurry over to the sink. I recalled from the days when I lived in Boston how fond roaches are of electrical appliances. When the toast popped up, a roach would often pop with it. And how often a TV show was enlivened by the cross-screen ambling of a roach that had emerged from the set's wiry innards! So I was not particularly disturbed by their presence. As long as they keep out of my bed I can tolerate them. Later in the evening, as I was about to brush my teeth, I was mildly put out to find that one little chap had made his bed of joy in my toilet bag.

In the old days there were many traditional ways to dispose of roaches: the spray, the fumigator, the whack with the shoe, emigration. Progress has been made, however, and all over the New York subways you can see ads, in English and Spanish, for a device called the Roach Motel. It's the size of a large matchbox, and you leave it on the floor near where your local roaches love to congregate. The cockroach is lured to investigate the box because, I assume, some delicious aroma emanates from within. The creature scurries up a little ramp and then down into the body of the box, but, poor fellow, his senses have deceived him and he is promptly poisoned and never seen again. It works. I've tried it. As the manufacturers of the Roach Motel justly claim: They check in but they can't check out.

THE HERB THAT'S
SUPERB

Those who inhabit great cities often know them least well. Each morning about two million commuters arrive in Manhattan by bridge or tunnel, by subway or car, and each evening they pour back into the boroughs and suburbs. Even Manhattan dwellers shelter against the walls of a few closely defined neighbourhoods. A young executive might frequent the more eastern reaches of the Upper East Side, where he rents or shares a small flat, the midtown turmoil of, say, Madison Avenue or Sixth Avenue where he works, and a few other parts of the city into which he will occasionally venture: Central Park on a summer weekend, the theatre district once or twice a year, the Upper West Side or Chinatown for a meal. As in all large cities, territoriality is intense and denizens of different neighbourhoods eye each other with suspicion, warily divided by unease as well as distance. City dwellers confer a strange value, part snobbish, part temperamental, on the area where they live. The visitor is at first unaware of these loyalties and divisions.

Greenwich Village became my neighbourhood. It's congenial, attractive, neatly proportioned, atypical of the rest of the city. The grid system which makes it almost impossible to get lost on Manhattan — with the numbered streets running east and west of Fifth and the huge avenues from north to south — breaks down south of 14th Street. As the island tapers towards its southernmost tip, the straight avenues either fade away or veer and collide. Although the southernmost part of the island — down by Wall Street — was the first to be settled and urbanization spread northwards, one doesn't experience the urban geography in that way, possibly because Manhattan's flame burns most intensely at its centre, from which the city pushes out towards the edges, north and south. This is historically false, yet psychologically it seems to be so.

The Village too, enjoying a layout so tortuous that it not only defies the grid system to the north but actually parodies it, seems remote from the rest of Manhattan. Its small scale differentiates it. The streets are lined by red-brick houses rather than the apartment blocks that loom over the Upper West Side and parts of the East Side. The houses of the fashionable East Side tend to be luxurious, often pretentious in their eclectic architectural styles, whereas Village houses are modest, uniform in style (though there are variations), undemonstrative. In themselves they say nothing about their occupants. A boarding house could be next door to a house subdivided into flats which could be adjoining a house still occupied by one prosperous family. Only the condition and the number of doorbells give clues. Many houses retain their original stoops, the short flight of steps leading to a solid fanlighted front door, and the stoops give the houses a distinct loftiness and formality.

Because, until recently, New York developers have blithely torn down houses if they thought they could build a more profitable structure on the same site, there are few streets in the Village that are stylistically intact. It is all very much a jumble, with small pockets of row houses inter-rupted by multi-storey apartment blocks, or by a mock-Romanesque fire house, or even by an eighteenth-century wooden house. Nevertheless the heart of the Village has a special quality of its own: the buttoned-up beauty of its red-brick shuttered houses, a domestic quality not found elsewhere in Manhattan, and even a tranquillity — away from the main shopping streets — that is at odds with one's image of this frenetic city. Almost everything here is modest in scale: the countless small restaurants, chic and shabby, Italian bakeries and butchers, antique shops stuffed with Art Nouveau baubles, and innumerable boutiques. There's the Erotic Bakery on Christopher Street, and on Seventh Avenue a shop displays the sign: EAR PIERCING. YOUR CHOICE: WITH OR WITHOUT PAIN.

The preciosity and self-consciousness of the Village — its image has become self-sustaining — are nothing new. For decades there have been those who haven't been able to stomach the place, who find its prettiness and charm outweighed by the trendiness, the bijou daintiness, the distasteful scent of money masquerading as small change. They say the Village isn't what it used to be, that its bohemian pretentions are essentially bogus.

'Greenwich Village is no more. My impression of this was confirmed by an old New York journalist: "Everything's fake in Greenwich Village — fake cabarets, fake news-papermen, fake poverty, fake genius." "Olde Tyme Innes" and peasant arts sprout at every street corner.' So wrote Paul Morand in 1930. Though his disdain is justifiable, the Village still has a vitality that coexists with the tranquillity of its more residential corners.

Early one evening I sauntered east towards Washington Square. The eccentric street plan prevents one from walking due east or west; one must zigzag until one reaches Sixth Avenue, where the grid resumes. I walked up West 11th Street as far as the crossing with West 4th Street which runs at right angles to it. Once one has come to terms with that geographical contradiction, the Village has been mastered. Washington Square lies in the heart of the Village and from its northern side springs Fifth Avenue. These lower stretches of Fifth have a midtown feel to them, since huge apartment blocks line the avenue. The small-scale Village, with its mews and courtyards, has been kicked to the side. I was heading for a classy bar called One Fifth Avenue, which has decor rescued from an old Cunard liner, the *Caronia*. It's Art Deco and very stylish. I strolled in at six and immediately recognized the man I was looking for.

Stephen is a journalist who keeps a cool eye on show business and reports his findings to a major city newspaper. Not that he's a native New Yorker. He's from California. But in these matters I like to adopt William Gass's 'pork chop principle', which states that if you take a prime pork chop and throw it in the garbage, it becomes garbage. Gass devised his theory to explain what happens to facts in novels, but it applies in a variant form to what happens to out-of-state people who reside in New York. If they're still there after a year, they've become New Yorkers. They adopt the attitudes, the affectations, the eccentricities, the turns of phrase, on which the natives pride themselves. Some go further and embrace the city with the ardour of the convert.

Stephen is too cool and fastidious to press the sweaty body of the city to his bosom, but it was clear that he'd adopted the city, and the city had returned the compliment.

He sat at a small table near the centre, and blended in so well with the sophisticated aura of the bar that he could have been mistaken for part of the furnishings. Hovering about the age of 30 (he'd have approved of Saki's observation that 'to have reached the age of thirty is to have failed in life'), he had red flocculent hair and a complexion that might become florid with time. He waved a greeting and I sat down opposite him and ordered a dry martini. He asked me how he could be of help, and I told him I hoped he would assist me to plunge into the cultural whirl.

'I'm not sure I'm going to be able to help you much there,' he sighed, and reaching into his briefcase he pulled out a bulging manila folder which he dramatically flung open. It was stuffed with invitations. 'Let's see, let's see . . . Mmm. No, that wouldn't be interesting . . . Let's see . . . A couple of invitations to Studio 54 any use?'

He mentioned a few other parties and openings I could attend, and promised to keep me informed should anything particularly intriguing come his way. He flicked through his diary.

'Ah, here's something! How about a screening of a new Bugs Bunny movie next week? You can come along to that if you like.'

'Bugs Bunny? I think not.'

'Really? It's about the only thing I'm looking forward to.' He sighed again. 'I'm really a very private person. I just want to retreat to my apartment, my cat, the pool, and not answer the phone. You know, I have to change my number every three months because people won't leave me alone. Old ladies come up to me in the lobby of my building, tell me how much they've enjoyed something I've written — and would I like to have coffee with them some time. No I wouldn't, thank you very much. All I want is my privacy.' He gave me his phone number.

As I scribbled in my diary, he insisted on ordering me another drink. 'What else do you want to know about New York?'

'Well, we foreigners think of it as such a dangerous place, but I can't say I've noticed. I don't actually feel fear in the city, and yet I can't help believing that fear and danger are part of the New York experience.'

Stephen clearly couldn't imagine why anyone should want to invite fear and danger, but he gave the matter his attention.

'Well . . .' he said, and looked around him. At the next table sat four smartly dressed blacks. 'Why don't you yell "Nigger!" at the top of your voice — that'll create a sense of danger all right.' He rose to his feet. 'Just excuse me while I move to another table.' But he sat down again. 'Or you could lie on your stomach on Christopher Street and wait to get raped?'

'I'll send my assistant.'

'If I were you, I'd stick to Bugs Bunny. Ah, I just thought of something. I have to go to a restaurant opening tomorrow. Come along. They'll have good food. Just mention my name at the door and say you're with me. If you can't make it, give me a call soon. Early in the morning is the best time. If someone else answers the phone, just ask her to pass the phone to me.'

We parted, and I walked the few blocks down Fifth Avenue to Washington Square, past the great arch that frames the view coming down Fifth, and into the large paved area of the square. There isn't much vegetation here (apart from packets of marijuana) and the square is a cheerless place, where people seem to hang out rather than enjoy themselves. In summer it's more convivial, though even in winter, on a bright day, people gather in thickets round folk singers that hail from Staten Island and grunt to the accompaniment of rapid scrapings across guitar strings. When I arrived it was dark, but the mild weather had brought the crowds. Around the basin in the centre of the park was the usual gauntlet of dope dealers, one of whom was hawking his wares with considerable invention: 'I've got the herb that's superb, the smoke that's no joke! Don't pass till you've tried my grass!'

I crossed the square and sat on a bench on the south side, watching the joggers circling the perimeter. There were some younger, coltish runners, erect and light on their toes, but they were atypical. There were quite a few old people crawling past who would surely enjoy their twilight years more reclining on a chaise longue clutching the cocktail of their choice. One man of middle years had his leg swathed in bandages, and he probably shouldn't have been walking, let alone pounding the pavement. Many men had pinched, unhappy faces, and appeared to be in pain, possibly because their shorts were too tight. There were hefty pudgettes, their breasts swinging out of control beneath their sweatshirts, their clumping progress mocked by tall men overtaking them, vain men with silvery chains that glittered against the sweat gathering on their exposed chests.

Would the youthful Henry James, who over a century ago had lived in one of the grand Federal houses on the north side, would that wise and knowing writer have tugged on his running shorts and trotted heavily round the square? No, he would not.

I'LL TAKE MANHATTAN

Manhattan, through its very constriction, corsets in tremendous excitement and vigour and pace. So much is immediately obvious. What takes longer to sink in is the sheer beauty of the city. Age textures objects of beauty with lichen on the stone or the associations of the past, but this leisurely and very European aesthetic is alien to New York. Its beauty has little to do with its churches and cathedrals, fine though they are, nor with the sweep of great boulevards, nor with the disposition of parks and squares, nor with the fretwork of lanes and alleys. No, the beauty of New York is sculptural and atmospheric.

It's a city of shapes that bang together and rearrange themselves as if seen through a kaleidoscope. Move 20 yards and the view changes. Even if the foreground hardly shifts, the entire background may have vanished and been replaced. No two views are ever the same. It's not always pleasing, but it's never dull. There's fascination in the details of the city's forms too, but they need to be sought out: the classical elaboration of the cast-iron warehouses in Greene Street, the radiator grilles in the Chanin Building lobby, the riotous encrustation of Alwyn Court Apartments, the restful indoor garden of the Ford Foundation building, the bright terracotta top of the otherwise unremarkable 2 Park Avenue, and the sensational collection of stone heads on the roof of the building next door.

The details are remarkable, but it's the vistas that remain unique. On a bright day cross the Brooklyn Bridge on foot, and halfway over look back towards Manhattan. You'll be standing on a boardwalk that runs above the traffic. The boards feel springy underfoot, gently vibrating as cars and trucks pound noisily over the metal plates that line the road surface of the bridge. Peer through the thicket of white cables that link the twin towers of the bridge and cage you within its grid. With every step the lines of those cables shift, so that you are glimpsing the city through a constantly changing geometric design. To the left are the towers of the financial district; the Statue of Liberty, behind which the sun will set, is away in the distance. Along the shore is the South Street Seaport with its parade of old clippers and trading ships of the last century. To the right, and further off, are the midtown skyscrapers, while closer to the bridge is the curious and unhappy cheek-by-jowling of the inhuman telephone building, rising windowless into the sky, and a fortress-like high school with fat cylindrical towers.

There you stand, with a stiff breeze scuffing your face, with the roar of traffic in your ears, and constant shuddering underfoot, and in front of you is this most glorious of urban views, romantic beyond belief, full of promise and excitement that are not in fact belied by the city close up. It scarcely seems possible that this vertical island, as frail as skittles, as solid as trees, could exist, and yet you know it's not just a fantasy of form but a living city. It changes not just because its permutation of relationships, one building to another, is close to infinite, but because the city itself is dedicated to change. With cannibalistic delight New York consumes itself, tearing down the old and then creating, and not always for the worse, a new structure in its place. New York, constantly surprising you, constantly tightening the screws of its own intensity, is the ultimate city of the world, the last word in urban existence; around the clock it will make its demands of you, never letting you go, rarely allowing you to relax, repeatedly assaulting the senses.

It's impossible to tire of New York. It will wear you down, but it won't wear you out. It can satisfy all moods. There's the stupendous drama of Manhattan, the downtown skyline, the walls of buildings lining Central Park, the swathe of Broadway; it's a drama that is monumentally present, dwarfing, bullying, pounding into submission. And on the other hand, there are the peaceful wooded slopes of Morningside Heights and Fort Tryon, the genteel charm of Greenwich Village, the silent warehouses of the Hudson shore, the Egyptian Revival lunacies of the Pythian Building

15

— all those myriad constituent parts. Yet, though it's possible to sit quietly in Central Park or to sprawl on the Bank Street pier and watch the sun luridly squatting over the industrial squalor of New Jersey, though it's possible to find rest and romance even in this most unrelenting of cities, you have to know where to look. The great cities of Europe invite you to rest and stroll as well as to work and prosper. Not New York.

You have to fight the city constantly, carving out your own space. When you're feeling jaunty and high, full of zest, Manhattan will back you up, opening the door to pleasure and wonder. But when your spirits are low, or when you're caught in a tangle of sadness and heartache, the city won't offer you any relief as it asserts that the race goes unwaveringly on even if you choose to stand aside for a while. New York can render you invisible, it can seem oppressive beyond endurance. In the summer especially, with the heat, already in the 90s, amplified by high humidity and the stifling air trapped by the buildings and the street tarmac softening underfoot, New York can become intolerable, and anyone who can afford to do so decamps to wooden houses in the hills of Vermont or on the rocky Maine coast, or to summer cottages on the Long Island shore. The poor have no possibility of escape, and for them the city in summer must be a cruel joke in which every street is a dead end and in which the sluggish rivers trap the island like a moat.

New York is not a place for the weary or the sick at heart. If you have the youth and the gusto to ride with it, it will carry you along, but it demands your fullest participation; slacken in your own effort, and Manhattan will drop you like a stone. Its exhilaration is also a kind of terror. New York needs to be paced, to be left and returned to, like a lover who asks too much. And when you do return, with what unfailing excitement you cross the Henry Hudson Bridge and realize you are back. To return to New York is to repossess it. After a year abroad or a day in the country, you hungrily reclaim the city, and the city responds, recharging you, awaiting your deepest pleasure.

New Yorkers love their city with a passion. With what ardour they point, not just to the scalloped crown of the Chrysler Building or the effortless white coloratura of the

Woolworth Building, but to some of the lovely newer buildings. There's the sleek Citicorp Building on the East Side, a smooth curtain of glass and silvery aluminium, and a razed top, sliced off at an angle, that gives this tall box a simple and unmistakable form that is recognizable from all over New York. Inside it is a seven-storey space filled with shops and restaurants, trees and shrubs, and even a sunken church. Above this atrium rise floors of offices, of course, but here below is a perfect urban space, protected from the weather, accessible, undemonstrative, impeccably designed, and packed with people throughout the day.

New Yorkers discuss heatedly the merits of controversial new buildings, such as Philip Johnson's AT&T Building on Madison Avenue, a pink granite pile that you either find exhilarating or pompous. From their offices New Yorkers will insist that you admire the view. They lovingly expose the classical detailing of the iron columns in their Soho lofts, picking out the acanthus swirls in gleaming paint. New Yorkers are alive not just to the flair of the city, but to its poetry, which is as subtle as wine, responding to changes in light and temperature and mood. Every decent bookshop has a section called NEW YORK, with rows of photographic books on every conceivable aspect of the physical city. At this moment no one has yet published a portfolio on the kerbstones of Murray Hill, but probably within a year someone will have done so, and very interesting it will prove to be.

It's a wintry night and the clouds are low. Walking through the midtown streets my chin is thrust into my coat, my hands are chilled inside my fur-lined gloves. Taxis swish by, bucking and veering over the uneven streets; office workers, heads down, hurry homewards. Pausing at a kerb, about to cross the street, I look up and see, slightly to one side, the graceful bulk of the Empire State Building, an underrated tower that grows more serene with each year that passes. The top is floodlit, and lights still burn in some of the offices. The clouds are brushing the radio masts and the peak of the structure; the powerful floodlights crash into the clouds, which seem to reel with the impact, swirling about the sky, rushing up to and bruising the stone and metal of the tower. There, way up in the sky, is this intense motion and activity.

The light spreads along the cloud cover, so that a whole portion of the night sky is a pale jazzy grey and orange. There's no one up there, but the restlessness of down below is duplicated in a cosmic tableau of light and vapour and wind. The scale of this aerial marbling is frightening yet the effect, in its lofty isolation, is pure magic.

DROP DEAD

Gold, which moves men to murder and sustains the wealth of nations, was, I discovered on seeing large quantities of it for the first time, a dispiriting and curiously lacklustre substance. In the vaults of the Federal Reserve Bank, a Florentine palazzo not far from Wall Street, are deposited a sizable portion of the world's gold reserves. Lumpish bars, each 'worth' $160,000, are immobilized behind grilles, locked into cages. 75 nations, their identity kept secret, hold their reserves here, and occasionally, in accordance with international transactions, bars are shifted from one cell to another. Bars within bars — there was a box of meaning to be unpacked!

The Fed admits small groups of visitors, herded through the building by guides. I don't know whether ours was typical, but she knew nothing. Perhaps I was duped by a subtle strategy designed to keep essential information from being made public. Yet I think not, since our guide compounded ignorance with an incompetence so all-encompassing that it became endearing.

'We are now on the third level, where our own police force is trained on its own firing range.'

'No, ma'm,' corrected the liftboy, 'we're only on the second level.'

'We are now on the second level, where our own police force —'

'No, ma'm,' muttered the liftboy, 'you want the third level.'

'Excuse me,' began a kindly schoolteacher, 'but how large is the Fed's own police force?'

'Err . . .'

'Roughly . . .' murmured the teacher.

Inspiration descended. 'The size of a small town police force.'

That was vague enough to satisfy us, and we all sighed with satisfaction. The lift doors — more like gates — parted and we saw another group with another guide, who was speaking as steadily and richly as evenly poured molasses.

'There's not supposed to be another group on the same floor!' thinly wailed our guide, and we all settled, with a lazy complacency, back into the fogs of her incompetence.

Not that the financial affairs of the city of New York have been run with any greater mastery over the years. If New Yorkers proudly speak of a 'renaissance', and they do, there's always an unspoken reference back to the dark days of 1975 when the city was almost broke.

High in a tower off Wall Street, the Banker looked back on those terrible years. In those days he'd been working in city government, so unlike most bankers he had an insider's knowledge of the city's mismanagement. His office was immaculate, as white and orderly as his shirt. Few papers were in sight, and there were few signs of mighty transactions passing through the junction box of his office. He was relaxed, enjoyed talking, dipping into his expertise, and gently criticized the insularity of his colleagues in his new profession.

The Banker had been involved in social services, and throughout the 1960s and early 1970s the city's spending on those services and on salaries and benefits had grown by leaps and bounds, in accordance with the ambitious policies that sprang from Lyndon Johnson's Great Society programme. In four years, spending on higher education and welfare in New York more than doubled. The city also supported over a dozen hospitals and its own system of colleges. New York, the most liberal and humane of American cities, looked after its own.

Consequently it continued to be a mecca for immigrants and the indigent. If you were poor, city programmes ensured that you would be less poor in New York than elsewhere in the United States. Federal law gave Puerto Ricans the right of entry into the country, but it was New York City that had to deal with their accommodation, education, and welfare.

In the heady days of the 1960s the city seemed eager to live up to its liberal reputation by expanding its programmes. In 1973-4 its per capita spending on social services was almost seven times that of Chicago.

There was only one small problem. How was this open-handedness to be paid for? The city is authorized to impose a variety of local taxes, and these local revenues, augmented by federal and state aid, constitute the expense budget, which pays for social services and salaries. Quite separate from the expense budget is the capital budget, raised through borrowing and bond issues, which is used to finance new facilities such as hospitals.

'Although those budgets are separate,' explained the Banker as he hoisted his long legs onto a coffee table in front of his chair, 'as expenses went through the roof, the city took to financing its daily operations by raiding the capital budget. Remember it's always easier, and politically less troublesome, to borrow than to tax. When we were short of cash, we'd resort to short-term borrowing. That's an expensive way to do business. The city's accountants kept thinking up new ways to raise money. They were legal but they were dumb. For instance, the city is legally empowered to borrow against receivables. Great. Trouble is, many receivables are uncollectable. But that didn't bother the accountants, with the result that we were borrowing against nonexistent revenues whose only reality was in a book-keeper's ledger.'

'Sounds like laying down mines in your own garden.'

'You can say that again. In the seventies federal aid dwindled, costs kept rising, yet the city failed to reduce its expenditure. So it borrowed more just to keep afloat. By June 1974 $3.4 billion worth of debts fell due, but the city had to borrow a further $7.3 billion to finance that debt. Early the next year the banks grew nervous.'

'Why did it take them so long? The tumble over the cliff seems to have been inevitable.'

'Well, banks like to lend — they get good rates of interest and clean up if they're smart. Nobody seriously thought the Big Apple could default. But by 1975 they started to think those thoughts. It was on April 14 that the city ran out of money. The banks would lend no more, and that was the day the shit hit the fan.

'Along comes the Governor, Hugh Carey. Mayor Beame took a back seat as the governor instituted bodies such as the Municipal Assistance Corporation that successfully restructured the city's debt with the help of the banks and the unions. 60,000 city employees were laid off and other austerity measures were slapped on. New York lobbied Gerald Ford and the federal government for help but it was a long time coming. Every New Yorker remembers the *Daily News* headline in October 1975 — FORD TO CITY: DROP DEAD. Eventually financial order was restored and gradually the city revived.' He waved towards the window, which looked out over half the skyscrapers of Wall Street. 'As you can see all around.'

'Could there be another crisis like that of 1975? After all, federal and state aid are declining.'

'True enough, and that's going to exacerbate New York's budgetary problems, but that's separate from the long-term nightmare caused by excessive short-term debt. That can't happen again. Our budgets are too closely monitored. But the Mayor has to balance the budget, and that means services will be cut further. Something else worries me. We're experiencing a boom in service industries, but will it last? A weak dollar meant that New York became a bargain for the rest of the world, and there was a huge increase in foreign investment.

'But there's no reason, other than mystique, why large banks and financial institutions *have* to be in New York. Wall Street is convenient for lunching with other bankers, and that's about it. With computerization expanding, banks don't need to remain here and some have already moved part of their operations to Delaware and South Dakota.'

A few blocks away at the city's Office for Economic Development, its deputy commissioner, a casually dressed, emphatic man on the borders of 40 called Lawrence Kieves, agreed with the Banker that there was no essential reason why major financial institutions should remain in New York, since costs would be lower elsewhere.

'What attracts them, and keeps most of them here, is the city's infrastructure and the quality of its services. In the early decades of this century we built our subway system, our bridges and tunnels. It's all been paid for. The new expanding cities of the Sunbelt, such as Houston, still need to build their transit systems, their sewers in the suburbs, and all the rest of it. That's hugely expensive. New York has a hard enough time maintaining its systems, but at least it's all there.

'All the economic incentives the city can offer are a waste of time and money if we can no longer offer the services. Not just the communications, but policing and hospitals and sanitation. Service industries stay in Manhattan because by and large they're satisfied with what we provide.

'Manhattan's going to remain a terrific place — but it'll be expensive. It will contain many rich people and a small number of very poor people. Gentrification will spread as far up as Harlem. Everyone wants to live on Manhattan.'

WONDERWOMAN
HAS A BALL

While the banks keep the wheels of New York's finances in motion, the smaller wheels and cogs that drive the city's cultural life also need to be oiled with lavish injections of cash. Fundraising has been elevated from a necessity to an art in itself. Consultancies specialize in raising money solely for the arts; it's not a matter that's left to amateurs. Patronage enhances social status. The Metropolitan Opera programme, for instance, lists every single contributor: benefactor patrons, sponsor patrons, supporting patrons, patrons, fellows. Hardly a night goes by during the winter season without at least one 'benefit', a fashion show or concert or celebrity-packed dinner. Attend enough benefits, or better still organize one, and your name will begin to appear in the social pages and on lists of New York's best-dressed, or some magazine will do a feature on how tastefully you've done up your triplex.

I wasn't going to be left out of this social excitement, and I too graced a benefit: the Writers Community Bowling Tournament. The Community's ill-written self-definition is that it's 'a non-tuition, non-degree program for persons who will benefit from professional training and participation in a group whose primary commitment is to writing' — what we non-writers call workshops. The Community hoped to raise $15,000 by persuading writers and other celebrities to bowl against teams from publishing houses and movie companies. Corporations 'buy' lanes for $500; supporters pay a mere $25 admission. What the PR handout called 'savage intramural competition for five golden trophies' would take place from ten till midnight, and then the lanes would be thrown open to those of us not on a team but eager to hurl shiny black balls at skittles.

What particularly attracted me to this gala was its location: the new Mid-City Lanes at the Port Authority Bus Terminal. They've cleaned up the terminal recently, and have built extensions and new facilities, but I remember it when it oozed menace. In the summer of 1965 I'd arrived on a bus from Mississippi only to find Manhattan equally sweltering. Clutching my two cases in each hand meant that my pockets were left unguarded and swarms of hopeful six-year-old hoodlums stuck to me like flies to meat. One of those four-foot-high locusts offered to carry my bags for me, and I realized I was better off agreeing: they were damn heavy and any nonsense from him and I would at least have two hands free with which to wring his neck and start a race riot. Loopy anorexics ricocheted around the main hall of the terminal, barbiturated into the next century. Religious maniacs hawked pamphlets and bewildered travellers just in from Nebraska with corn in their hair stood around the vast halls scratching their chins while urchins vacuumed their wallets.

It had all changed. For one thing the place was clean. Cops with night-sticks strung round their wrists weren't wending their way through the waiting rooms waking up bums posing as long-distance travellers. 'You gotta ticket, man? No? OK then, let's move it . . .' And where were the hookers? Plenty outside on Eighth Avenue, the only women left in America who still wear satin hot pants, but inside the terminal I couldn't see any. I didn't check out the lavatories, but I bet there was no action there either, no decaying pensioners breathlessly offering blow jobs to 16-year-olds aiming fresh Pennsylvania pee at New York urinals. The expansion of the terminal had brought more space: there were no crowds to threaten, no huddled groups of fledgling muggers keen to win their spurs.

The bowling alleys are stuck away on an upper floor. The teams were already warming up on the lanes, while a sizable collection of well-wishers and benefactors clustered around the bar. The Community was fielding three teams, each led by a distinguished writer: Ted Hoagland, George Plimpton and Galway Kinnell. Over the past dozen years, I'd had fleeting encounters with all three, insufficient to claim acquaintance, but adequate to crank up a conversation. Kinnell I had heard at a memorable poetry reading in

Connecticut at which he'd stopped reading his own work and started playing tapes of an Iranian poet reading in Persian, which nobody, including himself, could understand. Hoagland had contributed articles to a magazine I once worked for, and I had done my best to improve his prose.

I found Hoagland trying to tie up his shoelaces; he was wearing some snazzy bowling bootees that require the wearer to thread the laces through some twenty eyes, and Hoagland was not doing well. I reminded him of our former connection, assuming he'd want to thank the unsung editor who had once enriched his walkabout paragraphs.

'Oh yes,' he said, and returned to his shoelaces. There was only half an hour left before the tournament began and I could understand his desperation. I tried flattery.

'I love your hat.' It was scarlet, and a feather sprouted from one side.

'Thank you.' He was still face down, his nose near his toes.

'You still write for the *Atlantic Monthly*?'

'Not since 1972.'

'Ha! That means I must have worked on your final piece.'

Silence. A minute later, he surfaced with a gasp and surveyed one laced boot. At that moment, a raven-haired girl as tall as the clouds walked by wearing a Wonder-Woman costume — what there was of it. She was sensational.

'Who's that?'

'Er' — and it was only now that I realized Hoagland had a bad stammer which was doubtless being exacerbated by my inane questions — 'she's with the Warner Brothers team.'

Wrong again, Ted! She was with DC Comics, but we'll let it pass.

Hoagland bent down to restructure his other boot. Could it be that he'd rather be left alone? I wished him luck, slapped him on the back, and headed back to the bar. The Tournament had organized a wonderful system for free-loaders such as myself. On arrival I'd been handed a package containing a press kit plus two drinks vouchers, exchangeable for the tipple of one's choice. Earlier observation had enabled me to identify two barmen with opposed styles of pouring: one merely splashed the ice with bourbon, the other merrily filled the glass to the brim. I was on my way back to the latter when I spotted a dozy official rummaging through some papers that had been left on a chair; he was supposed to be keeping the place tidy, and had in his hand one of the press kits.

'Guess I should throw this out,' he said as I smiled at him.

'Not quite yet,' I returned, grabbing the envelope and peering in. I retrieved the two unused drinks vouchers, gave the envelope back to him, and said it was now his to do as he pleased.

I used the vouchers, and my memories of the next hour became blurred. As a reporter, I somehow lost my detachment, as I roved the hall waylaying beautiful women. Four drinks over an evening is hardly a bender, but when they're quintuple Jack Daniels you're getting close. Watching 20 teams bowl, even if they are studded with 'celebrities', is actually rather dull, and I was in search of greater stimulation. I decided to interview WonderWoman, who was taking a rest. I squatted beside her.

'I hope you don't mind if I ask, but do your nails' — they were scarlet and very long — 'get caught in the bowling ball?'

She laughed and replied, and I quote her verbatim: 'No, they don't.'

I had successfully devised the question to which there is no follow-up, and I drifted away, too timid to risk the non sequitur: 'And what are you doing after the show?'

I went back to watch the bowling and stood near a table pyloned with beer bottles. A youth picked up a bottle and started to drink.

'Hey!' I said aggressively, 'that's my beer!' It wasn't, but I was trying to be friendly.

'What do you mean? I just put it down.'

'I know. Only joking.'

'What a relief. I'm a TB carrier.'

'So? I have gonorrhea.'

You can see what a merry time we were all having at my first benefit. Benefit? *Pro cui bono?*

It was about one in the morning and I didn't want to keep Meryl Streep waiting, so I made my way out, saying goodbye to Todd and Alison and Sue and all the other wonderful new friends I'd made, and stole a cab. No, not literally. It's an old-established New York custom: when you see a luggage-laden traveller hailing a cab, you obstruct his passage while he's trying to haul his gear and jump into the cab ahead of him, laughing heartily as you do so. If he remonstrates, just give a traditional New York riposte, such as 'Beat it, asshole!' It's hard the first time, but you soon get the hang of it.

ZONING THE OZONE

Money obsesses New Yorkers, perhaps because consumption is so conspicuous. Why live in a cornucopia if you're unable to sample the fruit?

Money is needed, above all, to pay the rent. There's a shortage of residential property in Manhattan. On West End Avenue a handbill taped to a lamppost offered a $200 reward to anyone who could find a 1/2 bedroom flat for the advertiser. Because of the physical constriction of the island, space equals money. Real estate, consequently, is one of the biggest businesses of them all.

The entire United States contains 700 million square feet of office space, and 280 million of them are located in Manhattan (not to mention the 40 million in Brooklyn and additional space in other boroughs). Financial institutions alone rent 68 million square feet, which is more than the total office space available in London. Despite this acreage of space, commercial rents in Manhattan remain high, up to $60 per square foot in Park Avenue. High rents notwithstanding, the vacancy rate of commercial buildings is low. Despite the recession, Manhattan is enjoying a building boom that is only just beginning to level out.

The boom has political repercussions. It's in the interest of the city to encourage property development. It increases the tax base, it adds to the glamour of the city and helps draw in the rich people who will boost the local economy. There is an 8% sales tax in New York City, so every time someone buys a bar of soap or a case of wine or a Matisse, the city grabs its share. To encourage property development, the city offers tax abatements which in effect absolve developers from payments of taxes on new property for a certain number of years. If you're a major developer you regard this as a business incentive; if you're a taxpayer, it may look suspiciously like a handout, welfare for the wealthy.

However you look at it, property and politics are laces that tie up the same shoe. Of roughly $8 billion in city taxes raised each year, about half comes from levies on 850,000 parcels of property. A balance has to be struck. If taxation rates are too high, tenants may be forced out. Should that happen (as it did in the 1970s), the city's tax base, and hence its revenues, will shrink, setting off a downward spiral of dwindling services. On the other hand, if taxation levels are lowered, then the city can't afford to maintain its level of services.

Strict zoning laws specify the permissible bulk, height and use of any proposed structure. Laws, however, are made to be broken, and there may often be good reasons for allowing the law to be bent. There is a complicated procedure for assessing applications for 'zoning variances'.

One kind of variance became prevalent in the 1960s and affected the physical appearance of New York. The city devised a system whereby, in exchange for a variance allowing a structure larger than permitted, the builder would provide some kind of public amenity. In 1960 the Chase Manhattan Bank erected its headquarters downtown, and offered the public a 'plaza', a traffic-free area where pedestrians could stroll and sit. Soon everybody was doing it, and plazas sat like small rugs at the foot of monolithic buildings all over New York. Some were embellished with sculpture and fountains. Chase Manhattan Plaza sprouted a large zany Dubuffet rearing up in black and white; Marine Midland Bank Plaza on Broadway contains a striking cube by Isamu Noguchi. These are exceptions. Most plazas are no more than wind-swept slabs of concrete with a token tree or bench.

There are other ways in which developers can compensate the citizenry. The tall sleek Olympic Tower on Fifth Avenue next to St Patrick's Cathedral offered no room for a plaza, so instead the developers provided a public arcade that tunnels through the building. It's a tall, cool space, with an elegant Rizzoli news-stand, an excellent patisserie, a bar, and seating for weary shoppers. Clever use of mirrors and trees enlarges the space, and a three-tiered waterfall splashily blocks out street noise.

These zoning regulations and variances only affect sites that are vacant or ripe for development. Most prime sites are already occupied. But that needn't stop a skilled entrepreneur! If you can't buy the site, you may be able to buy the fresh air above it instead. So great is the pressure for space on Manhattan that well-situated oxygen can be worth millions. If the zoning laws permit the erection of a 30-storey building on a site and, 40 years ago, a short-sighted builder only put up 20, then there are 10 storeys of fresh air that could legally be built on. These are called air rights.

Let us assume that I own a historic building that can't be altered or demolished. It's 10 storeys high, but the maximum height on that site is 30, which means I have 20 storeys of air rights to play with. Not much use to me, but of enormous interest to Mr Capone next door, who is tearing down a small office block and planning a more spacious replacement. Under the regulations he, like me, is only entitled to build 30 storeys, but if he can persuade me to sell him my air rights, he can add my spare storeys onto his 30. Result: I become very rich overnight, and Mr Capone builds extra storeys which will yield additional rents to make him rich too.

This chicanery can have beneficial aspects. Major landmarks such as Grand Central Terminal and St Bartholomew's Church on Park Avenue can justify their inefficient existence by selling their air rights. But the system is devised as an aid to development, not as a means of conservation. Gordon Bunshaft's elegant Lever House on Park Avenue, one of the loveliest of city skyscrapers, may be demolished because the structure is extravagant in terms of the site.

In the war between developers and conservationists, the Municipal Arts Society has led the fight for conservation. It helped to set up the first zoning laws in 1916 and persuaded City Hall to establish the Landmarks Commission in 1965. The MAS is usually assisted in its fights by local community boards and civic groups. Get a few dowagers and rock stars on your side, and any developer or mayor will tremble.

Margot Wellington, the executive director of MAS, is feisty and garrulous, proud of what the Society has accomplished. 'We have no power, of course. We're just a self-appointed watchdog. But we'll use any means available to exert pressure: publicity, law suits, rallies. We win some, we lose some. Our most recent triumph was in getting the Upper East Side designated. Frankly, I was amazed that we won, because we were battling while the property boom was at its height and rents were out of sight. You know why I suspect we won? Lots of developers live in that neighbour-hood, and they were finally persuaded that it wasn't in their personal or professional interest to wreck it.'

Playing devil's advocate, I asked Miss Wellington whether the MAS was in danger of 'freezing' the city, of stifling the process of change that keeps it vital.

She dismissed the notion. 'Listen. Developers here have so much power that the MAS can't even neutralize it, let alone counter it. We're not opposed to change, but we do insist that if the city allows the destruction of the qualities and amenities and buildings that make New York special, then it will no longer be the mecca that makes it so attractive to developers in the first place. That's what we try to convince them of. Without our efforts, developers would be left undisturbed to Houstonize New York City.'

The MAS recently moved into the north wing of the splendid old Villard Houses on Madison Avenue. Miss Wellington showed me round, she showered me with the phone numbers of people I should talk to, she was lavish with offers of help.

Gratefully I scribbled away. I looked up with a smile that says a thousand thank yous, and it was then that I noticed the less tender smile on her lips. 'All I ask in return,' she said brightly, 'is that you join the Society.'

'Er . . .'

Her smile broadened. 'No rush. But if your subscription cheque hasn't crossed my desk by the end of next week, I'll instruct all those people whose numbers I've given you not to cooperate.' Just a little joke.

I forked out on the spot.

Just a few weeks later, the *New York Times* reported: 'Margot Wellington will resign March 31 after seven years as executive director of the Municipal Arts Society.' A great loss to the Society, and I'm sorry for its sake, but it really doesn't pay to squeeze money from well-connected working journalists . . .

AT THE MEZZARINE

The phone rang.

'Hi.' It was Stephen. 'Been raped yet?'

'Alas . . .'

'Keep trying. In the meantime, do you want to come to a backers' party tomorrow?'

'Sure.'

'Good. See you at the Westside Arts Theater at 6.30.'

The Westside is a small theatre seating about three hundred people; it's enclosed within the bare brick walls that certify an authentic small theatre. In recent years about a dozen such theatres have sprung up on 42nd and 43rd Streets to the west of Ninth Avenue, all part of the redevelopment scheme which is successfully reclaiming the area back from the massage parlours and the pimps.

I pushed my way through the wine-sippers in the lobby to the front of the auditorium, where I found Stephen seated on the side. I had only the vaguest idea of what happens at a backers' party and I asked him to explain.

'I'm not exactly sure myself. In fact, I've never been to one of these before, as they don't usually like the press to turn up while a play's still struggling to get off the ground. The producer has put together a cast and a director, he's planned his budget, and now he needs backers prepared to buy shares in the show, in this case 50 of them at about five thousand bucks apiece. If enough angels dip into their pocket books, then they can mount the production and try to make some money. So what they're going to do in front of this carefully selected audience is perform an abridged — my God, I hope it's abridged — version of the play. Then after an hour or so and some heavy prompting everyone is supposed to reach for their cheque books and at that point we run like hell.'

The producer had provided documentation. Everything had been estimated: ticket prices, sales forecasts, subsidiary rights sales, salaries, publicity expenses. And profits.

I looked around me. 'So most of the people here are rich?'

'Quite a few.'

'How can you tell a rich person from 50 yards?'

'Fur. See that lady in the fur hat? She's extremely rich, often gives money to new productions. She often asks me to her parties. One day I said yes and found I was the only person there under 80.'

'*She* looks very rich,' I observed, nodding in the direction of a tall blonde wearing a full-length silver fox.

'No, no, you don't understand. She's kept. *He's* rich.' And he pointed at the svelte man by her side.

Once the audience was seated, the producer welcomed us, the author rashly took a bow, and then the director hopped onto a stool by the side of the stage. He told us what a great show it was, about its commercial potential, how any investor would be certain to clean up. He then introduced the cast, who were clutching their scripts — no point learning your lines until they've raised the money.

It would be unkind to identify the play or to say anything about it beyond the fact that for a full hour Stephen and I squirmed under a barrage of sentimentality and nostalgia that must have strained the endurance of even the most stereotypical New Yorkers, who beneath that tough coppery surface melt like butter once their bounteous supply of emotion has been resourcefully tapped. During an especially nauseating boy-meets-girl scene — you know the kind of thing: teenagers scrabbling on floor searching for mislaid bibelot come face to face and look deeply into each other's eyes, realizing for the first time what their hearts etc — Stephen whispered, 'Wanna fuck?' The director shuddered. After the first act the lady in the fur hat left. There went ten thousand bucks.

After the show we went to chat to the star of the piece; she accepted our patently insincere expressions of delight and soured her look to let us know that she wasn't enraptured either. She berated Stephen for not having included her in a piece he'd written about New York actresses.

'You had no stars! You quoted from all those people who've only been in New York for a short while!'

'I know, you're quite right,' capitulated Stephen, meekness itself.

'Nobodies! You should have quoted *me*.'

'Yes, you're right. I should.' (Over dinner he told me the nobodies included Meryl Streep.) During a brief pause in her flow of chatter, he introduced me. 'He's from London . . .'

'I've been in London a lot. You must have seen me over there.'

'Er . . .'

'I was in the West End for all of 1977.' She named the show.

'Yes, of course.' (Never heard of it.) 'Missed it, I'm afraid. What a shame.'

'Other shows too.'

Stephen intervened. 'We're going to Charlie's for dinner. Come with us.'

'Darling, I'd love to. There are a few openings I want to go to' — and digging into a capacious handbag she pulled out a wad of engraved cards — 'but perhaps I'll join you later.'

On the way to the restaurant, one of those legendary establishments frequented by theatre people and specializing in mediocre food, I thanked Stephen for coming to my rescue.

'Oh, she let you off lightly. Usually by that stage she's taken out the press clippings.'

After our meal, we made our way to the cloakroom to collect our coats.

'Mine's the mink,' said Stephen.

The girl replied: 'I'm out of mink, how about the chinchilla?'

As she handed us the coats, he pressed two dollar bills into her hand — 'Let's not be shy about this . . .' — and we left the restaurant. He invited me back for a drink, but he was obviously exhausted and I declined. What a terrible thing, to see a New Yorker drained of energy, submitting meekly to the castigations of an actress, picking at his food, moping, grasping feebly for the barbs and lashes that give conversation its zest. I let him go home to restore himself.

Having watched a producer, director and author sweat it out at a backers' party, it seemed miraculous that any play ever made it onto the stage. Do producers have an overwhelming passion for the theatre or is their profession a business much like any other, with its risks and rewards?

Ken Waissman ought to know. As the producer of *Grease,* which holds the record for the longest running musical on Broadway, he clearly had a shrewd commercial instinct. But that winter Waissman had two successful shows running which were 'straight' plays and far from sure-fire winners: *Agnes of God* and the brilliantly performed *Torch Song Trilogy,* which went on to pick up Tony awards for Best Play and Outstanding Actor.

'In the old days you had the angels, who put up the money, and the producers, who were imaginative, theatre-wise, knew their way around,' began Waissman, speaking rapidly, with a nervous, edgy energy. 'Now the distinctions are blurred. These days major angels and many theatre owners like to style themselves as producers. Some shows don't appear to have a traditional producer at all, just a lot of people backing it, and it's a mystery to me how shows like that get themselves onto the stage.'

'And money?'

'You need to raise a lot, but you can't begin to finance a play until you've fixed a start date and can assure investors that the show's going into rehearsal. It takes real expertise and salesmanship to raise money. You have to be able to tell who's riding you along and who isn't. You develop a sixth sense for who likes to be courted but isn't going to invest. Costs keep rising too. There's no such thing as mechanization in the theatre — it's still a hand-crafted product.'

Waissman's manner suggested that restlessness was a feature of his professional life, that sitting behind a desk made him fidgety. His office was curious, with cheap furnishings that pinned down a carpet of virulent blue like a large stain that would never wash out. A whole wall was filled with framed photographs that featured without exception the smiling face and curly hair of Ken Waissman, who resembles Gene Wilder in repose. Next to him stood the stars he'd been associated with over the last dozen years, but the most remarkable feature of this gallery was that a smaller figure who appeared next to him in almost all the photographs had been blotted out with a black circle.

It was a woman, the same woman in each one, and it wasn't hard to deduce that she was his former co-producer and ex-wife; they had split up not long before and she was now an independent producer herself with an office in the same building. I tried to picture Ken Waissman staying late at the office extinguishing her features in a hundred photographs, and found it hard to associate such studied rage with the spry wide-eyed man behind the desk. By obliterating her likeness he had of course drawn attention to her in a way that was, in the richest and most flamboyant sense, theatrical, combining wit and anger. What, I wondered, did the picture wall in *her* office look like?

I ran into Waissman again some weeks later at an eggnog party, where he made his entrance in a full-length fur coat. At that moment I was deep in conversation with a pixie of a box-office manager, and I was asking him whether the audience changes in the course of a long run.

'There's a big difference,' he sighed, 'a qualitative difference.'

'How do you mean?'

'They laugh in different places, respond in different ways. You see, most of the audience we get now *Evita*'s been on for years is, dare I say it, from New Jersey. Apart from tourists, everybody in Manhattan who wants to see the show has seen it by now.'

'How can you tell the difference between a New Yorker and someone from New Jersey?' I innocently asked, throwing him a cue.

'Well, when a New Yorker comes to the box office, he'll ask me whether we have two front mezzanine for next Friday. They know what they want. When a Jersey person comes up and asks for two seats and I offer front mezzanine, they invariably say, 'Wassa mezzarine?' There are other ways you can tell. Women from New Jersey wear Hermès scarves, carry a Gucci bag, and have fur coats on —'

'Don't New Yorkers?'

'But the difference is that the Jersey ladies also chew gum. Loudly. I remember once I'd had a simply ghastly Saturday evening with a very late closing, and I had to arrive early at the box office for the Sunday matinee. I admit I was not my usual gracious and lovely self. A New Jersey woman came up and asked for two matinee tickets. I told her we were sold out, as we were. This she refused to accept. I repeated what I'd said, and then she went: "*Arrrgh!*" Really, just like that. Frightful noise. To which I responded, "Madam, that is an animal noise. Here we prefer to communicate with words." Well, she was so furious that she attempted to stab me through the aperture with her umbrella.

'And we adore stolen credit cards. Get them all the time. The nerve of the thieves is incredible. One morning I look through the window and I see this black guy pushing some plastic towards me. It's signed "Manny Greenbaum" and he wonders why we're suspicious. But the most blatant attempt I remember is when another black guy tried to convince me he was a Chinaman called Bill Wu. Unfortunately for him the signature on the card was in Chinese script and there was this man painfully trying to copy it onto the voucher. "You *must* be kidding," I said, and he looked *most* offended.'

NEW YORK CONSUMED

'Gimme a pound of rum truffles, willya?'

'I'm sorry, ma'm, we're out of rum, but I can let you have our whisky truffles instead?'

'OK. Wrap em up good, willya?'

And the girl behind the counter at Confiserie Namur on East 66th Street hands over a box in exchange for $28. This trade sustains any of two dozen or more midtown chocolatiers. Godiva has two branches on Manhattan, and one November the great French chef Michel Guérard flew into New York specially to open his 'comptoir gourmand shop' at Bloomingdale's, featuring chocolates of his own making. Chocolate has become an emblem for luxurious consumption. The opera or the races are an acquired taste, but almost everybody loves chocolate and, if statistics are to be trusted, each American consumes nine pounds of the mush each year. Of course most of it is dreadful commercial stuff, far worse than its run-of-the-mill European counterpart, but discerning New Yorkers are prepared to pay inflated prices for these dark globes of richness flown in regularly from France or Belgium.

New York strews in your path every dreamed-of gratification. Chocolates offer an instantaneous rapture which lingers lovingly on the taste buds. The vogue for handmade chocolates, and the passion with which they're devoured, became for me a trivial but potent symbol of the avidity with which New Yorkers consume all culture. Ballets, musicals, gallery openings, they all vanish into a great communal maw in a delirium of ravin. Time and again I found New Yorkers unable to recall what they'd seen or whom they'd heard recently at the opera or concert hall. Like a sweetmeat, culture is devoured and then forgotten. And what would come of fashion without this helpful amnesia? Clothes designers are hyped as though they were Baskin Robbins' flavour of the month; restaurants are elevated to the gastronomic aristocracy by such reviewers as Mimi Sheraton or Seymour Britchky, and then mobbed for a month until a new prince is born.

Yet some favourites or fads do become institutionalized, and New Yorkers cling to those that win their hearts with a tenacity that is deeply sentimental. The soprano Beverly Sills (justly known as Bubbles to her fans), never lost her grip on the marzipan hearts of New Yorkers, whom, I suspect, responded more to her irrepressible personality in the face of personal tragedies than to her screech of a voice. Restaurants as notoriously bad as Sardi's and Elaine's are full every night because celebrities, who have no more taste and discrimination than the rest of us, like to be seen there. Yet for the most part discovery is equivalent to contamination. The delightful Heartbreak Club was declared, by a knowledgeable acquaintance, to be no longer an acceptable night-spot. Originally patronized by the discerning few who flocked loyally to this large and characterless luncheonette in TriBeCa which at night turned the lights down low, substituted beer for coffee-to-go, and hosed down the dance floor with an undiluted stream of fifties and sixties rock music, this splendid club was, he assured me, 'ruined ever since it became known that Bjorn Borg had been seen there, and now every Saturday night the hordes descend from New Jersey'. Well, they didn't get in my way and I stomped my tiny feet off for three hours without stopping until dwindling batteries prompted my companion to whisk me away in a cab at 3 a.m. for other pleasures of the night.

Munch, munch, stomp, stomp — whatever the activity, New Yorkers ingest it with a relish and forgetfulness that seem unique to that city. To see avid consumerism at its most frenzied, comic, and determined, step inside the doors of Bloomingdale's, that large, externally nondescript department store on an unfashionable stretch of Lexington Avenue. It's as disorienting as Hampton Court maze: with its panelled mirror ceilings, shifting floor levels, and fragmentation into boutiques and units, it's designed to keep you lost and wandering for hours. Bloomingdale's has a Main Level, a Middle Level and a Metro Level, an Arcade and a Loge, not to mention seven floors above that lot. The whole store is an incitement to confuse. Even the boutique names tease and puzzle: Sleeper of the Year (dressing gowns), Top Billing (T-shirts), Brief Encounters (underwear, hoho). At the top of an escalator, you are likely to be assaulted by leggy girls with trays full of new products, such as musical toothbrushes and sprays of new scents. As I stood there enraptured while Valley Girls spritzed me with fragrance, fearsome ladies with lacquered hair and matching furs bashed me with their carrier bags bulging with bargain duvet covers.

Let us flee this madness, this funfair, this palace of mayhem, and walk a few blocks further up Lexington to a far smaller shop where, in a different way, consumerism is every bit as rampant. We're at Canine Styles, a hole in the wall that provides New York's pooches with such indispensable accessories as Pet-Sac sleeping bags, doggie boots and smart leather doggie coats for 50 dollars, fake foods (sausages, tacos), Dogette nail enamel, and Puppy Piddle Pads.

While the many consume, a few are consumed. Close by Rockefeller Center, a short plump man with thinning orange hair stopped me in the street.

'Excuse me, I won't keep you long.' He was standing very close, so that any move on my part to escape would have appeared abrupt. 'No, I won't keep you long, but I can see that you're a kind man, you have a kind face, has anyone ever told you that?'

'Only when they want something.'

'My story will not detain you for long. My name is Sam Cohen, and I just got back from the Temple. My father Rabbi Cohen is dead, may he rest in peace, and I have nowhere to live. I'm homeless. Can you help me out?'

'Actually, I'm just visiting the city . . .'

'You may be a visitor' — with great dignity — 'but you're also a yumanbein. I'm just a Jewish boy who needs some help.' His voice rose as I dug into my pocket; he couldn't let go now, and he kept pinning me down with his cascade of words. 'I'm not actually homeless. I've found a place but it's

$160 and where do I find that kind of money? If my father Rabbi Cohen were alive I'd go to him, ask for $100. But as it is, I'm on my own.' And on it went, gushing over the stones and pebbles of my dilatoriness, until I finally settled on what I felt was an appropriate sum. I hadn't believed his story, least of all the graphic bit about returning from the funeral, but — reason not the need. I handed over some coins and he blessed me, as I knew he would.

Sam Cohen may not be homeless, but social workers estimate that up to 35,000 city dwellers may be. There are about 6000 bag ladies alone in greater New York. The problem is far from hidden. I'd seen dozens of men sleeping under the iron canopies in the meat-packing district and lying on the gratings which allow warm musty air to rise from the subways to the street. Above all, the homeless occupy the subways at night, taking advantage of the warmth and of the fact that the stations never close. From time to time they'll be picked up and taken to city-run shelters, but there they are prone to detention or molestation, and many of the homeless prefer to live and sleep on the streets. Tramps in rural areas often make a conscious choice to live on the road, but this is different; this is poverty and despair.

From 1965 on, thousands of mental patients have been released from hospitals; commendably, since so many people had over the years been needlessly institutionalized. However, no adequate provision had been made for these ex-patients, who were ill-equipped to make their way unaided in a large and hostile city. Many poor and solitary people found spartan and sometimes verminous accommodation in single-room occupancy hotels. The sumptuous façades of dilapidated hotels such as the Clinton and Wolcott near the garment district conceal mean lobbies guarded by signs to warn off non-tenants. Outside the Wolcott is the notice: NO ONE FROM OUTSIDE IS ALLOW [sic] TO USE THE WASHING MACHINE. Grim these places may be, but they at least offer some privacy and a roof. However, as property developers continue to snap up large buildings with a view to converting them into flats and offices, many of these shabby old hotels have closed, and their occupants, many of whom scrape along on welfare payments, are forced onto the streets.

Shelters have sprung up all over the city, offering refuges and some basic services to the homeless. Many are sponsored by local churches, aided by financial subsidies from city agencies. One I visited caters to over 100 people a day, mostly regulars. By no means all are actually without a home; quite a few of those who use its facilities live in cheap hotels. Men and women do stay overnight at the shelter, but no beds are provided and they must sleep on chairs. At four on a Saturday afternoon the place was crowded and noisy, with two TV sets blaring at either end of the medium-sized hall, where shabbily dressed people sat drinking coffee, chatting, reading magazines, or just immobile and silent. There's a kitchen here, and a laundry and showers for delousing; volunteers run discussion groups on poetry, art, the Bible, and play-reading sessions.

Upstairs, near the laundry, is a depository for old clothes. Here there was plenty of activity, as men and women rummaged through bins of dowdy knitwear and slithered hangers along the rails in search of a jacket or dress that might fit. Betty was talking to herself nonstop as she selected clothes which, if they met with her approval, she tied round her head. Martha, an old woman sturdy as a Bulgarian peasant, hovered near the mirror trying on cardigans. Her stoutness was partly explained by her habit of wearing layer upon layer of these old clothes, some of which she would take away and sell. A volunteer told me she knew what Martha was up to but she turned a blind eye: 'It's not for me to moralize, and how else is Martha going to make ends meet? She's unemployable.' The activity was observed languidly by a beautiful Hispanic woman lolling on a sofa; she was aloof, self-conscious, silent. She looked perfectly capable of surviving outside a shelter, but I learnt that she, like so many others there, kept tripping over the wires of mental disorder and breakdown.

Mr Quinn approached, a small, dapper, and very precise Bostonian who still spoke with a west of Ireland lilt. His grey hair was closely cropped, he could have been a priest or a scoutmaster, but what gave him away was the extraordinary combination of ill-matched clothes he'd studiously chosen to wear. He had a courtesy that was oppressive, calling me sir all the time, profuse with his thanks while mindful of his dignity. A volunteer had picked out a cardigan in his size and insisted he take it. Stepping up close and standing stock still, Mr Quinn began in his beautiful soft voice his litany of gratitude: 'My dear, that will be a great help. It will be very helpful to me. I must thank you very much. It will be a great help. You must let me thank you for your kindness to me. You too, sir, have done me a service — And do you happen to have a pair of mittens as well?'

When later that evening I was searching through 23 pockets for the one containing my house key, I was reminded of what a friend had told me as he explained why he'd left New York for pastoral New England. 'The trouble with New York was that it took up too much of my limited energies. I used to get up in the mornings, shower, check the weather, dress accordingly, make sure the windows by the fire escape were closed, lock up, wait for the elevator, check whether the mail had arrived, say hello to the doorman. By the time I actually hit the street, the day was over and it was time to go home again.'

His exaggeration cloaked a truth. Getting from apartment door to street can easily swallow up five minutes of the day and five minutes more on returning. I have calculated that if the average New Yorker makes three excursions each day, then 3.3% of his or her waking existence is spent getting in and out of an apartment. There are not many doors in New York with fewer than four locks. To add to the difficulty, American locks turn in the opposite way from European ones, and the reflexes of a lifetime have to be reversed. A friend in the Village has a huge iron bar soldered into the floor of her living room; its top end slots into a groove on the inside of her front door, and she assures me it's impossible, without the aid of a tactical nuclear weapon, for anyone on the outside to force an entrance. My own door was equipped with an ingenious little number, a lockable chain welded to the door frame; it could also be locked from the outside. To do so, two fingers had to be inserted between door and frame and the what's-it at the end of the chain inserted into the bit on — in other words, unless you have fingers the width of knitting needles, you can't get the damn thing to work. What used to trouble me was that, while I was absorbed in struggling with keys and tugging and pulling at a recalcitrant door, an enterprising axe-murderer could creep up behind me and cut me down to size.

Having locked up, your troubles are just beginning. You walk down the lonely corridor to the lift and press the button. Eventually the lift arrives and you step inside, but not before checking the discreet mirror in the far corner, which will reveal whether Charles Manson is lurking in a corner where he wouldn't be immediately visible. Then it's down to the lobby, and time to greet the doorman. This takes skill, since a large building may have four or more doormen on shifts, and you must master their names and their accents.

Doormen are not all old widowers enjoying a cushy job. They tend to be, in my experience, men of letters. Mine was a Romanian writer who published his own books, which told me more than I wanted to know about his sexual fantasies. The writer James Atlas told me his doorman is a literature graduate who, every time James reviews a book or writes an article, feels compelled to discuss it with him; while another doorman in his building is a doctor from Puerto Rico who exchanges diagnoses with James's wife Anna, also a doctor.

It was James, too, who urged me to extend my experience of New York's mores. Singles, he informed me over dinner at the Museum Cafe on Columbus Avenue, were supposed to frequent singles bars, and he was astonished that I hadn't yet made a tour of them. He expatiated on these alluring establishments that he, as a married man, had heard about but never experienced. After dinner he pointed me in the direction of Ruelle's a few blocks down the Avenue and off I went.

Ruelle's was a stylish place. Its small restaurant upstairs had a balcony from which diners could look down enviously as adoring women in teams flung their satiny bodies at men like me. Unlike many American bars, which have all the charm of dungeons, Ruelle's is brightly lit. Immense windows provide frames for spotlit hanging plants. Most of the women round the bar seemed to be in pairs, but on the far side sat a gloomy young woman who appeared to be on her own, and she glanced at me once or twice in a desultory way. I picked up my courage and my glass and strolled over. On closer inspection I changed my mind. The appraisal was clearly reciprocated. I returned to my seat. In sheer boredom I turned to the man sitting next to me and attempted to converse. He wasn't interested. He did manage to tell me he'd majored in management techniques, at which point I decided I wasn't interested either.

I fared no better some weeks later at Rascals on First Avenue. This is real singles territory, and lone wolves scour this stretch of the East Side for prey. A few blocks south are the richer pastures around Sutton Place which are populated, according to a friend, 'by women with very short haircuts and very slim bodies, being dragged along by huge dogs, and by tall svelte men in expensive coats being dragged along by packs of small terriers'. Rascals was less elegant than Ruelle's, darker and noisier. Opposite the crowded bar, a band with a gutsy-voiced female lead belted out old Stones and Motown numbers. I bought a drink and stood about feeling foolish, then left. On the way home I stopped in at Peter McManus's, an old neighbourhood bar on Seventh Avenue at 19th Street, a scruffy corner of Chelsea. Ah, this was better, no sexual searchings here, everyone far too pissed for that. At one end of the long bar, hunched men hypnotized a TV set showing a football game. The furnishings were plain and woody, and McManus's was far more publike than the classier uptown bars. As I nursed a bitterly cold 'beer' (as Americans call the pale tasteless liquid they serve in bars), I heard a man to my left celebrating the joys of love as he swung a heavy uncertain arm round the thick waist of an equally blotto woman who had already drifted far from the shores of youth.

'We are now incorporated,' he proclaimed. 'INC. We are definitely incorporated. That's 'cos we're INC, her and me.'

Happy man! I walked off down Seventh, passing as usual the St Vincent's Hospital skips. I tried to peer over the edge to ascertain exactly what it is that hospitals throw into them, but it was too high. So was I, and I headed for home.

When I got in I found a message on my recently acquired answering machine. The excitement of it: my first caller! On my recorded message I had referred eagerly to my 'brand new answering machine'. I switched it on. The voice was female, gentle and languid, not unlike Laurie Anderson's. 'Hello,' she began brightly but slowly. 'You have a brand new answering machine.' Pause. 'And I have a brand new wrong number.' She sighed. 'I'm sorry. Goodbye.'

NEWSBREAKERS

PREZ IN FLAP OVER BREZ RITES

That's what it said. As I threw a pile of newspapers onto the park bench which I proposed to occupy, the *Daily News* unfolded itself and revealed that headline. Swift perusal of the story unravelled its tightly told message: Reagan had decided not to attend Brezhnev's funeral.

The dignified *New York Times* in contrast employed verbs and syntax in its headlines, while the sensational *New York Post* probably neglected to cover the story at all, preferring to concentrate its journalistic powers on spot-lighting some gruesome attack on a crippled widow.

The magisterial *Times* prides itself on its motto 'All the news that's fit to print' and that's what's wrong with it. What's fit to print is often remote from the whole truth. The *News* was once a conservative working man's tabloid, but it's now engaged in a curious balancing act. It seeks to retain its traditional readership with its snappy headlines, such as NAB 2 ON L I CIG SCAM, and, when police rejected a new recruit who'd once posed for a centrefold, SHUTTERS AT HIRING OF NUDIE-PIX COP. But it was also trying to broaden its base by printing pomegranate recipes and concert reviews that were often more detailed than those that the *Times* ran.

Rupert Murdoch had taken over the liberal *Post,* then an afternoon paper, in 1976, and pushed it relentlessly downmarket. Circulation increased once Murdoch started issuing morning editions, but the new-style *Post* has lost many of the advertisers who'd regularly taken space in the earlier model. Anxious to retain leading accounts Rupert

48

Murdoch, it is said, gave a lunch party and made a direct appeal. The head of Bloomingdale's rose to his feet and said: 'Mr Murdoch, the trouble is that your readers are our shoplifters.'

At bus stops and subway stations there's a large ad which shows a colour close-up of a bleary-eyed man with grey sideburns. Thanks to poor colour printing, the whites of his eyes are piglet-pink, as if he's being flayed by a terrible hangover. A block of type moves down the left side of the poster:

He's charming
He's exciting
He's caustic
He's outrageous
He's informed
He's controversial
He's involved
He's emotional
He's New York

Who, I wondered, is this paragon of animals, so infinite in faculty? Norman Mailer? The Mayor? Read on:

He's Tom Snyder
He's on Eyewitness News. Tonight at 11 pm.

Of course! I should have known! A man who reads the news. Americans seem to have a trust that's total in the men and women who make fortunes by reading telecues. It used to be said that if Walter Cronkite ran for President, he'd win hands down; and that seems entirely possible. A few years ago, an ad on a New York TV station showed a pleasant-looking man taking a walk through Central Park, looking about him, pausing to pat small children on the head, and in general radiating benevolence. The voice-over extolled his humanity, his care, his concern. Ah, I thought, an ad to boost the fortunes of a would-be Senator or Mayor. Not a bit of it: another damn newsreader being hyped by his station.

The ads these days emphasize the team as much as the individual. So arduous is the effort of reading a few lines of script that it takes a team of three or four to accomplish the feat. One poster shows the entire Channel 4 news-team, about eight in all, stepping out of a subway car, with the cute caption: '*The* New York Local.' Beneath the ad someone had scrawled: 'We don't really ride the subway but the ad director thought this would be a good place to pose.'

Of course these nonentities — Channel 2 ads call them 'news-breakers' — have to be transformed into personalities because the three principal networks are locked in battle for high ratings and hence high advertising revenues. TV news is big business in New York. Each network runs solid news programmes between five and seven, and these are followed by 30 minutes of national and international news from the nationwide networks. In addition they run midday and late night local news reports. Soon the time spent covering and relaying 'news' will be greater than the time-span in which that 'news' has occurred.

One afternoon I visited the Channel 2 newsroom because I wanted to see what Michele Marsh really looks like. She's another newsreader whose features fill an entire poster: with her dark sultry complexion and black hair and eyes of rare liquid beauty, her image must fuel the erotic fantasies of half the male population of New York. When I saw her on the news one night, however, I didn't recognize her. Animation broke the sensual image into fragments of ordinariness. Here was a mystery I could only resolve by personal confrontation.

She was off sick.

Stubbing out my disappointment, I wandered about the newsroom, which looked exactly like the newsrooms made familiar through watching American sit-coms. Channel 2 has two separate though related news programmes every afternoon, one from five to six, and one from six to seven. Even with thirteen minutes of ads per hour, it was clear that the producers had difficulty filling the hours with anything that could remotely be called news, so they provide 'service features' to pass the time. Segments were either prerecorded or shot on location, or spoken into camera from the studio, and so there was little for me to observe in the newsroom itself.

Dutifully I peered into cubicles, read private memos, chatted to two flirtatious raven-haired receptionists with horseradish voices. I leaned against a wall to make some notes. A man in his shirtsleeves came by, a sheaf of papers under his arm.

'You checking up on us?'

'Sort of?'

'You a reporter?'

'In a way.'

'Who you with?'

I explained.

'Gee. Be sure to mention me. My name's Shelley, S-H-E-L-L-E-Y. That's an English name. Don't forget now.'

'I shan't.' OK, Shelley, this is it, this is your mention. The big time at last.

At five I wandered into the news director's office to watch the broadcast on his monitor. I'd imagined that my hours in the newsroom would give me some insight into the way the city sees itself. That it regards news about itself as of major importance was clear, but most of the stories were trifling in themselves: a barroom brawl, a Christmas party for old folks, a subway rescue, a murderer sentenced. The big political story was the attempt to avoid a subway fare increase, and that got full coverage and analysis. There were the nightly Princess Di story, a Santa Claus spot, and snippets about personalities: Nancy Reagan's minor surgery, the death of 'piano great' Arthur Rubinstein. Only the most vegetal viewer would actually want to sit through all two hours of local news, and most people watch one segment only. But it still seemed abundantly clear that there just wasn't enough information to be relayed to an expectant citizenry. Mini-features by greengrocers and car mechanics looked like the visual equivalent of landfill: they were time-fill. There were too many live reports about lost babies and animal rescues, broadcast at the expense of the more detailed analysis that some of the topical stories required.

The fabled newsreaders and anchormen and women struck me, on all three networks, as disappointing in various ways: some were clearly stupid, however lovely their cheekbones or their smile, others had all the appeal of a bloodhound, others had a glassy cheeriness that soon became vapid. Channel 7 had the most engaging team, but then their approach to the news was more frivolous. No bad thing; a lacing of irreverence is indispensable when the material is as immovably dull as most 'news' stories tend to be.

Far and away my favourite reporter was a self-parodying New Yorker called Myra Wolynski, who each afternoon had a mike thrust into her hand and was sent out into the streets to find anything of interest. One night, shortly before Christmas, she simply stood on Fifth Avenue and opened her mouth. Gleefully she described the chaos, the pavements clogged by street vendors, Salvation Army troops with collecting boxes, office workers, tourists, shoppers, and window-gazers.

'What you're seeing,' she drawled as the camera lingered on a sea of humanity congealed by sheer numbers, 'is not just slow mo, but no mo. The trouble really comes from all these out-of-town people' — a xenophobic snarl, winningly followed by a smile — 'cos they're just not familiar with the moving and manoeuvring mannerisms of us New Yorkers.' She paused dramatically, peered at the camera. 'Did you know that, with the exception of the Japanese, New Yorkers are the fastest walkers in the world?'

VILLAGE PEOPLE

As Myra herself might have observed, walk 80 yards in any direction in Manhattan, and you'll find a greengrocer. They are all alike. They've been taken over by Korean immigrants who, together with their families, work up to 20 hours a day in their shops most of which never close. Should I wake at four in the morning with a craving for papayas, I could satisfy it by walking 20 yards from the door of my building. Yet spoiled New Yorkers still lament that it's hard to find really fresh, farm-grown vegetables. To satisfy them, farmers' markets have been established at various open spaces throughout the city, and early on Saturday mornings battered old vans and trucks trundle in from the furthest reaches of Long Island and from upstate New York bearing fresh produce for urbanites who long for veggies that still have clumps of loam adhering to them.

Greenmarkets, they're called, and I went to the one at Union Square just north of 14th Street. My friends LuAnn and Elene, both admirable cooks, were going there one morning and wanted me to join them as a restraining influence. The market, which occupies two sides of this large square, was bustling, and I could see why. Not only were there plentiful supplies of apples, leeks, cabbages, home-baked cakes, honey, cider, and fresh fish from Montauk, but the prices were low. Shoppers were beside themselves with delight as they veered from stall to stall, comparing quality and prices. LuAnn bought enough leeks to coat all Fifth Avenue with vichyssoise. My enthusiasm for this friendly jostling market dwindled as my arms became laden with her purchases. To make the most of Green-market, it helps to be gullible. A pretty hand-lettered sign offered hand-made pretzels all the way from Lancaster County, Pennsylvania, good old Dutch country, full of cross-eyed Amish sisters driving around in buggies and refusing to send their children to school.

Then too there were the health food stands: all those dense loaves of wheat-infested breads, shapeless cookies with bits of unrecognizable goodness protruding from them like teeth, blocks of indigestible carrot cake. Beneath a sign on top of a van for Hawthorne Valley Farm, which baked bread and made cheese, were the stern words A Bio-Dynamic Farm. Thanks, but I'll take my food without magic.

While I was happily wandering about, dodging the roller skaters and the loony ladies mumbling to themselves, my charges had been stocking up with eggs and root vegetables. LuAnn thoughtfully suggested that we could do worse than go eat these fine examples of the farmer's art. So back we went to her Village flat, and I rested from my labours while LuAnn turned her attention to omelettes. How gratifying to see these two good friends, both with doctorates in comparative literature, hard at work in the kitchen while I offered culinary advice in between bottles of beer.

Later we walked through the Village to the Caffe Kabul, a basement dive on St Mark's Place. Even in a city that prides itself on yoking together unlikely constituents to produce a bizarre outcome that then, through its mere establishment, acquires a sense of inevitability, the Kabul must be unusual. The owner is an Afghan — man not hound — and is wedded to an Italian; the culinary consummation of this marriage is a cuisine mercifully unlike any other. I looked around me at the plates on which crouched chunks of lamb and yellow mounds called 'Afghan omelettes'. I ordered coffee. The waitress, pretty and blonde, smiled as we caught her attention, smiled as she took our order, smiled as she returned with three coffees.

'Do you think there's something, well, a bit strange —' began Elene.

'Yes.'

'She looks too happy, far happier than the circumstances warrant.'

'Definitely. Do you suppose —'

'Yes. After all, it's Afghanistan's primary export.'

54

The Kabul attracted the kind of clientele you would expect: talkative NYU students, tall women in jeans and heavy coats with those large knitted bags that seem to have too many handles, unshaven men wearing a single earring and smoking rapidly while making notes on yellow pads, young teachers getting together to discuss over a bowl of grains and sour cream how to construct a civics seminar that their students can relate to. On the bare brick walls hung coats and other items of peasant-wear, presumably for sale, but business was slow; many of the customers were already wrapped in sheepskins and padded jackets.

St Mark's Place is my least favourite street in the city; it's a street where the different strands of Village life are twisted into an awkward braid. It has cafés and bars for students and unemployed actors and writers. There are boutiques and bookshops, which look tawdry till you draw close and realise many of them are surprisingly expensive. Other shops cater to what New Yorkers think of as punk: bright plastic jewellery and thin leather ties in savage pinks and greens. One basement shop window is stacked with leather caps and jackets that could adorn either a sado-masochistic homosexual or your common-or-garden East Village thug. At one end of this short street is a gay bath-house, a blank façade with only a discreet plaque on the door to identify it. It was on this seedy street that W. H. Auden chose to live in 1953, and here he stayed for many years in a building that Trotsky once occupied. At any time of the day or night St Mark's Place spells Drugs. There are always a dozen or more people looped out on some weed or powder; they sit on the stoops or huddle in small groups on the corners. Some of them are young girls favouring a New Wave mode: black leather blousons, pink hair and silly eye make-up, striped jeans, spiky boots. They look cold, unhappy, and sixteen. A puffy-faced boy in a green flak jacket and an inane grin approached and said, over and over again, not just to us but to anyone within earshot, 'Got a cigarette? Got a cigarette?' Two minutes later he was back, same grin, new cry: 'Got a light? Got a light?' Two hours later, at dusk, he was still there, still at it.

At the eastern end of the block you cross Second Avenue, and here the atmosphere changes. There's a substantial Ukrainian community here, and a few doors down from the offices of the Ukrainian Liberation Front is the Ukrainian National Home, a club which, in its furthest recesses, houses a good restaurant, plain and dingy yet dignified, depressingly dim in its decor and its elderly clientele, who tuck into cheap pirogi and Pilsener beer. A few yards further south is the more convivial Kiev which serves Russian food 24 hours a day. The shops round here are Russian too: barbershops and shoe repair shops with Russian notices in the window, and two Ukrainian souvenir shops crammed with books, dolls, records, painted eggs, and religious objects.

I kept walking east along East 6th Street, which, within half a block, contains about twenty Indian restaurants, the cheapest in the city and extremely good. New York has taken to Indian cuisine with that connoisseurship and unflagging expectation of quality that keep the city's restaurateurs on their toes. Here flock devotees to gorge themselves for under 10 dollars on samosas and dhansaks and biryanis. On Saturday night queues snake onto the pavement outside the establishments with the highest current reputations.

The logic of the grid system would lead one to suppose that First Avenue is the easternmost of the Avenues. Not so. Here, below 14th Street, the island bulges eastwards and the city planners, presumably to avoid minus signs, switched from numerals to letters, and dubbed four more avenues A, B, C, and D. This neighbourhood, unapproachable by subway, an isolated tumour on the flank of Manhattan, is known as the East Village or Alphabet City. Call it what you will, it's one of the worst slums in the city. In its centre is Tomkins Square, 16 acres of blighted greenery between Avenues A and B. I'll walk just about anywhere in daylight, but I stayed out of Tomkins Square.

Not that it was deserted — far from it. There was a choice collection of drunks and bums and pushers, the wretched occupants of the half-abandoned tenement houses to the east of the square. This is the city's human dump, populated by addicts and cripples and derelicts. Almost every rubbish bin is attended by a toothless dotard in a coat of many dribbles, searching for scraps of food. Between Avenues B and C an indescribably filthy man was sitting between two rubbish bins, which he'd been rifling, and on his head, as if to encapsulate his life, was a black garbage bag. Moreover, the East Village is dangerous. A large proportion of its population cannot survive without a daily intake of hard drugs; crime is plentiful and crude.

As I walked down the dirty, tenement-lined streets, passing one or two undertakers, a few secondhand clothes shops, and a grocery, my anxiety nestled not in any fear of premeditated attack, but in the strong sensation that nobody's behaviour in this area was predictable. There were old droolbags, high on meths or some other tipple, just standing in the street or in a doorway shouting incoherently at the world. There were young men, amiable enough in gait and appearance from the distance, who as they approached could be seen to be wearing a fixed grin. They may have been retarded, they may have been high, they simply may have been happy, but I couldn't tell which and they made me nervous. Then too there were people of all ages who weren't walking in a straight line. They weren't overtly menacing, but I did fear that some electrical connection in what was left of their brains could short-circuit or play some other neuro-chemical trick which would snap the frayed wires that linked them to the world of rational, predictable behaviour.

Returning along 7th Street, I passed the large Ukrainian Catholic Church. On Sunday mornings the pavements here are crowded with head-scarved churchgoers coming and going. Now it was quiet, but McSorley's Old Ale House opposite was packed, even at four in the afternoon. A sign in the window reads: *We were here before you were born,* quite an understatement, since McSorley's was founded in 1854. Like a Heidelberg bierkeller, it doggedly maintains its antiquated character. For a dollar you buy a mug of decent ale, light or dark, and that's it. The bar, a simple room lined with framed photographs and foxed prints, hasn't altered in decades and doesn't propose to.

Avenue A on a pleasant afternoon is seedy but unthreatening, but I was keen to experience it at night. Thanks to Maria I was able to return late at night a few weeks later. For all her beauty and other sterling qualities, I feared that she might not be an ideal nocturnal companion, since she has the deplorable habit — it's her Southern upbringing —

57

of going to bed early and rising at dawn. But Maria insisted she was game, more than game, and one night we said goodbye to her cats and parrot and took a cab down to Avenue A, just south of 7th Street. There are a number of bars and clubs in the area, all attracting the same unsavoury clientele of skinheads and punks. With the help of our obliging and amused cab driver, we ended up at the right doorway, paid our five dollars, and entered.

The front room of the Pyramid Club was small and crowded, with a long bar up the right side. We pushed through the mob into the back room, which, since it was still early (about 11.30), was not too crowded. At the far end was a stage for musicians, and to the left and right were raised areas behind balustrades where one could sit and drink and watch the action — nothing happening right now — on the dance floor. Commandeering a free table, we sat down and ordered some beer. While waiting for the room to fill up, we talked of cats and life. By midnight the sound system was in full throttle: the New Wave music was good and loud, just the right side of deafening.

When the club had filled with slouching youths, white make-up smoothing over the pimples, a spotlight picked out on the stage our 'hostess' — her word — Ann, a bargain-basement Bette Midler. With great pride, or so she said, she wanted to introduce an act all the way from Germany that would be making its New York debut this very night. The name of this group — if two women can be said to form a group — was either Audrodeck or Autodreck; I favour the latter. The two artistes, Helga and Carmen, were built like Panzer tanks and wore short, clinging tunic dresses. Their act was either called Explosion or Explosition. Does it matter?

No it doesn't. For two people, even the size of Helga and Carmen, it was a big act, and they took up a lot of space — the stage and most of the dance floor. Because of the background music it wasn't always easy to hear the words, which were additionally muffled by their Teutonic accents, as thick as dumplings. The action consisted of strutting to and fro and shouting inaudibly. From time to time the two gals would collide and mime stabbing each other, accompanying each lunge of the imaginary knife with ghastly shriekings. Then more strutting. Out of the swamp of music and yells, we could pick out a few words and phrases: 'Zare is blood . . . vat terrible torchas . . . feel ze pain, feel ze pain . . . look in ze face of ze corpse . . . a great iron spike . . .' The two bruisers hurled themselves about the place enacting rituals of violence and torture.

But it wasn't over. An allegory was creeping up. Carmen, or was it Helga, dragged a kind of antiquated print-out machine onto the stage and sat astride it; as she cranked out the endless roll of paper, she sprayed it with green paint, while Helga, or was it Carmen, did a war dance as yard after yard of paint-spattered print-out whitened the floor. 'Last message!' they shrieked in unison. 'Last message!' Of course! the death of the word, end of communication, *und so weiter*. Then the two *blümlein* started tearing at the paper and pounding on the machine, till eventually the whole performance collapsed in an exhausted heap.

'Machine is dead?' whispered Maria.

'By George, she's got it. Well, that was a treat.' And we clapped and cheered as the two idiots left the stage. Then the disco music came back on and the mob that had been waiting in the front bar while art was taking place surged forward and took over the dance floor.

Some were dancing solo, especially one or two suave blacks; vaguely punk girls in very short black dresses were leaping about, and one curious creature in a long black coat was doing a number straight out of a Feiffer cartoon with great stretchings of his arms down to the floor, like Narcissus reaching for the water. Scrubbing-brush hair-dos in many colours were favoured, as were skinny ties and spiky heels. I looked at Maria and she looked at me, and moments later we were showing the rest of them what dancing's all about. She was wearing a striking metallic green dress, a relic of the fifties, flotsam from the attic of her ole Virginia homestead, and entirely appropriate for the occasion.

After an hour or so Ann the hostess returned to announce the live band for the evening, a dreary collection of inadequate musicians collectively called Excuse Me, Sir. We listened for a while, attempted to dance to their incoherent rhythms, but eventually gave up. 'Excuse *me*,' we said, found our coats, and left. The Avenue was still buzzing: on the opposite corner lurked a gang of about twenty-five people, their shaven heads gleaming under the streetlights; I could hear their distant chanting. They were either waiting to get into another club and singing racist songs to keep warm, or they were practising a war chant before strutting off to casserole some terrified local residents.

So taken was I by the Pyramid Club that I returned there some weeks later to watch the film classic, *Wrestling Women vs. Dr Assassin,* which was screened, for one night only, in the back room to a packed audience.

WAKE UP LITTLE SUSHI

For every miscreant arrested in the city, there's a lawyer to prosecute him and another to defend him. The pusher or thief or swindler gets a spell in jail and the lawyer gets a fee. That said, the rewards for criminal lawyers are spare change compared to the fortunes corporate lawyers can stash away in fees for enriching the rich. When in the early 1960s Richard Nixon became a Wall Street lawyer, a corporation wanted his advice on whether France would remain a safe country in which to invest. Nixon pondered and replied that as long as De Gaulle was alive, France would remain stable. For this analysis he received $25,000.* And that was 20 years ago.

Law diplomas not only open the door to wealth but to political success. A law practice is an almost indispensable passport to public life. Most politicians are, or have been, lawyers, perhaps because it's a profession one can slip in and out of with reasonable ease. It's always seemed to me that lawyers should be debarred from becoming legislators if only because there is a conflict of interest in having lawyers decide what ought to be legal or illegal. The eminently sensible no-fault insurance schemes became permissible some years ago over the fierce objections of many in the legal profession who feared that by simplifying insurance settlements, litigation, and hence legal fees, might be reduced.

Lawyers, too, make so much money that they can afford to take time off for political adventures. I am talking, of

* Lewis Chester, Godfrey Hodgson, & Bruce Page, *An American Melodrama* (NY: Viking, 1969), p. 238

course, of big-time city lawyers, not of amiable, slow-moving, cigar-chewing country lawyers who haven't opened a law journal since college and earn a modest living from conveyancing and wills.

Since Manhattan is the nerve centre of the world's business community, it follows that it's also the base of the American legal powerhouses. Of the 25 largest law firms in the country, 11 are in New York; in contrast, only two are based in Los Angeles, a city almost as large. The smallest of the 25 largest firms employs 235 lawyers; the largest has 622 on the payroll.

There's great competition to enter this elite. A top law firm, and there are no more than 35 or so nationwide, may recruit up to 20 new associates (the lowest rung on the ladder) each year. Unless you're attending one of the finest law schools, you won't even be interviewed, let alone admitted.

Sharon had made it — this far. An associate of a few years' experience in a top New York firm, she was well groomed and wore the smart black suit that is a uniform for professional women in the city. She was also pale — the sun is something she sees from her window but rarely feels on her flesh. Looking older than her years, she sat primly behind her desk, some documents arranged neatly in front of her. Like most lawyers, she is intensely orderly. For good reason too, since the pursuit of her career entails working long hours on complex applications of a system more intricate than the Summa Theologica, work that offers occasional tingles of intellectual satisfaction but for the most part consists of drudgery. Some lawyers who specialize in antitrust work have been tangled in the same case for years.

'Well, Sharon, the view's nice. But do you have enough work to keep you occupied?'

She smiled ruefully.

'Good. Let's move on from your work to your career, which is what this is all about. Thousands of young lawyers are drooling with envy because you're sitting here and they're not, but let's face it, you don't want to be an associate for ever. What's next? When will they make you a partner?'

'Mind if I close the door?'

'Not at all. I wouldn't want to stand in the way of indiscretion.'

She shut the door firmly, returned to her spot behind the desk, her black-clothed back screening the sunlight. 'This firm, which is more or less typical, has 250 lawyers. About 65 are partners, and they're the ones who share in the profits. Associates like me are salaried and we work the crazy hours. Partners can slow down a bit and the senior partners, four or five of them, don't do much *legal* work, but they bring in the major lucrative clients.'

'Sharon, I want to know when they're going to make *you* a partner.'

Her eyebrow rose like a soufflé. And dropped. This was no joking matter. 'Associates are eligible after eight years. But that doesn't guarantee you'll make it. There may not be a vacancy. Here all our partners are under 50, and there are unlikely to be any vacancies for years.'

Appointing new partners means that the pie of profit has to be divided into ever smaller slices, which is fine if the firm's profits keep climbing. To keep them soaring, though, you may have to hire more associates to do the work, and that in turn means higher overheads, and so the spiral circles in on itself.

Hence the elephantine dimensions of some big city firms. Sharon's firm of over 250 lawyers employs a back-up staff — messengers, secretaries, paralegals, word-processor operators — of 750. The firm burrows through the innards of a prestigious skyscraper. The overheads are colossal, but it's the client who pays.

'What happens if you don't get promoted?'

'You remain an associate. Some firms have invented a new layer, called permanent associate or junior partner.'

'Sounds like the kiss of death.'

'Can be. You get tenure but you also stay put.'

'Can't people leave to start their own firms if they're not making progress in a big firm?'

'A few do, but small firms tend to handle legal problems on a domestic scale. Here we work on tax, antitrust, real estate, business reorganization, that kind of thing, and we're trained to put together deals of enormous complexity. I know how to handle a major bankruptcy but I'd have trouble with a child custody case.'

'If there's no room in your own firm for you as a partner, can't you move to another firm?'

'It's hard. By the time you've been here for a few years you're making so much money that it becomes very costly for any other firm to hire you. You have to have something very special to offer to make it worthwhile for them.'

'What a dilemma.'

She laughed. 'Yes, they pay us a great deal, but we do work hard for it. I'm expected to bill about 50 hours a week. That's standard in New York. Not every hour I work can be billed, of course. There are vacations, and non-business meetings, such as this one.'

Good God, I thought, she's donating me time when she could be clocking up another $100 worth of billing. 'One department here billed *on average* 300 hours per month per lawyer.'

'That's an average of 75 hours a week!'

'That's right. There are lawyers in that department who are here every night till midnight. And the client pays. If I lunch in and order up a sandwich, it's billed to the client. If I'm here after eight, the client has to pay for my dinner and a taxi home.'

'What are your rates?'

'Associates bill at least $75 per hour. A partner, depending on ability and reputation, bills at between $200 and $300.'

'Well, I'm not coming here for my next divorce.'

Sharon gave me a mirthless smile. 'You can see why our clients tend to be big corporations. Not long ago we had a client in real estate, and we negotiated a flat fee of a million for his case. If you bear in mind that this one client cleared $18 million profit as a result of the deal we helped put together, our fees don't seem that outrageous.'

'And what do you get paid for your labours?'

'Starting salaries here are over $40,000.'

'So by now — in your mid to late twenties? — you're making considerably more than that?'

'Yes. I feel embarrassed when I see my monthly cheque.'

'Only you have to spend your weekends in the office, the pressure never lets up, and you have no social life.'

'Right.'

I left, bought a pretzel from a street vendor, and sat on a

bench in the sun for half an hour, munching away and reading the paper. A modest pleasure, but one that Sharon can't afford to indulge in.

'This one's tuna, that's smoked salmon of course, the one in the corner is sea clam, and the streaky one is fat red tuna — that's a real delicacy — you only get it at the best places like this. And we're in luck. Not only have we got salmon roe and herring roe but this one here is a real specialty — not even this place has it every day — it's sea urchin roe. You do like sushi, don't you?'

'No.'

My dislike for the stuff is regarded as an aberration in New York, where during daylight the chief topic of conversation is where to get the best sushi in town, and after dusk you discuss where to find the best Szechuan shrimp. My guest had recommended Kurumazushi on Madison, and I gallantly agreed to try it. A mistake: the wet blobs that bounced down my throat threatened to bounce right back up again. I anaesthetized myself with sake, and later took a walk down Lexington, staring with longing into the windows of pizza parlours. Later, after equilibrium had been restored, I cooled the spirit in that most sumptuous of museums, the Frick on Fifth Avenue. Formerly a private house, the Frick is small enough to fend off aesthetic indigestion, and when one is eventually sated by so unrelieved a diet of beauty, there's a peaceful courtyard in the centre of the building where one can sit quietly and listen to the splashing of the fountain before returning to the surge of the New York streets.

I left the Frick at four, allowing plenty of time for the thirty-block walk to the Algonquin, where I was to meet the Literary Editor for a drink. I'd known her 10 years ago when we'd been working for rival magazines, so I shouldn't have been surprised that, when I phoned her up a decade later, she had no idea who I was. To my suggestion that we meet for a drink she responded with the eager words: 'I suppose so,' and we agreed to meet at the Algonquin. Where else?

It's not hard to see why the Algonquin remains one of the favourite bars of the New York literary set. You don't have to sit impaled on bar stools or huddled in dark booths; the lounge of the Algonquin is a museum of stuffed chairs and sofas, small tables with decorous lamps; columns and large plants and screens add Victorian clutter. It's Bournemouth come to Manhattan. It's comfortable, reasonably private, and small enough so that without too much neck strain you can see just about everybody else in the bar. The Algonquin is supposed to be packed with celebrities, but apart from myself I've never spotted a soul.

I once spent 10 days there before trading in my tiny room for a vast suite at the same price at the Royalton across the road, and so I knew from experience that a table and two chairs are hard to secure in the bar.

Although I was meeting my guest at 5.30, I turned up shortly before five. There were indeed some empty tables at this hour, but they all had RESERVED signs on them. Luckily I found one that didn't — it had just been vacated — and sat down. The maitre d' promptly rushed over and shooed me out, explaining that it was also reserved, I would have to wait, and as a nonresident I would have to wait longer than most. After 10 minutes I outflanked him by spotting another freshly vacated table, with an excellent view of the entrance, which was necessary since I wasn't sure the Literary Editor would recognize me unless I spotted her first. The maitre d' looked exasperated when I laid claim to the table, but I successfully gave the impression that it would be more trouble to evict me than to let me stay. I ordered a bourbon and watched with satisfaction the lengthening queue of anxious literati in search of a table.

The appeal of the Algonquin, apart from its long-faded reputation as the home of the Round Table and its musty charm, is the sheer difficulty of getting in. The 'reservation' business is nonsense: the maitre d' simply slaps a RESERVED sign on *any* table that falls vacant so that he then has the power to dispose of it as he thinks fit. Perhaps those with infinite patience are ultimately rewarded with a table, but I am not among that number and prefer my own technique of mercurial aggression. Even more preferable is to avoid the place altogether and go round the corner to the Century Café or some other smart little bar where they don't regard your presence and custom as an affront.

The Literary Editor arrived on the dot, looking much as I remembered her. She was swaddled in expensive woollens that could have come off the walls of a weavers' collective.

What fun we had, she and I. I would ask her a question, and she would respond with short bursts of speech, orchestrated with odd whoops and scoops and rallentandi of sudden languor. ('If you're going to pick an affectation,' remarked a friend of mine, 'why that one?') When I offered an observation of my own, her eyes would glaze over or drift away. She was strong on deflation too, and when I mentioned that I had recently dined with another literary editor, she said, 'Oh, it must have been *thrilling* having a conversation with *her*.' I seemed to be boring her into a stupor, but that didn't stop her from pinging the bell that sits on every table to summon the waiter and ordering herself another drink.

By 6.50 I was getting nervous. In 10 minutes I was expecting what I can only call a Blind Date, and since I was going to be at the Algonquin I had suggested that she join me for a drink before dinner. I had assumed that the Literary Editor, who had accepted my offer with such reluctance, would have been long gone by seven, but not a bit of it. There she sat, happily sloshing the bourbon around the ice cubes. I explained the situation, but she paid no heed. She looked increasingly sour, as if I were somehow deserting her instead of whisking her off to Lutèce for three courses of *cuisine grosseur*.

At 7.05 the Blind Date arrived, cleverly identified me, and explained that she had a limo waiting outside. I began to panic. The Literary Editor was pointedly looking in the other direction, and I could scarcely rush off and leave her to pay the bill. I returned to the table and pinged away, while the Literary Editor looked ever more surly and the Blind Date stood about looking increasingly exasperated as she thought of her limo double-parked on 44th Street. I willed my guest to drink up. Eventually I managed to pay. I helped the Literary Editor climb into her tapestries, exchanged unconvincing assurances of how delightful it had been to meet again after all these years, and then she swept out. By this time my Date had dismissed her limo and instead joined me at my table. I basked in the envious glances of other drinkers admiring my ability to spend half the evening nursing a drink at the Algonquin while elegant women in relays streamed in to see me.

'Do you always travel by limo?'

'A lot of the time, yes. It's raining and I couldn't find a cab. So I spotted a couple of limos outside a hotel. The drivers have probably got to sit there for an hour or two until their passengers re-emerge, so one of them can make a few bucks on the side by taking me where I want to go. He'll be back in time to pick up his passenger at the hotel. Easy.

'And now where are you going to take me for a wonderful dinner?'

THE CORMORANT
BELLY

Walk down Greene or Wooster Street late at night, and it would not be immediately apparent that you are in one of the most fashionable districts of New York. Until 20 years ago, SoHo (an acronym for South of Houston Street) was a scruffy commercial district in the no man's land between Greenwich Village and the civic centre below Canal Street. Substantial old cast-iron buildings, floridly decorated with fire escapes and large windows, housed printers and small manufacturers. As New York began to decline as a manufacturing centre, much commercial space became vacant, and some artists and writers, no longer able to afford the increasingly chic Village, began to take over former light-industrial premises. For low rent, an artist could move into a floor of one of these substantial buildings and acquire at least 1,000 square feet, which could then be converted into a joint studio and living space. In those days it was pioneering: there were few shops down in SoHo and after office hours the streets would be dark and deserted. Buildings might lack decent plumbing and heat, and many residential conversions of these buildings into 'living lofts', as they're known, were technically illegal, though the city later changed the law to acknowledge what had become a *fait accompli.*

Nowadays Greene and Wooster are still dark, and it's possible to trip over a jagged kerb into a deep gutter or to stumble across the patched cobbles of the street itself. But look up and you will see dim lights in the broad windows and the symbol of the living loft: hanging plants.

On the cross streets, Grand and Prince and Spring, the gentrification is more obvious. Here, and also down busy

West Broadway, are the restaurants and art galleries and specialized food shops. If the character of SoHo has not been spoiled by the influx of wealth and fashion, it's largely thanks to the marvellous architecture: those grand, ornate, and seemingly indestructible cast-iron façades, all alike but hardly two the same, marching down the narrow streets. In New York as a whole display is discouraged, and the buildings still look like commercial premises. The display is internal. The bravura effect of stepping from a freight elevator into a room that may be 50 feet deep can be overwhelming. The problem of making these factory floors habitable by deploying partitions and paintings and floor levels is a challenge that their occupants, prosperous artists and professional people, are eager to rise to.

Nowadays an artist in search of a studio couldn't afford to live in SoHo, and will probably look further south in TriBeCa (Triangle Below Canal) or across the river in Brooklyn.

Thronged with visitors every weekend, SoHo's streets form a showcase for the upmarket avant-garde. One mighty six-storey structure on West Broadway has a different art gallery on each floor. I wondered what effect these huge galleries have on the production of artists and sculptors. So immense are some of these spaces that an etching would be scarcely visible, and no canvas smaller than eight feet square would be fitting. On Broome Street I wandered into an exhibition entitled *Women Who Have Mastectomies Go Public,* and stood in front of a pile of filled black garbage bags, which the artist had coercively entitled *Discarded Breasts.*

On Prince Street Back in Black is crammed with Art Deco-ish jewellery, and nearby Artwear sells imaginative craft jewellery. Other shop windows were filled with wooden frames that support immense Japanese woollens, clothes so sculptural and flamboyant it was hard to imagine anyone actually wearing them.

'You can try anything in SoHo,' said a friend who's well tuned in to the higher consumerism. 'If you've got a great idea, rent a storefront and try it out. Within two weeks everybody will know about it. You may fail, your idea may be terrible, but if you succeed, you can succeed mightily in SoHo. All you need is one Italian clothes designer who goes crazy over your stuff, or a quarter-page feature in *New York Magazine,* and you're off and running.'

SoHo, and also parts of TriBeCa, are dotted with some of the most stylish shops and restaurants in New York. Wings, for instance, is a large deep room decorated entirely in pink, a lustrous and very beautiful pink. A restaurant like that demands the aesthetic cooperation of its clientele: a blue suit would be a visual disaster, and even the chef must think carefully before devising a new sauce. Dean and DeLuca on Prince Street is an absurdly expensive food shop on the ground floor of a loft building. The quality is superb, and the prices preposterous, yet people drive in from the boroughs to shop there. In nearby trendy hi-tech Turpan & Sanders, you can buy a mop for $8 and a torch for $23. Members of the staff, like high priests of fashionable living, advise loft-dwellers on their conversions.

Even the bums over towards Sixth Avenue have style. 'Young man,' began one, flatteringly, as he approached me, 'I know you've heard it a hundred times before, but have you a dime that you can spare?' I smiled and he promptly capitalized on his success: 'Or any multiple thereof?'

If the character of the neighbourhood leans towards the grandiose and overarching, this is bitten into by an attendant preciosity. On Hudson Street in TriBeCa is a bijou food shop, with a single long counter that curiously features very little food. What morsels there were looked tempting: Moroccan olives, truffles flown in from Italy, an array of virgin olive oils, goose liver pâté, home-made salads. It's as if the owner of As You Like It, for that is the shop's name, has travelled the world and selected these few choice items for your exclusive pleasure. Further north on Bleeker Street is an even more exquisite shop, Bleeker on Perry, which is not a mere grocery but a shop that offers 'fine foods, service, and event coordination'.

Catering for the well-off but kitchen-shy is big business in Manhattan and the desire for novelty is intense. It won't do to have one's guests groan, 'Oh, no, not kumquats stuffed with macadamia nuts again!' If, however, you fancy that particular dish, Bleeker on Perry will supply you with a dozen, or with hearts of palm in a salmon roll. If their range is insufficient, then check *New York Magazine,* which regularly lists 'gourmet services', provided by A Sense of

Taste Inc., La Petite Soiree, Posh Nosh, Wine Tastings Unlimited, and, for the calorie-conscious, Thinderella.

No gustatory hybrid, however, is quite so bizarre as Miriam Mizakura's Shalom Japan in SoHo. Yes indeed, New York's first and only kosher Japanese restaurant! Miss Mizakura, 100 per cent Japanese, was born to parents who had converted to Judaism. Her menu features wonton kreplach and nippon borscht for starters, and as you ingest the Japanese-style gefilte fish, Miss Mizakura, who is also a chanteuse, will sing to you in 12 languages, all part of the invaluable service she offers to numberless Hasidim with a passion for sushi.

As Shalom Japan confirms, Jews, in many ways so tasteful, so refined, so sophisticated, so appreciative, do enjoy the most dreadful food.

Kosher salami should be towed out to sea sooner than eaten; most cold cuts make ideal roofing tiles. Israelis, I'm told, look on edible matter as a form of matériel, which is why their cuisine is acclaimed as defiantly awful. Even the generous spreads thrust at customers in New York's legendary delis don't do much for me, and I shall live content all my days if I never again taste a dill pickle, pastrami on rye, or rugalach. I suppose it's less to do with being of Jewish origin than of being of East European origin: Polish Jews like Polish food. Hungarian Jews, on the other hand, such as my reliable friend Julie, turn up their noses at knishes and kreplach and instead make a beeline for the Dobos torte. When she suggested that we expose ourselves to Sammy's Rumanian Jewish Restaurant, I resisted. But I never stood a chance.

Chrystie Street is parallel to the Bowery, to the very worst stretch of the Bowery. Nobody comes here at night except to forage in garbage, mug, peddle dope, consume dope, find a cut-rate prostitute, or cut someone's throat.

We got off the bus low on Second Avenue and started walking — fast.

'Do you think this is safe?' wondered Julie.

'I *know* it's not safe,' I replied. 'Just keep walking, and let's cross the street to avoid that vacant lot. I don't want to be jumped on by a squad of thirsty meths drinkers or the Scottish football team.'

Clattering along in high heels that reverberated on the empty pavement, she followed me across one block to the Bowery itself. For company, at the corner of the block, were three young ladies in skintight jeans and garish jackets to protect them from the cold. They were standing a few feet out from the kerb, watching for passing cars and trying to catch the eye and the desire of drivers. As we approached I could see their hard scarred faces, powdery white and buffed chocolate, their lips and their jaws set against the wind.

'I'll be right back,' I told Julie. 'I think I'll go and interview them.'

She grabbed my arm. 'You're staying right here. It's your job to protect me.'

On we went, past the alluring ladies of the street, who must be at the foot of the ladder of prostitution if their turf consists of traffic coming down the Bowery. Who, I wanted to ask them, is driving that way at seven on a Sunday night? And how much do you charge? And can clients get their money back if they're not satisfied?

Next came the rat scene. I made a promise not to put in the rat scene unless it truly occurred. Every page ever written about the Bowery, fact or more probably fiction, includes the statutory rat, scuttling malignantly across the pavement into a doorway or down a drain or into a decaying mattress festering in a gutter. I saw it, I truly did. Julie did more than see it: she went into a tailspin, shrieking and clutching and commenting: 'Yech!' It wasn't her imagination; there really was a plump little rat, scurrying happily across our path in search of its playfellows. Skillfully I steered her past the rat, and past the bums that almost seemed like street furniture. Drunks, though, didn't feel threatening: they were too blotto to do much harm, except for the odd wino with a kitchen knife under his coat and a passion for the colour red (Julie's hat).

At last in the distance we saw the signs that told us, beyond any doubt, that we were nearing our destination. Like harbour beacons, limousine tail-lights twittered redly behind the Cadillacs double-parked outside the restaurant. From New Jersey they'd come, to celebrate Manny's birthday, or Ruth's silver wedding, or the opening of yet another dry-cleaning store. 'My people,' I murmured, as we descended the steps that led into the restaurant. We had a reservation for seven and Julie did all in her power to get us our table, including running up to the owner, Stan Zimmerman, and flinging herself into a rapturous clinch, dislodging his cowboy hat as they threw their arms around each other.

'Soon,' he said, and that meant an hour.

Sammy's is a large room. Decor it has none, unless you count the Polaroid factory-full of colour snaps pinned to the walls, showing Manny and Ruth and Sherman and Louie and every cousin in the diaspora seated happily round a table laden with steaks and kreplach and pickles and rye bread. It was, it appeared, impossible to eat at Sammy's without leaving behind a fading replica of oneself with which to adorn the walls. There weren't diners at Sammy's; there were parties. Eight or 10 people squeezed round most tables, shouting and guffawing, not because they were drunk, but because they were having one hell of a good time. For wasn't a moist-eyed singer heaving over a mike at the far end of the room, unreeling yards of melody from *Fiddler on the Roof* while the band played on? Wasn't Stan just a few feet away, giving an encouraging slap to the bottom of a pretty waitress as she rushed towards their table with fresh supplies of chops or fried onions? Wasn't it wonderful to see Aunt Marta on her feet after all those weeks in the hospital, and enjoying herself again, God bless? Better she should beach like a whale at Sammy's than have to spend another day at Beth Israel, though the nurses were fabulous.

Enough! I'm hungry. Stan has found a table for four — that's about the smallest they do — and we're seated not far from the window, which is to say, as far as possible from the band, which is exuding the musical equivalent of chicken fat. Speaking of which, there's a glass pitcher on the table, and exterior as well as interior is drenched with chicken fat — the finest! The waitress, crisp as an ear of Iowa corn, smiles as she approaches with the menus, exchanges rapid courtesies with Julie — who excels at small talk and engineers many a social bridge across gorges of discomfiture — and flings down a basket of bread. Nobody has to tell me what to do. Ancestral instincts rush back. The viscous fat Niagaras onto the heavy bread, dousing it. I've eaten two thick slabs by the time our kreplach arrives, followed by wonderfully tender Rumanian tenderloin steak roofed with chopped garlic. I'd decided against the rib steak, which, the menu warned, weighed almost two pounds. Julie settled for the stuffed cabbage. Sammy's food is excellent because although it's Jewish, it isn't Kosher.

As we munched we listened to the entertainment. The maudlin singer had mercifully retired for a spell to refill his tear ducts and was replaced by a 'walk-on', a diner who in between mouthfuls of chopped liver comes up to join the band in a number or two. She was terrible. A black woman (diner? professional singer?) followed her and gave us her rendition of *Send in the Clowns,* which we were now hearing for the second time that night. She had flipped the switch called Emotion, and her singing was larded with pauses, husky special effects, and gulps. One or two insensitive diners attempted to continue their conversation, but were shushed by the reverential audience who, forks briefly laid to rest, recognized sincerity when they heard it.

Julie was still harvesting her cabbage when the restaurant began to thin out as sated diners rose to point their bellies and their limos in the direction of New Jersey. A bearded singer, who'd been yawping Yiddish songs earlier, came by and obsequiously asked if he could sit down. An artiste! At our table! Why of course. Under his arm he just happened to have a pile of records, all perpetuations of his art. He wasn't, he deferentially explained, trying to sell us his records, but merely wanted to know if we had enjoyed his singing (we had, we had, said Julie shamelessly). 'Then perhaps you'd be kind enough to mention me to your friends. That's all I ask of you two nice people. Well, I won't detain you. I hope you had a wonderful evening and that you'll come back soon.' I thought he was about to cry. I was about to puke.

'You can't go till you've had the egg cream,' declared Julie as I was calling for the bill. She caught the eye of Iowa, who returned with a carton of milk. They showed me how to create this New York delicacy. Into a tumbler I splashed some chocolate syrup (a bottle of the stuff had been glued to our table next to the pitcher of chicken fat), added milk and soda water. The waitress whisked this mixture with a spoon and bade me drink. One taste was enough.

'Fetch me my hat, fetch me my cane, call me a cab,' I moaned, clutching my throat, now lined with molten Hershey. Julie laughed so much I made her pay for the taxi.

LOVE THAT SPUTUM!

The tall trim man with peppery hair rose to his feet and strolled to the rostrum. Time had skied down Lew Rudin's long face, leaving deep furrows and a cleft in his chin, and he had the air of a dignified bloodhound. Before introducing the guest speaker, he wanted to let us know that an association for homeless people had contacted him.

'They've raised a quarter million dollars to buy a shelter, so if anyone here knows of a suitable building would they please get in touch with me afterwards.' One or two people scribbled a note, presumably to remind themselves when they got back to the office to check in case they had a spare building lying around.

Then Rudin introduced the speaker, and about forty of us pushed aside our croissants and tepid coffee and leaned back in our chairs to listen and doodle. The executive committee of the Association for a Better New York (ABNY) was at work. It was 8.30 in the morning and I sat there in my vintage suit pretending to be alert.

Lew Rudin and other men of property had founded ABNY in 1969 in response to the worsening image of the city. For years it had been portrayed as a criminals' paradise where hapless tourists were mugged in hotel corridors, where gushing fire hydrants failed to cool racial tensions in the hot months, where parks could only be enjoyed from afar, where filth and fumes filled the cavernous streets.

This spectacle, of the great city choking on its own lack of self-esteem while at the same time its politicians laid down a cellar of financial trouble, pained many prominent citizens. To Rudin and his friends, New York was eternally the Big Apple, and they asserted their pride in their bruised city by sporting on their lapels enamelled or jewelled Big Apples.

That's touching, but let's not be too sentimental. Lew Rudin and his brother own real estate worth $750 million, and their continuing prosperity is umbilically tied to the city's. By 1975, 30 million square feet of commercial space was unoccupied, and that was bad news for men like Rudin. His Association welded a coalition of different interests that met regularly to ponder the problems that affected them all. Union bosses, politicians, tycoons, administrators, lawyers, community leaders, would routinely gather over breakfast to hear a brief talk on some pressing issue and then discuss what, if anything, could be done about it.

'When ABNY was founded,' Rudin told me, 'the city was dispirited, business was fleeing. But we've been turning around the city's image, and slowly confidence, self-confidence, returned. There's a changed perception of the city, and that's why people, foreign business in particular, are once again investing heavily in New York.'

As I stepped into Rudin's offices on the 33rd floor of a Park Avenue tower, I could have been mistaken for thinking I was in the Mayor's suite. It was easy to see why Rudin has been called 'the unofficial Mayor of New York'. Framed photos showed the Rudin hand clasping the hand or shoulder of politicians by the dozen — Ford, Reagan, Kennedy, Bush — and of influential entertainers such as Bob Hope. In one photograph the very Jewish Rudin was intently pinning a Big Apple onto the lapel of a bewildered Anwar Sadat. A certificate proclaimed Rudin an honorary CBE ('for obtaining landing rights at Kennedy for Concorde,' he explained). In addition to founding ABNY, Rudin was not shy to inform me, he sponsors the New York Marathon and twice persuaded corporate taxpayers to prepay a share of their immense tax bills to help the city with its cash-flow problems.

'Remember,' said a friend of mine, 'when you're standing in Lew's office, he doesn't rent that place. He owns it. That building isn't mortgaged to a bank. It's his. Every fucking inch of it. It's odd, Lew doesn't seem too strong on smarts, but as very rich men go he's kindly and he's genuinely committed to helping the city.'

He was also keen to help me, and sent me a mantelpiece-full of invitations to ABNY breakfasts, which is why I was seated that morning in the sumptuous Drawing Room of the Villard Houses, the same mansion where Margot Wellington (alas, poor Margot) had held court at the Municipal Arts Society. The lovely mansion is now the Madison Avenue front of the Palace Hotel, erected by Harry Helmsley, a tycoon even richer than the Rudins (it'll take five billion to buy him out).

Before we all sat down to eat, I'd found myself in desultory conversation with a tall lizardly man so immaculately dressed that not a fibre in his light wool suit was out of line. I asked him who joined ABNY and why.

'Most of our members are people of means,' he drawled, looking over my head, which from his height wasn't hard. 'I guess we come here both to learn about the city's problems and to try to find solutions to them, and' — his eyed roamed the room — 'it's also a meeting place for prominent people in different walks of life.' Sniff.

As breakfast was served, I looked around me. There was Basil Patterson, a dapper black politician; and Harry Van Arsdale, a red-faced white-haired puff-chested rooster of a man (and former head of the New York AFL-CIO, roughly equivalent to the TUC); and bow-tied pipe-smoking Jack Bigel, a lawyer who is also the grand strategist for the municipal unions. I sat next to Fred Papert, the brave chairman of the 42nd Street Development Corporation which is reclaiming that famous street from seediness and the vice industry.

Papert's corporation presented an illuminating contrast with Rudin's. His is nonprofit and sinks all its earnings into new projects. 'That means we can't pay our phone bill right now. We're always getting bogged down in the city bureaucracy and some of our projects grind to a halt.'

He grew reflective. 'It's awful being a landlord. You can't be a landlord unless you're a shit. The Corporation has property worth 10 or more million — but it's all rented on long leases to theatres at low rents. So we make nothing. You know, sometimes it's so tempting to throw the turds out and really make some money. We could do what other landlords do, cream the zoning laws, just add on extra floors to buildings and hope no one notices. I used to believe that landlords were shits and tenants were wonderful maligned people. Now, show me a tenant and I'll show you a river you can shove him into.' He laughed, rather miserably. Misanthropy clearly went against the grain.

A few seats down from us was a charming Abe Beame doll, beautifully crafted. Beame is the diminutive mayor who presided over the collapse of the city in 1975. With his accountant's mentality, Beame had always seemed an unimaginative and humourless little man, completely out of his depth. Since he is only three foot six in his socks, it must have been easy for him to sink beneath the waves of disaster. *Autour de moi, le déluge.* Clearly the real Abe Beame, who is alive and well, is too ashamed to appear in public any more, but I thought it fitting that ABNY should commemorate his reign by placing this grim warning at its breakfast table.

The speaker that morning was David Axelrod, the New York State health commissioner. He asked us to consider how to finance improvements to the system. Much of the state's plant is clapped out, he told us, but renovation costs would run to $300,000 per bed. That's some bed. Part of the difficulty was that the competitive spirit between different medical institutions obstructed a more rational spirit of cooperation. To clinch his case Dr Axelrod quoted from Tennyson's *Idylls of the King.* Nobody flinched.

Questions and statements from the floor followed. One speaker pointed out that maintaining standards of hospitals and treatment was essential, otherwise New York would lose its reputation as a 'medical mecca', a status that pulled in out-of-town folks, mostly private patients with money to burn. In other words, good medicine benefits the local economy.

Medicine is money. Most hospitals, being private institutions, can't afford to take a loss: an empty bed means a financial hole. In a sane world, more and more hospital beds would be regarded as a *failure* of a health care system; but in America a bed financed must turn into a bed occupied. Hospitalization is encouraged since institutions stay in business by keeping bodies in beds, pumping them with costly drugs and wheeling them in to face the knife of a very expensive surgeon.

One brave soul at the breakfast did make this point. 'People are occupying beds they don't need, mostly because the system needs their money. The problem,' he declared, 'is not so much financial as systemic.'

Someone lamented the falling number of GPs in the city. Jack Bigel worried aloud about the rise in hospital insurance premiums. To my astonishment the tiny Abe Beame doll moved its jaw and well-formed platitudes issued forth. As it spoke the head swivelled to face Dr Axelrod, and on finishing it nodded and resumed its former position. Cute, but technically less versatile than Kermit. Next Van Arsdale jumped to his feet like a boxer on the count of nine, and gave a stirring irrelevant speech about the decline in the quality of life and the need for jobs. Who could disagree?

And the outcome? Rudin suggested setting up an 'ongoing dialogue' on health issues in the form of an ABNY subcommittee.

So much for theory. A few weeks later I was standing in a chest ward at Bellevue Hospital, accompanying the doctors on their round of patients in various states of wheezes and hacks. Bellevue is a famous hospital, the first municipal institution of its kind in America. Its fame derives largely from its psychiatric wing, which has become part of the city's mythology; commitment to Bellevue is a much-loved threat to elderly relatives who won't retreat quietly to old people's homes. Bellevue's emergency room is equally famous. Should a limb be parted from your body, take it along to Bellevue and at least they'll have a shot at stitching it back on.

Bella Rapaport, a Bellevue administrator with an energetic manner and one of those New York voices you can substitute for rocket fuel, explained the Bellevue way. 'We charge a per diem rate of $350. That includes everything. Go up to University Hospital or any of the other voluntary — that's to say private — hospitals, and you'll pay the same per diem, but on top of that you'll pay extra for medication, doctors' fees, X-rays, operating room. Two weeks in a voluntary hospital for major surgery's gonna cost you at least 30,000. At Bellevue two weeks will cost five. Trouble is, we can't always collect. The voluntaries get it back from the insurance companies, but about 30 per cent of our billings are uncollectable, and the city makes up the difference. There are about 15 municipal hospitals in the city, and we share our revenues. Sounds fine, but that means our efficiency isn't rewarded. The system isn't well run. They ought to fire all the jerks round here and hire some people whose neurons connect. I shouldn't be saying this, but I don't have much time for the unions either. They complicate procedures and decrease efficiency. We have another problem too. As medical technology improves we have to keep up with it, and that can be very expensive. At the voluntary hospitals they just pass the costs on to the patients. We can't do that. We have to provide a service to the city, and we have to keep up our standards.

'Let's say you're in an accident, God forbid, or are really sick. They take you to a voluntary hospital. The first thing that happens is that you or whoever brings you in fills out forms at the registration desk, and if you don't have the right insurance or can't put 50 bucks on the table, you know what they say?'

'?'

'Go to Bellevue! They know we never turn anyone away. We don't ask questions. We get illegal aliens in here, and we know they shouldn't be here, but we treat them anyway. People know this is a great hospital. If the cops have been shot up, or a UN diplomat gets sick, they all come to Bellevue. They brought John Lennon here after he was shot. If you have a complex medical problem that needs urgent attention, then Bellevue is the best hospital in the world. If you have a stomach ache and need a little stroking and TLC, go to a small hospital in the suburbs. Don't come here. But for anything major, this is the best.'

In the ward I was visiting, we talked to a Hispanic woman with pneumonia. She lived in a hotel room with three small kids and no husband. She expressed anxiety not about her health but about her children. Dr Vincent, with whom I was doing the rounds that morning, spoke enough Spanish to get by, but sometimes communication could be a problem.

'We have one Chinese lady with TB,' said Dr Vincent, 'and she speaks no English. One day we got an interpreter in, but it turned out that he spoke a different dialect. So now when we go in to see her we just smile a lot.' We did just that.

'What do you do with TB cases? You can't keep them here for nine months, can you?'

'No, we treat them with drugs for two weeks, then we send them home. The problem is that many of them are alcoholics or unreliable in some other way, and can't be depended on to follow instructions, so we daren't send them away.'

The other beds in the ward were occupied by a TB patient so deaf we had to communicate with scribbled notes, and a prisoner still with two years to serve. There were cuffs on his feet, and sometimes, Dr Vincent told me, he was chained to his bed. A guard sat outside thumbing a paperback, though the prisoner didn't look as if he could make it to the door unaided, let alone out of the hospital.

In the corridor a Groucho-like figure was approaching, like Doctor Hackenbush in his white coat. Dr Vincent introduced us, and I held out my hand. Dr Epstein, however, had his files in one hand and a tray with specimen slides in the other, and couldn't reciprocate.

'Hi,' he said brightly. 'How are you?' Then he thrust the tray in my face. 'Want some TB?' I recoiled. 'I'm so happy. I was able to make the diagnosis immediately from this sputum. Definitely TB. Oh love that sputum! Eat it up!'

The three of us stopped in at the nurses' station. Dr Vincent explained that the nursing ratios were low and that Bellevue is under-equipped and understaffed as a result of spending cuts. A doctor came past wheeling a stretcher patient.

'See that?' she snorted. 'That's not unusual here. You spend $40,000 putting yourself through medical school, and then you spend a good part of the day wheeling stretchers and fetching blood samples. It's crazy, a bad use of skills.'

In came a nurse. Dr Vincent smiled at her, turned to me. 'Rose is someone you must meet. She's been a senior nurse here for 30 years. She's one of the best anywhere.'

'Why have you stayed so long?' I asked Rose, a strong, slightly bedraggled woman who could clearly turn a patient and prop up the pillows with a single flick of the wrist.

She shrugged modestly. 'Guess it's the dedication.'

'Arr, come *on,*' groaned Epstein. 'Don't give us that, Rose. It's the money, isn't it? Admit it.'

'Money's not so good,' growled Rose, 'never has been.'

Epstein put an arm round her shoulder. 'I know what it is. It's guys like me that keep you here.'

The doctors took me down to the prison ward in the old wing of the hospital; rooms open off a high grubby pink corridor, heavy grilles against inaccessible windows. The doctors were on their way to tap a couple of criminal chests, but weren't sure how to get me past the security.

'We can say he's with us,' said Dr Vincent.

'That won't do. Our word isn't enough. I know — let's say he's a British doctor doing the rounds with us.'

Dr Vincent looked me up and down. 'Mmm. Could be. Looks the part in that suit. We'll give it a try.'

'Here,' said Epstein, thrusting his stethoscope round my neck. 'On second thoughts, stick it in your pocket with the ear pieces dangling out — then you'll really look like a doctor.'

The guards were still suspicious, and only some skilful talking from the doctors, affecting loose acquaintance with correct procedures, and some plummy vowels from me persuaded them that it was all right to let me in. I was glad the prisoners were ill: many of them were massive men with glowering faces; they looked at me as if they were Samson and I was a pillar. The doctors greeted their patient, Mr Clay, who had dozed off over *Sports Illustrated*. They exchanged a few words, then moved on.

'You didn't examine him?'

'No, there's nothing wrong with him.'

'So why's he here?'

'He's a material witness in a big case. The police didn't want to keep him guarded in a hotel, so a few weeks ago they simply got a court order and threw him into Bellevue. You see, we're the ultimate dumping ground. He's safe here, he's no trouble to the Police Department, and the city will pay the $300 a day it costs to keep him here.' She shook her head. A male nurse who was walking through with us commented: 'Don't think we indulge the patients down here, though. We know Clay's got to stay, but we keep a careful eye on the rest of 'em. Remember the old medical saying: if you're breathing, you're malingering.'

Dr Vincent took me along to the emergency room. There are four sections: a walk-in clinic for minor ailments, a pediatric emergency room, the Adult Emergency Service (for drug overdoses, fits and seizures, gashes and bruises), and the actual emergency room, equipped with nine beds

(including intensive care units) and a trauma unit. Dr
Vincent put her head around the door of the unit and waved
me in. Standing there were four beautiful nurses straight out
of a hospital movie.

'The only thing these nurses deal with is very severe
injury. Their job isn't to operate or heal. Their sole function
is to keep you alive until they can get you to the operating
table. We're all terrified of these nurses' — they smiled
sweetly, dangerously. 'They're fantastic, but put one foot
wrong and they'll eat you alive.'

The walk-in clinic was full of mostly black and Hispanic
women and a sprinkling of men; they use the clinic, even
though it's in the emergency area, as though they were
visiting a GP. Bella Rapaport explained: 'Visit a doctor in
the city and you get charged $75 the moment you walk in the
door. Poor people can't afford that. So they come to our
walk-in clinic instead. We charge a minimum of $8 and it
goes up according to your ability to pay.'

Dr Vincent had to return to her patients, so she left me
under the wing of a doctor in the AES. I hung about, trying
to be unobtrusive. The receiving area is surprisingly
cramped and there was a constant bustle of doctors and
nurses and straying relatives. It was a quiet afternoon.
Bellevue is at its liveliest at about midnight on Christmas
Eve, but I had better things to do that night than count the
mangled bodies. One or two surly men were brought in
handcuffed and foot-cuffed, with cops in attendance. A
pretty Hispanic girl was interviewed by the doctor; she'd
been vomiting and fainting at work.

'Are you pregnant?'

'No.'

'How do you know?'

'I don't fool around.'

Embarrassed, the doctor murmured: 'I'm sorry, I've
embarrassed you.'

'That's OK.'

In the receiving area two doctors were arguing about a
case. The more senior of the two advised against doing a test
the younger doctor wanted to conduct. 'In my view, it's
inappropriate. It's going to use up 45 minutes in emergency
when there are dozens of people waiting outside for
attention.' The other doctor gave way. The senior doctor

was Italian, but I only knew that by reading his tag. His mannerisms, his speech patterns, even his dark moustachioed features, were Jewish, and it struck me how in New York the population unwittingly leans towards Jewishness as a kind of cultural norm. 'I assume,' confirmed a friend, 'that everyone in New York, if they're more or less white and not Oriental, is Jewish until proved otherwise. One could argue that Jews sort of look Italian, but nobody in New York would ever make that assertion. So you're right in mistaking Italians for Jews. Anyway,' and he gave a very Jewish shrug, 'what's wrong with that? This is a Jewish city. A man I know told me he was going to a Gentile dentist. I laughed. It's ostentatious, it sounds good, but let's face it, it really isn't practical.'

My reveries were interrupted by a nurse sourly demanding to know who I was and what I was doing lurking in the emergency room. I told her. The little runt then reported me to a head prefect, who sent for me. I mentioned that I had spent the day with doctors who had taken me into the emergency room and left me in the care of another doctor there. He was now examining a patient, which was why I was quietly standing about unattended.

'Those doctors,' fumed the prefect, 'are out of line!' Who were they, he wanted to know. I refused to tell him. He ranted on: I was supposed to have proper authorization before visiting the hospital, and so on and so forth. If I wanted to stay I would have to go along to the PR office for clearance and —

'PR!' I adopted my stunned-with-disbelief pose. 'You're the worst thing that's happened to public relations since herpes. Goodbye.'

BLOOD AT THE OPERA

Seen from Columbus Avenue or Broadway, the Metropolitan Opera at night itself becomes a stage set. Separated from the street by a sizable plaza, the opera house is glass-fronted and the passerby looks onto bustling stairways and balconies and bars. To either side of these public areas are the two immense murals which Chagall executed for the Met. Neither the architecture nor, some would say, the colourful murals bear close examination, but on a fine evening it hardly seems to matter. The Met is projecting itself at the outside world, proclaiming its own glamour while keeping it at a safe remove from the Broadway hoi-polloi.

Excitement is coshed by disappointment the moment you walk in to the place. New Yorkers keep telling each other how beautiful the opera house is but, like the building itself, they're putting a brave front on it. It's ostentatious, fussy, tacky, the High Culture equivalent of a Las Vegas casino. The ushers who collect your tickets are decked out in full-length cloaks with red velvet collars, an absurd costume, breaking a cardinal rule: never mimic the audience. The spaces of the auditorium and the lobbies are grand enough, but the detail is as cheap as Hilton Ballroom Rococo: twirly light fittings, distracting wall textures, vulgar chandeliers that have to be raised before the curtain goes up otherwise they would obstruct the view from the galleries. During the intervals you can buy overpriced 'champagne' which is served in shallow plastic 'glasses'.

Indeed, the whole notion of opera and opera-going in New York is essentially vulgar. Singing of the most hectoring kind has always been welcome at the Met. New Yorkers prefer great voices to great singing. They applaud lavish productions rather than good ones. They value display, putting on a show, hitting high C. The stridency and musical insensitivity that characterize the Met at its worst seem to be exactly what the audience most adores. This is not to say that I haven't seen fine productions and heard marvellous performances at the Met, but they often seem to be achieved in spite of the values that prevail there. The badness is not so much a lapse in standards as a built-in consequence of putting value on those elements in opera that are most meretricious.

At least the audiences aren't constrained from expressing their opinion. Peter Hall, a very fine opera producer, came to the Met to mount a new production of Verdi's *Macbeth*. At the first night there was booing and laughter at his brave but misguided attempt to reproduce a 19th-century *mise en scène*; the next morning the *New York Times* declared that this was probably the worst new production to have been mounted at the Met in decades. It wasn't quite that bad, but it came close. The production had its supporters, though, and there was a rousing battle of noise between clappers and booers, one side trying to outdo the other, neither prepared to let the other have the last cheer or snarl. The audience successfully upstaged the performance.

This they failed to do during a performance of *Tannhäuser* a few weeks later. Soon after Maestro (as pretentious New Yorkers call their conductors) James Levine raised his baton, almost the entire audience, myself included, fell into a heavy doze. This reflects no discredit on Levine. It's just that we'd all had a heavy day and were in for a very long evening at the opera, and we simply needed a rest before the protracted musical exertions of the next few hours. A few of us woke briefly to hear Tatiana Troyanos' beautifully sung Venus, but that didn't keep us awake for too long, and we slumbered on for the rest of the act. In the interval, thoroughly refreshed, I wandered down from the Family Circle to the lower parts of the house. Why the gods are called the Family Circle I can't imagine. There were no more families up there than anywhere else. Perhaps Gallery or Upper Circle sound too distant. Americans always like to disguise the least attractive elements as something more acceptable. Family Circle is a neutral term; it doesn't immediately suggest the cheapest and worst seats. It's rather like the American egg. There is no such size as 'small'. On the other hand, the Met, unlike older British opera houses and theatres, does permit the rabble to mingle with the rich and powerful downstairs. The patrons and benefactors disappear into private bars, where they form a mutual admiration society instead of exposing themselves to the public view. I looked instead at the ordinary folks, such as a tall bearded operagoer with a Walkman headset and an elderly man in a Black Watch tartan suit. Tasteful. As were the wonderful groups of tiny old ladies with bleached pinkish blonde hair piled above their anxious lined faces, feminine counterparts to the much-loved Abe Beame doll. They appeared to be swopping bagel recipes. Up in the Family Circle the crowd was practising for Saratoga, since at least half the audience was bent under the weight of huge binoculars strapped round their necks.

At least the Met doesn't go in for the shameless sentimentality of the promotion department of the superlative New York City Ballet. At its home next door at the State Theatre, the lobby shop peddles NYCB jigsaw puzzles and cufflinks as well as more routine T-shirts. Inoffensive enough; but unfortunately the company's distinguished founder, Lincoln Kirstein, has had the preposterous idea of using the sobriquet New York Kitty Ballet, and a whole new line of goods and trinkets has been developed to match, thus appealing simultaneously to balletomanes and cat fanciers. I much preferred a series of witty lapel badges designed by Edward Gorey, portraying ballerinas in a succession of uncomfortable positions. Less tempting were sweaty pairs of ballet shoes, autographed by the dancers who had used them and worn them out. Eight dollars will buy you the tatty pink footwear of a principal, while a mere five bucks will secure the shoes of a promising lesser dancer.

Back at *Tannhäuser,* the next act was enlivened by a blue balloon that belonged to David Hockney's beautiful designs for *Parade*. It came floating across the stage just after *Dich teure Halle* and cheered us up no end. As the act came to a welcome conclusion I reached down under my seat to retrieve my programme and felt a fierce pain. I had jabbed the jagged corner of a light fixture. Withdrawing my hand, I noticed a scarlet streak gathering force as it flowed down my finger. Wrapping the finger in a handkerchief, I asked an attendant to direct me to the dispensary, which is backstage. As I swanned in a door marked No Admission, I was hauled out by a guard, who told me I couldn't go in there.

'I'm looking for the dispensary.'

'Why?'

'Because,' I said grimly, holding up the now bloody rag around my digit, 'my finger is a geyser of blood.'

'Why didn't you say so. Come with me.'

We found the doctor on duty. The dispensary was crowded with his friends who had stopped by for a chat.

'It's not serious,' I said apologetically, as he bathed the wound, which was in fact quite deep. 'I just don't want to get blood everywhere.'

'Oh, I'm used to blood.'

'It's not you I'm worried about. It's your beautiful auditorium.'

There was some mild amusement when no one could find a plaster (Am: Band-Aid), since the appropriate cabinet was locked and the key was missing. Eventually someone rooting about in a drawer found one and my finger was bound up.

'So I went through medical school for this?' murmured the doctor, echoing Dr Vincent. He told me he'd had an eventful day. Earlier, a 12-year-old member of the chorus had come in with a broken arm.

'Bad break?' someone asked.

'Oh yeh. Pretty serious.' Everyone sighed with relief.

Bellevue's walk-in clinic costs $8 minimum, so for a real bargain next time you need emergency medical care, try the Met dispensary: excellent service and not a penny to pay.

A few days later, my wound healed, I returned to the cultural trail. A famous poet was scheduled to give a reading at an Upper West Side bookshop and I was tempted to attend. Only tempted, since I am bad at being a captive audience. I decided to compromise by turning up towards the end, so I could savour the ambience, hear the poet declaim a final poem, perhaps greet an old friend or two, and then slip away relatively unscathed.

I took the uptown subway at 14th Street. I sat next to a

grizzled and dozy black man. I took out a book and read. Somewhere in the Sixties he turned to me, his eyes bloodshot, his jaw slack with weariness.

'Say, we goin' uptown?'

I nodded.

He shook his head ruefully. 'Oh no.'

'Where do you want to get to?'

'Far Rockaway.' In furthest Queens, about 50 stops in the opposite direction.

'Definitely going in the wrong direction.'

'Yeh, sure am.' And he laughed, chuckled to himself for a while, and went back to sleep.

By the time I arrived at the bookshop the reading was over. As I walked in I could see the poet standing in a corner chatting to his publisher. I moved into the shop, and it was at that moment that I spotted Sarah, tall and slim and with an intense smile directed shyly at the floor. As lovely as I remembered her — remarkably unchanged!

But I retreated. She was married now and a relationship that still yielded pleasant memories to me had doubtless been confined to the attic of her remembrance. Feeling oddly disconsolate, I walked off alone down Columbus Avenue. I walked and walked. The incident, trivial in itself, suddenly changed my perceptions of the city. A number of places I had come to think of as mere sights were restored as memories. A familiar corner became not just an intersection, but a spot where I had anxiously waited for her all those years ago. Places, bricks and mortar, rang with an emotional resonance they hadn't had before.

The next day I went on a pilgrimage, up to the places near Columbia University which we used to frequent. On the clifftop of Riverside Park bulges Grant's Tomb, a pompous structure modelled on the mausoleum at Halicarnassus. It's now embellished with graffiti, which, in this instance, usefully pull it down a peg or two. Surrounding this grandiose pile are sets of wonderfully garish mosaic benches, with backs that undulate crazily around three sides of the tomb. They're inspired by Gaudi's mosaics in the Parque Guell in Barcelona, but these have a distinct New York quality to them, since they depict the cars and animals and faces of the city. These benches are so different in style and mood from the tomb that they seem barely related to it; they commodiously lounge back from it, as if luxuriating in a knowledge that they reflect, brightly and crudely, the life of the city far more than the lugubrious Grecian sepulchre only a few yards away.

Nearby stands a small urn fenced in on the edge of the small cliff that sheers down to the parkway and the river. The inscription — the more touching for its restraint — reads: *Erected to the memory of an amiable child, St Claire Pollock,* who, in 1797, came to an untimely end when he fell over the edge. I wouldn't have known about the grave had not Sarah made it a frequent stopping point on our walks along the Hudson. Another resting place was the Riverside Church, a huge French Gothic-style edifice, with an immense tower that even dwarfs the bulky church below. Built in 1930 with Rockefeller money, it's a Baptist church, though the interior, dimly lit with deep red-and-blue imitation French glass, has a more liturgical feel to it than I associate with preachy Baptists. Riverside is inappropriately comfortable; were the light better, it would be ideal for curling up with a book on a winter's day when the wind whiplashes Riverside Drive. Beautiful in its way, it lacks austerity. Jesus, one suspects, might be turned away at the door if he weren't wearing a jacket and tie. A worshipper would come here for reassurance rather than self-examination, let alone self-improvement.

On the other hand, the Holy Ghost has surely descended on the extraordinary Cathedral of St John the Divine, about a quarter of a mile away on the escarpment that overlooks Morningside Park. Already 600 feet long and 320 feet wide at the transepts, it remains incomplete. The apse and choir and crossing were built at the turn of the century in a Byzantine style, but the nave and aisles and west front were built later, between the world wars, in a lush Gothic revival. Perhaps because of the immense scale of the building, the clash of styles doesn't jar; everything is absorbed into the mightiness of the space. St John's is a disquieting building in a way that Riverside is not: deep aisles hide shadow and darkness that resonate with mystery and emotion. St John's has a nave pyloned with immense, deeply moulded and ribbed piers that bear the great weight and sustain the space. In a side chapel is an awesome monument to some city firemen who were killed in an accident. Its rusty form grasps within it the charred timbers taken, one must assume, from the scene of the fatal fire. Riverside is magisterial but dull; St John's is mighty and moving, a monument to anachronistic ambition.

Absorbed by St John's, I forgot about Sarah. I took the subway back down to the Village, getting off at Sheridan Square. Emerging into this unsatisfactory apology for a park, I had another jolt, as I recalled a cool summer morning when, for some reason now entirely forgotten, she and I had sat there. Sheridan Square, scruffy little oasis that it is, was, like those other places in Riverside Park, dragged back from the past and reinstalled as a focus of unjustifiable but inescapable affection, reminding me that places in themselves may be beautiful to us, but that places shown and hence given to us through the mediation of someone we have loved, those places alone become precious.

GET KNOTTED

Snow had fallen and the city was transformed. The bumps and excrescences of the streets — cars, skips, trash-cans, dogs — had been evened out. The white blanket was the great unifier, obliterating all distinctions of colour and putting the brakes on the pace of the city. Traffic did move, but slowly, with headlights picking out the fat white flakes that continued to fall. The speed with which an East Coast blizzard can coat and incapacitate cities is extraordinary. Earlier in the evening, the sky had been threatening, and so had the weather forecasts, issuing 'travelers' advisories' and out-guessing each other with estimates of 'precipitation'. Now, a few hours later, a few thousand of us were spilling out from Lincoln Center, clomping in galoshes and holding our coats high against the collar to keep out the swirling flakes. Cabs were in short supply, and the few that were visible had steamed-up windows.

Yet there was much laughter in the air. Blizzards are an invitation to anarchy. When the city breaks down, and a blizzard inevitably shreds all the routines of getting about, it's a joy to see it with its guard down. The mechanisms of bustle and traffic are snagged. The webs of communication fray or snap as buses break down, stations are closed, and the airports shut down for two days. The inhabitants of the city gleefully take possession once again, stepping onto the quiet streets, walking unchallenged down the middle of a road that would normally be clotted with traffic. On the cross streets cars are stuck, and there's a whirring of tyres skating ineffectually over hard-packed snow that turns to ice as the rubber compresses it. Fluffy clouds of breath rise from the scarved heads of helpers trying to push a recalcitrant car away from the kerb. A gust of wind drives a few flakes onto the tongue as one opens one's mouth to speak or breathe, and a delicious freshness invades the moist caverns of mouth and throat. There's laughter too at the prospect of the disruption to come. Offices will close early or not open at all; the radio waves the next morning will be thick with lists of school closures.

After a good night at the opera, and exhilarated by the wonderful transformation of the city, I gathered up my courage and went to the 'baths'. This decision was not entirely spontaneous. I had never been to one of these legendary establishments and was curious to see what they were like — but such was my unease, even fear, that I had procrastinated, and it took the unshackling of the blizzard to make my resolve firm. The misnamed 'baths' are meeting places for homosexuals in search of instant sex, warrens of purposeful promiscuity — what better way to spend a civilized evening? For my part I was determined to indulge a curiosity of the most shamelessly voyeuristic kind.

I'd done my homework. *The Gay Source* listed the eight or so bath houses in New York. Some catered to the four-leaf clovers of the sexual garden, such as S&M baths, or were almost exclusively black. I wanted a cosy, unassuming, middle-of-the-road place, with no more than a token freak doing something unspeakable in a corner. I chose accordingly. The still functioning subway took me downtown and I walked a couple of blocks towards a dark canopy, flapping in the blizzard, on which the name of the establishment was clearly lettered. It could have been a restaurant entrance, though there was no menu outside and no stickers listing acceptable credit cards.

Dipping my chin into my coat, I pushed open the door and walked in. I took one look at the queue of loitering men in the poorly lit lobby and turned on my heel. An angel of prudence urged me to return to bed, with a bottle of wine, to watch the late-night movie, but the angel was knocked smartly off its perch by the cherub of unsavoury voyages, who told me to relax and step right in.

There were a dozen men ahead of me, all swathed in coats and parkas. Up-to-date homosexuals look like Real Men, and I felt out of place without a moustache and Western boots. Indeed, if anyone had been looking at me I'd have

94

been identified at once as an effete, smooth-shaven heterosexual. Most of the men were in their 20s, a few were older; we shuffled forwards in silence, as if all had to shelter our identities until we'd been formally admitted. A few men had come in couples and exchanged the odd word or laugh, but by and large the discomfort — or perhaps it was no more than boredom and impatience — seemed to be shared by all. Worse, we all looked seedy, as if we were queuing for a doss-house rather than a labyrinth of delight.

I was assailed by a new worry: they knew the ropes and I didn't. For instance, what was I to ask for when I reached the cashier's? I could have a locker, a single room, or a double. A double? Was that for a private orgy? That was out for a start. It also cost $20. $12 would secure a single room and a refuge if I needed one — but then if I needed a refuge that badly I could just as easily leave. The problem was solved for me: no rooms left, only lockers. It cost me $5 — a bargain! Up in Times Square, men were paying as much to see hardcore films, but here the same sum allowed me to slip through the screen and mingle with the actors. I handed over the money and was given a key and a towel, left a deposit and signed for it. Then in through the swing doors and up the stairs to the locker room.

I stuffed my opera-going clothes into the locker and inexpertly wrapped the white towel around my waist; it was as if I'd shed my personality and become just another naked man encircled by a towel. I felt more at ease in this undressed state, content with my bland condition as a body to be appraised, disdained, admired, ignored. Since, however, we take our sexual pleasures in different ways, an elaborate code of signals has evolved in the silent world of the baths to communicate sexual preferences. Since the only equipment at hand is a white towel, the code hinges on how you knot it.

My scholarly investigations informed me that, for instance, if you knot the towel behind you it signifies a preference for being fucked. Unfortunately, my books said nothing about how to knot the towel so as to show that one is a tourist, ignorant of the language of the country. I settled for a fetching three-quarter angle to suggest nothing in particular, or perhaps a sexual confusion so perplexing as to deter any aspirant for my favours. When I plunged into the

95

melee, I couldn't discern any code of knots in operation. Indeed a code seems superfluous — intentions and desires can be made clear in far more explicit ways, such as the grope simple or the grab direct.

There are no baths at the baths. The primary function of the establishment is to provide a place, free from harassment, where gay men can meet and fulfil any and all sexual urges, provided, of course, that they can find compliant partners. This is no brothel; no money changes hands after you've been admitted.

A few recreational facilities were provided for the blasé and the detumescent; the rest of the building was devoted to sex. There were nine floors. The first floor was the entrance, the second contained offices, the third the lockers; the next three floors housed the 'rooms' and a TV room and gym; the floor above consisted of a communal shower and sauna; up more stairs to the Truck Stop, and the top floor contained so-called Fantasy Rooms (even pricier than a double).

If 'baths' is a misnomer, so is 'rooms'. They were no more than cubicles, a double row of them encircled by a corridor, at least 30 on each floor. On the outer side of the corridor was blank wall — no windows anywhere, one was boxed in, secluded, secure — and the occasional uninviting lavatory and washroom. A cubicle was only large enough for a mattress and a chair. Most of the doors were closed, either because the tenant was busy elsewhere or because the room was occupied by a couple at work.

But some of the doors were open. In some cubicles the dim light exhibited a man languidly staring out into the corridor while he fondled his penis or otherwise displayed his best features to those who passed by. Some of these men looked battle-weary, but they must have been game for another bout, or else they'd have closed the door and taken a recuperative nap. In others men lay on their stomachs baring their buttocks. I was puzzled by the constant availability of the inmate of one cubicle. He was a lithe creature, with a mop of very dark hair and a shapely bottom — but his door was always open and it was clear no one wanted him. *Chacun à son gout,* of course, but he seemed a good deal more desirable, qua meat, than some of the other morsels that were more readily snapped up. Perhaps the cruisers knew something I didn't: piles or an unattractive disposition.

Although these sexual invitations are transparent enough, they are not of course entirely open. The prospective partner lingers on the threshhold and the two men look each other over and decide whether or not to commit unnatural acts. The succession of opening and closing doors implied considerable sexual athleticism, a determination to cram in as many sex acts as your body can take and muster. The silence in the air was punctuated with the grunts and cries of the compatible, but was also filled with the stillness of the undesired, hopelessly exhibiting their negligible charms to a parade of passers-by. In odd recesses stood couples of more exhibitionist inclination. One youth, with an ineffably bored expression, leaned against the wall gazing down onto the mobile head of another man who was energetically sucking him off. It spoke of a vast sexual indifference that was, if anything, more dispiriting than the meat market around the cubicles. Look on, stranger, I'm only making love.

The TV room resembled the corner of a small students' union. No sexual activity, just men lounging about on padded banquettes watching the large screen. It was a place for recuperation rather than trysts, and most of the men were decently clad in their towels. The gym too was no more than a gym, in which naked men did strenuous boring things with barbells and chest expanders. Gay men are 'into' their bodies — it wasn't hard to understand why — and great energies are expended in keeping them fit and trim. There was more exhilaration in the shower room, which was circular, allowing about 10 men to shower simultaneously. Here towels were jettisoned while bodies were displayed in a variety of dripping poses.

On to the Truck Stop! In the macho cult that seems increasingly synonymous with being gay in America, it's good to be fucked but it's better still to be fucked by a lumberjack or lorry driver. Hence the symbolism. There was indeed a large truck up there, but it was no more than a mock-up, a neatly realistic stage set, a butch emblem. The action took place in two rooms at either end. I walked into one of them and, even though the lights downstairs had been far from bright, it took me a minute or two to adjust to the darkness within. Gradually the contours of the room limned out of the gloom. It was furnished, like a youth hostel dorm, with bunk beds and a few single beds. The corridors and rooms had been carpeted in cheap red cord, but there was no carpeting in the Truck Stop. This is the factory floor of sex. All the beds were occupied, mostly by couples contorted in copulation. Standing between a row of bunks, I could touch, had I wished to do so, eight heated bodies. In the darkness it must be hard to discern who your partner is, and that, I dare say, is the point.

The Truck Stop is where you go for a group grope or an anonymous screw. Little danger that if, a week later, you run into your partner at a stockbrokers' lunch, you'll even recognize him. There wasn't room for everyone on the beds and other couples explored each other's orifices while standing in corners or idling in the spaces between the bunks. A few sweat-irrorated buttocks took in a succession of cocks in a passive passion of insatiability. Other men stood about and watched, forming circles round active sexual virtuosos. It's hard to remain sexually indifferent while a regiment of men is priapically interlocked all around you, and many onlookers were lazily masturbating as they gazed at the entertainment.

In a space near the entrance a group was observing a pair engaged in oral sex; further stimulation, for performers and spectators, was provided by a man obligingly popping amyl nitrate under neighbouring nostrils. Instead of wine, women and song, here in the Truck Stop there were drugs, men and silence. In Jerzy Kosinski's novel *Blind Date* a delicate political discussion is held in the corner of the orgy room of a New York bath house — perhaps this very one — because of the privacy and anonymity of the location. But it is hard to conceive of a less likely place for such a talk, not because of its incongruity, but because no one talks at all in the Truck Stop. Even propositioning is a matter of gesture, and though the room is full of noises, there is no speech and no sweet airs. The concentration is too intense. Yet the lubricity was too pervasive, since surfeit was the norm. The erotic lies more along the edge of expectation, and here was only the grossest of fulfilment, as subtle as a hurricane.

Still, there was an odd courtesy in the atmosphere. There was no sense of compulsion, no hint of rape. Even violation was an advertised commodity, and any sexual violence was, presumably, by mutual consent. Anyone can say no. I peered through the darkness at all those rutting couples, those silent cruising men in white towels. There was no love in that cave of a room and I pondered whether that disturbed me. I decided it didn't: sex without love is better than no sex at all. It dawned on me that what was unsettling was the darkness cloaking everything that gives human beings their individuality. You become your cock and the curve of your ass. The sweetness of your smile, let alone of your disposition, counts for little or nothing. Love, which was so markedly absent here, is what differentiates us, whereas sex alone points to what we have in common, and it was that brute commonality that was being celebrated in the workshops of the Truck Stop.

Perhaps in the privacy of cubicles there were gratified men lying peacefully in each other's arms, but not here, where each painful coupling spoke only of isolation, where an essential loneliness was temporarily assuaged by invading the flesh of another. The body was allowed to sing while the soul remained dumb.

In the other room the spectacle was, if possible, even less edifying. It was darker still, but I could make out that the room was funnel-shaped. The deeper one was drawn into the V, the less was the feeble light by the entrance able to penetrate. It was impossible to make out anything more than the contours of bodies. Hands reached out into the blackness, I grazed past restless bodies propped against the walls awaiting a fortuitous encounter and other bodies moving with the regularity of sexual activity — though one couldn't see or say what. Here's purity! — a context in which it is literally impossible to tell who or what you are touching. I could differentiate black from white, short from tall, but not young from old and certainly not beautiful from ugly. Sex here was crucibled into its most basic constituents: cocks and holes. I retreated.

The tour was not yet over. Up more stairs to the 'fantasy rooms', five chambers leading off either side of a single broad corridor. All but one of the rooms were occupied, so I had to guess what they contained. The one open door revealed a room about 10 feet square and padded on all sides; on the floor sat a burly man dressed like a football player in winter. I have no idea what his speciality might have been — possibly some strenuous athletic activity on the lines of an intimate rugger scrum. To lose oneself in sex is a metaphor I understand; to lose oneself and become another in order to be able to have sex baffles my understanding.

Now I'd seen all that was on offer, I began to feel more relaxed. There was no coercion of any kind other than the urgings of one's own body. If there was silence, apart from the gruntings of the sexual marathon, in the Truck Stop and in the gloomy halls of the 'rooms', there was more animation around the TV room and on the well-travelled stairs. Men greeted each other, exchanged a few words, and passed on; it was, paradoxically, a club of anonymity.

Shortly before I left, a pleasant-faced man, whom I'd seen at various times as I wandered about, smiled warmly and said, 'Hi, how're ya doing?' He wasn't asking me for my score card, as I at first thought; he must have observed me standing on the sidelines and concluded I was unwanted, and he wanted to cheer me up with a friendly word. 'Not too bad,' I lied, as a small blaze of macho pride was ignited. I smiled back, he grinned, and then he loped cheerfully off.

I returned to the lockers. It must be late now — about two in the morning — but people were still arriving. Some men spend the whole night at the baths. What would the place be like at seven in the morning? Perhaps a few joggers would drop by for a spot of additional exercise before breakfast. I changed, returned my key to the desk, and strolled out into the cold night. The streets were deserted and the snow had blanketed the city. It was a dangerous time to be out alone on the streets but it didn't feel that way. How sweet even the grimy night air of New York seemed, how fresh and pastoral after the sour sweat-heavy atmosphere of the baths. It struck me how oppressive had been, back there, the constant searching and roaming.

Tramping down the whitened street, I felt a sentimental sadness at having observed a place where there was pleasure but no trace of innocence. In that amiable American fashion, everything was open and available and almost free for the taking. There was a certain charm to it, but no sense of innocence or guilt. All the fine shadings, the great treks across uncertainty and hesitation, that make the sexual relationship so difficult and so powerful were missing.

Noisily crunching the snow underfoot, I headed for the Avenue and the welcome sight of an empty taxi swishing along the street.

TRUE CONFESSIONS

The Russian artist and designer Erté is scarcely a New Yorker, but he is regarded with some justification as the Father of Art Deco, that restless, surging idiosyncratic style that pervades the city. So his 90th birthday was cause for celebration. Nobody seemed quite sure which day was the actual birthday, and the festivities were generously spread over a number of days. There was an appearance on the *Today* show, openings of retrospectives at three or more galleries, a new and very lavish book from Dutton, and well-publicized but impenetrable dinner parties in his honour.

An acquaintance offered to take me along to one of the openings, a sumptuous show at the Dyansen Gallery in SoHo. Later she informed me that she herself might not be able to make it, but I should just turn up at the door, say I was a friend of hers, and there would be no problem. I timed my arrival for what I hoped would be the liveliest hour, just after nine. Wearing such finery as I possess, and with a trench coat to shield my splendour from the vulgar gaze, I tramped through the Village to SoHo. I had no trouble finding the Dyansen, since there were at least 200 people queuing on the street to get in the door. This was no mere opening; this was the paying of homage. Slowly, very slowly, the queue of peacocks shuffled down Spring Street, until 40 minutes later, I was inside. Nobody checked my credentials, I just walked in. I fortified myself with a couple of glasses of *méthode champenoise* and advanced.

Somewhere in the large space of the gallery was an exhibition, but fine as it was, an even more splendid display had been mounted by the beau monde that filled the room. Since I was never in possession of an invitation, I hadn't realized that the prescribed dress code for the evening was 'Erté-inspired'. New Yorkers are never reluctant to dress up, and those two words told them that no effort should be spared. Men, dozens of them, fluttered in wing collars between women in turbans and elaborate headdresses, ostrich feathers arching up and dripping down. Less formally dressed men sported luminous metal bowties and hand-knitted sweaters of witty design. Lace and frills were ubiquitous, the occasional monocle was spasmed into place, long silk-lined cloaks swept an inch above the floor. Many of the women were painted — not made up, but painted; some ethereal men had their thinning hair slicked down, as if they'd just walked off the set of *Brideshead Revisited.* Some dismally uncompetitive people were merely dressed in black tie or routine long dresses, while some slightly braver souls wore discreet Paisley smoking jackets. But if prizes had been awarded, the outright winner would have been the elderly lady who turned up wearing a lustrous green dress allegedly designed for her many decades ago by the hero of the evening.

And Erté? He'd left long before. For an hour or so he had held court, but fatigued by the throng, and possibly wearying of the unrelieved diet of adulation, the famous gnome had been put in somebody's pocket and taken off to dinner.

It had been quite warm that day, and it was stifling in the gallery, but I had no idea what to do with my trench coat. Before taking it off and slinging it over my arm, which would put that limb out of service, I decided to make a few notes, and slunk into a corner and proceeded to scribble away. I perceived someone standing directly in front of me. I looked up: a short, dark, and very pretty woman was staring straight at me.

'Hi. You look like Colombo about to make an arrest.'

I laughed. Wish I could come up with opening remarks like that. 'Yes, I feel stupid standing here in this coat, but I don't know what to do with it.'

'There's a cloakroom downstairs.'

'I had no idea.'

'I'll show you.'

She took momentary leave of the sombre couple she seemed vaguely attached to, and led me to the stairs.

'Isn't this amazing?' I said. 'One hardly ever sees costumes like this in London, even at openings.'

'You're from London?' She stared at me. I had said the right thing: London for her had the magic that New York held for me. But my preening was cut short when she continued: 'Funny, I thought you were from Brooklyn.'

'How insulting,' I retorted, eager to ally myself with the most glittering Manhattan circles.

'Not at all. I'm from Brooklyn.'

'Oh in that case . . .'

'I was only joking, you know . . .'

'I know.' Nothing like a little mutual embarrassment to throw the first frail communication cables over the oceanwide gap.

Her name was Lenore. She'd come with her oldest friends, Dick and Harriet, because she herself owned a couple of Erté prints already (I gradually learnt that half the population of New York owns at least one). She seemed in no hurry to get back to her friends.

'Do you mind if I latch on? I don't know a soul here.'

'Not at all.' And we wandered around, admiring the lovely graphics and gouaches on the walls. Given the artificiality of the style, the strength of Erté's line, it was extraordinary how much variety he could cram into an art that was essentially repetitious. It was an art of ornament and elaboration, and every nuance of colours in combination was exploited. I was duly dazzled. We ran into Dick and Harriet, and not wishing to be a leech, I drifted off on my own for a while to study some of the more intriguing pictures.

When I rejoined Lenore and her entourage, she was deep in conversation with an older man; the gestures suggested confidences were being exchanged. Unwilling to eavesdrop I struck up a desultory conversation with Harriet, who tactfully evaporated when the older man moved off and Lenore returned to my side. She was gazing intently at me, and those large eyes were unsettling. I didn't know what to say; she still appeared preoccupied by her previous conversation. Then she spoke.

'My husband left me.'

'I'm sorry to hear that.' Didn't want to overdo the sympathy, she and her husband being total strangers, and yet that kind of self-revelation demanded a middling level of concern. It really seemed to be true that in New York you raise your hat to a lady and she responds with the story of her life. 'Recently?'

'A few months ago.' Sympathetic shaking of the head. Deep exhalations. 'Three kids.' Further exhalations. The protracted silence that beams empathy. 'Wonderful man.'

'How terrible for you.'

'Yes. After 18 years he leaves. Can you believe it, he'd been fooling around with my best friend, moved out so he could be free to see her.'

'The classic story. Male menopause?'

'Guess so.' Despondently. The experience was evidently still too fresh for her to dab on a glib label.

'And the kids? They upset about it?'

'Yes, they worshipped him.' She stared at me, looking weirdly sexy as her air of abandonment wafted ever more heavily about us. Silence.

'What should I do?'

Good grief. There I was, armed for no more than gallery chit-chat, and with no notice I had to impersonate an agony aunt. Under the circumstances any advice would have been more welcome than a refusal to offer any, so I launched my verbal lifeboat.

'Gather your strength. Keep going. Don't hang about hoping he'll come back. Get on with your life.' Slip away with me to a quiet restaurant. Tell the babysitter you won't be back till the morning. Put your house and kids up for sale.

'Yes, I suppose so. But it hurts a lot.'

'I'm sure. I do understand. I've been through something similar.'

'Your wife left you?'

I blushed at my hypocrisy. 'Not exactly. But these things are always more complicated than the mere facts suggest.'

She mercifully ignored this specimen of bland pomposity. 'We had 18 happy years. No signs of discontent.'

Her song, my song. 'I had 5. Then bang — it all goes.' Enough of these self-pitying exchanges. Get on with the advice. 'Any money problems?'

'Not at all.'

'Well, that's something.'

'You think it'll get better?'

'Of course.' Deep breath, followed by cadenza: 'Let me

tell you, you certainly don't look like a woman who's been married for 18 years.'

Her eyes swam behind a descending curtain of moisture. My shameless flattery — though indeed she was decidedly attractive — scored a bull's eye, propping up, however temporarily, her battered self-esteem.

'That's nice of you.'

'Well, it's true. So don't worry. Things will get better.'

'They will?'

'I'm sure.'

Our conversation was beginning to loop in circles. I had dispensed magisterial reassurance to a woman I knew nothing about, had buttered her ego on both sides, and felt it was time to leave. Lenore was going back to Brooklyn with Dick and Harriet. In spite of her forlorn and confidential manner, I had no reason to think our brief contact would flower further. It was as though we'd stepped into the boat but left the oars behind. So I said I too had to go, and clutching her slender bare arm, I emitted a final burst of not entirely insincere coloratura, insisting that all would be well, she seemed to be a wonderful resilient woman, wishing her every luck, and so forth.

Slipping into his coat, Colombo brushed through the plumage and frills that still thronged Dyansen even at this late hour and emerged onto Spring Street, into a cab, and away to West 54th Street. Studio 54, as the world knows, is *démodé*. The night people have deserted it for the Red Parrot, or the Roxy, or the predominantly black Paradise Garage. The days when stars of stage and screen had to genuflect on the pavement outside and beg to be let in are long gone. The Studio may no longer be chic, but it's still a good place to dance for a few hours. It's favoured by its size; a converted theatre, it has a large stage area for dancing, balconies for resting and smooching, and lobbies with bars and couches for the weary. The auditorium has been left as a large space where you can hang about clutching the drink you've purchased from unsmiling but efficient bare-chested barmen. The hinter areas, the stairs and the upstairs lobbies, are dark, atmospheric, and relatively tranquil.

The technological interest is greater than the human. The twirlings and cavortings on the stage are much like twirlings and cavortings anywhere else, but the manipulation of the lighting is likely a stately dance. Multi-coloured neon lights fitted onto slats are suspended from the flies overhead; these slats rise and fall and swivel, and can also be lowered flat over the heads of the dancers. Lights and strips of silver foil are attached to tubes that move up and down, and hand-operated swivelling spotlights and strobes splash down onto the stage. The motif is flux: the slats and the illuminated tubes are constantly moving, shifting, the lighting goading on music that is so loud, downstairs at any rate, that it's impossible to make yourself heard unless you perch on the earlobe of your companion.

If the decor hasn't changed much since the Studio's most glamorous days, the crowd has. Few people, myself included, showed any sense of style. Clothing was unima-ginative, apart from a few men in wing collars and skimpy bowties (more refugees from Erté parties?) and some teeny boppers in rara skirts. There was more than a hint of party frock in the air, as if hours before, in the rococo splendours of New Jersey boudoirs, petticoats and hair lacquer and flounces and new tights had been applied in a frenzy of beautification. I'd come on my own, but was that any reason to leave on my own? At the very least, I wanted to dance.

'You ask, you get,' they say in New York. I went to work. Up in the balcony sat a wonderfully pretty girl. I had a shrewd suspicion that she probably had the brains of a ptarmigan. But she was lovely: mangoes and cream and curves that had no larding. I sat down next to her; she didn't shift away. After a while I turned to her with my sweetest leer and asked her if she'd like to dance.

'Nah. It's too loud.' I was right! The mammothrept did have the brains of a ptarmigan.

Another Botticelli turned me down with equal ineptitude, and then I walked down to the edges of the dance floor. Here the noise was so loud that there could be no reason for hanging around in that area unless one's intentions were terpsichorean. I spotted a fresh victim; struck; very sweetly the angel said no. I smiled, shrugged, walked off. Two minutes later I was passing her again (I bore her no grudge) and this time she leaned forward and said, 'I'll dance for a bit if you like.' I don't know what made her change her mind — what disappointment I anaesthetized — and I didn't care.

We boogied away for 10 minutes, then she smiled and said thank you (I almost thought she was going to curtsy) and returned to where she'd been standing before. Perhaps her date was late, and she feared being stood up? Who knows? But our vigorous stompings to the beat of *Gloria* and *YMCA* demonstrated that you didn't need a partner. There'd been no rapport between us and I could just as satisfactorily have danced solo. Indeed, towards the rear of the stage the entire female 16-year-old population of Syosset, Long Island, was hopping and twitching in a solid group.

My dancing fever burned away for the night, I downed a Heineken to cool off and went to fetch my coat. It must have been about 1.30 in the morning, a Saturday morning, and the folks were just arriving. There was a mob straining towards the cloakroom counter, and I was almost smothered between walls of mink and fox. After at least 10 minutes, I retrieved my coat and made for the exit. I stood on the pavement as the taxis disgorged more ambulatory coats. A car raced up the street and screeched to a halt outside the Studio. A woman lowered the window and yelled at the doorman.

'Hey! You seen my friend?'

'The blonde?' He was yelling back.

'Yeh.'

'She left in a cab.'

'What! Where did she go?'

'How the hell should I know?'

'This is her car. What am I supposed to do with it?'

'Sell it.'

It was late but I was thirsty, with a sudden craving for a tumbler of milk, and somewhere near Times Square I walked into an all-night coffee shop and sat down at the counter. I ordered the milk and looked around me. Strange, most of the other customers around the oval-shaped counter were young women, most of them black and heavily made up. Behind them were a few men, also black, slender and dressed in narrowly cut suits in various peacock shades. Some of them were wearing large scarlet or black hats. I noticed one of the young women strolling erratically in my direction; she sat on the stool next to mine. She might have been pretty but it was hard to tell behind the obscuring layers of bright red lipstick and silver eye shadow. It had begun to cross my mind that her interest in me was not so much the natural gregariousness of friendly New Yorkers as a commercially motivated curiosity.

Lurching drunkenly towards me, she said: 'You like pretty black women?'

'Yes, but not tonight.'

She looked affronted. 'Who said anything about tonight, man? I was just askin'. Do you like 'em?'

'Yes.' I took another slug of milk.

'Bet you like to have your dick sucked.' And to illustrate her declaration she laid a hand on my thigh and slowly slid it in the direction of the organ in question. I removed the hand. Again she hazarded her guess and once again sought to warm her hand between my legs.

'You may not believe this,' I said, 'but I came in here to have a glass of milk.' It did sound improbable, I had to admit.

Pouting, she removed her hand though she continued to lean against me, not because she was irresistibly drawn to my person but because without my support she would have fallen off the stool. The gentlemen in the broad floppy hats were beginning to take an interest in our discussion, and I took this as a cue to drink up, fling 50 cents on the counter, and make an unhurried but determined departure.

THE ORIGINS OF ENGLISH CULTURE

One afternoon I was visiting a friend. As we were talking, she glanced at her watch, then grabbed the phone. I heard her ordering a taxi to collect her 10-year-old son from school, about six miles away. This struck me as an extravagance, but she explained that, since both she and her husband were usually busy during the day, it was simpler to reel in young Christopher in a cab. Like most other children from professional families in Manhattan, he attends a private school. If you can afford private education (about $5000 per annum), then you can probably afford to have him fetched from school rather than waste an hour a day driving uptown to collect him.

Curious to see exactly what Christopher's parents were paying for, I went to visit his school, reputedly one of the best in the city. Collegiate School was founded in 1638, has an enrollment of 550 boys and a teaching staff of 90 plus 30 civilians (librarians, administrators, and so forth). The school buildings were well-equipped and maintained, and the 25,000-volume library stocked among its periodicals such journals as *L'Express, Business Week,* and the *Congressional Digest.*

The head of admissions, Mr Jacob, was giving prospective parents a tour of the school, and I latched on. Because competition for admission is fierce, it appeared as though the parents were on trial as much as their toddlers back home. I wandered through the corridors of the Lower School. Well-groomed boys were making their way to and from lessons. On the walls of the corridor teachers had pinned up essays written by seven-year-olds on the theme, *Who Am I?* The kids had written about themselves, their parents, their favourite foods and games. Most of the children were either Wasp or Jewish, but one essay began: 'I am different because I am a Pakistani.' In another classroom the boys had constructed their family trees. One pedigree Wasp had traced his family back to original settlers such as William Bradford and Miles Standish. The Jewish trees ran out of roots in the mid-nineteenth century.

The pressure that will persist throughout their future professional lives begins at an early age for these boys. To get into Collegiate they have to take verbal and performance tests, and kindergarten reports are scrutinized. Mr Jacob admitted that the school was high-powered. 'Boys tend to be able when they arrive and we aim to keep them that way. The school does have an image of being an intellectual pressure cooker but we also give them access to many other activities, some of them extra-curricular. They just eat up the things we give them to do.'

After the touring parents had left, I asked Jacob whether he was afraid of accusations that Collegiate was encouraging elitism.

'No. It's true that most of the boys come from families living on the Upper West and East Sides, but we do encourage enrollment by minority boys who often live in the boroughs. 10 per cent of the boys are on full scholarships. The sad fact is that public schools have had to cut back on what they can offer educationally. They just can't compete with a school such as ours. We offer a wider range of courses, more athletic programmes, more languages. We have better ratios, better tone, better discipline. That's important to parents. And our record of college entry is as good as any school in the country.'

As in college, the boys take courses for which they are given credits if their performance is adequate. The course catalogue is intellectually luxurious, with quite demanding courses on the Modern Middle East, the History of Psychological Thought, and The Literature of New York City. I was charmed by a course on Speaking Shakespeare, and it seemed fitting that the next generation of leaders should be offered sessions on Public Speaking.

I also wanted to see what the bottom of the heap was like. Were the public schools, the city's high schools, quite as awful as was claimed? Was it true that some teachers are afraid to walk down the stairs alone for fear of being assaulted by unruly students? Was discipline so poor that it was impossible to teach these city kids anything?

Travel north through Harlem on the west side and keep going, and you'll reach Washington Heights. It's the quietest of the residential neighbourhoods of Manhattan, and streets lined with modest apartment houses climb up and down the steep slopes of the Heights. To the west there are fine views over the Hudson to the Jersey Palisades, and the Heights also accommodate two of the finest and least frequented of the city's parks, Fort Tryon (home of the Cloisters Museum) and Inwood Hill. Slightly seedy but tranquil, Washington Heights keeps to itself; it has the feel of an inner suburb. The population is mixed, with many elderly Jews living on the western side, and a large Hispanic presence further east.

George Washington High School is strikingly situated on a slope in the Hispanic section. Set in surprisingly spacious grounds, the buildings are handsome in an institutional way. It was built to accommodate 5,000 students, but with the end of the baby boom enrolment dropped to 3,000. The principal gloomily told me that actual attendance was far lower: 'There's a large truancy or absentee rate, about 30 per cent. It makes our job so much more difficult when the kids don't even show up.' It's not simply the traditional preference of kids to go fishing rather than to school; parents often keep children at home to baby-sit or they need them to help out in the family store or business. The educational problem is exacerbated by the departure each year of about half the student body; an unstable student population disrupts the continuity of their education and undermines the social cohesion of the school. As for discipline, the principal said: 'My options are limited. I can hold a parent conference, I can order suspension, or I can have a student transferred. But these days I'm required to observe "due process". I have to hold hearings and notify parents by telegram.' He shook his head despondently.

I made my way to the drama department. Count Stovall, an actor from Lincoln Center, is a 'teaching artist', visiting various schools to give practical drama classes. Tall, slender, handsome, he oozed charm and smoothness. His easy manner seemed to win over the students, who were attentive and relaxed. But they were an unprepossessing bunch. They were dressed any old how, some were unshaven, others sported droopy bandit moustaches; they looked more like a street gang than a class. But they could act. The sketches focussed on a few revealing themes: drugs, drink, relations with parents, inadequate fathers, and cheating at school. Two or three of the students showed formidable improvisatory talent, and scarcely one was less than competent. It was, however, an 'elective' course, so only interested students were participating.

The next class was a good deal less relaxed. Miss Diaz, a young woman with an unyielding manner, was teaching English as a second language. 70 per cent of the kids at this school are Hispanic, but in this class and others like it there are also immigrant children whose first language may be Arabic, Urdu, Haitian patois, or Russian. Miss Diaz was teaching her daily class (none of whom had more than three months' tuition in English) the names of clothes.

She tapped a poster on the wall with her classroom ruler. 'Shirt.'

'Shirt,' mumbled the class.

She pointed at a picture of trousers. 'Panse.'

'Panse.'

Next. 'Swedda.'

'Swada.'

'No. Not swada. Swedda.'

'Swedda.'

'Maria, what is this? In English.' Unsmiling Miss Diaz.

Maria, unbelievably pretty, a wedding ring on her finger, tittered. 'These ees a panse.'

'No, Maria, that's not right.'

'O, es complicado!'

'No es complicado!' retorted Miss Diaz, unmoved.

Mr Cordero was also Hispanic, nattily dressed in black slacks and a lilac swedda. He wore tinted aviator glasses that glowed oddly against his swarthy face. He was teaching a history class to students whose ages ranged from 15 to 19, with different levels of language and academic skills. He taught almost entirely in Spanish. In New York's schools Hispanic students are entitled to bilingual education and can elect to take some courses in Spanish; but they must also take ESL courses to improve their linguistic ability in English.

Cordero was reviewing the homework assignments for the week. About 25 kids sat in a large circle around the room, notebooks on their laps or on desks in front of them. The assignment was, unbelievably, on the Origins of English Culture, subdivided into Early History of the English Monarchy, and Contributions of English Culture to the Culture of the USA. Quite an assignment. While he was talking rapidly in Spanish, Cordero wandered round the room checking the students' notebooks. Looking at me, he said, 'They don't study,' and shrugged before adding, 'Guess that happens everywhere.' The kids were moderately attentive; there was no disorder but there was a constant buzz of chat until Cordero launched into a cogent account of the effects of nuclear war. That interested them, and they listened in silence. Returning to the subject of British contributions to American culture, he offered the class an example: the Beatles — and asked them to think of others. As he spoke, he carried a globe round the class asking his charges to point to Great Britain. Very few had any idea.

After the class I told Cordero how astonished I was that he was teaching medieval European history to a class that had only the dimmest idea of where Europe was.

'It's true,' he said, 'but I'm legally required to teach certain subjects, even though I agree that it's meaningless to most of these kids given their background. It's very difficult. Some of these kids are married, some even have kids, and they're still in school. But they just don't realize how vital an education is to their survival in this city, in this country. Many of them have severe problems — they've only been in this country for a few years perhaps, it's unfamiliar, their families are dislocated and spread about, unemployment is pervasive. As far as teaching them is concerned, it's like the blind following the blind. The kids don't know what they need, and I'm not sure either. They follow what I teach, they're 100 per cent good kids, but they don't always do the work. The truth is that they have only the vaguest idea of what this is all about.'

I sat in on other classes and had a ghastly lunch in the cafeteria. The teachers struck me as dedicated and competent; they kept a firm grip on their classes without forfeiting rapport with the students. Nor were the students the monsters of depravity I'd heard about; many of them certainly looked evil, but on closer inspection turned out to be amiable and easy-going. Yet one teacher apologized for keeping me waiting by explaining that he had had to deal with 'a serious discipline problem upstairs'; and classrooms are kept locked during classes 'to keep out intruders'. The city schools are patrolled by over a thousand security guards, expelling intruders, disarming students carrying meat cleavers under their jackets, and trying to prevent violent attacks both on other students and on teachers. Middle-class parents insisted that it was discipline and safety rather than inferior education that obliged them to send their children to private schools.

'I, and everybody I know, sends our kids to private schools,' said the Banker, 'because of disorder in the public schools. My kids are frightened of black youths. Sadly, they've come to use race as a convenient if crude sorting device. If they're being followed down the street by three black kids they're on their guard, and with good reason. If there are three Chinese kids behind them, they don't worry. My kids are empirical bigots, though they do have plenty of black friends.'

THINK MIRACLES!

The Lower East Side, like Harlem, conjures up images even in the minds of people who have never set foot in New York. It's no longer the dumping-ground and breeding-ground for wave after wave of impoverished East Europeans. 70 years have passed since these streets housed 600,000 Jews, yet in wandering around the area, it only takes a modest use of the imagination to picture the place at the turn of the century. The old tenements, clustered together and defaced by rusty fire escapes that dangle over tacky shopfronts, are still there, still inhabited, though the tight city blocks are broken now by grubby empty lots. In the more easterly parts of the neighbourhood there are tall red-brick blocks of low-income housing, many of them funded and still maintained by trade unions.

North of Delancey Street a huddle of tenement blocks now houses Spanish-speaking immigrants. In the chunks of habitation between the burnt-out buildings along Rivington Street, and along Clinton and Stanton, the names on the shopfronts may be Jewish still but the language in the air is Spanish. The narrow streets are packed; small groups linger on the corners. Young men lounge in the doorways of cheap clothes shops, luncheonettes, tacky gift shops. Doors leading into tenements are ajar — no uniformed doormen in the Lower East Side — giving passers-by a glimpse of dark hallways and even darker stairways. Sharp whiffs of mari-juana hit the nose. The empty lots are waist high with rubbish, the usual tip of disemboweled mattresses, cartons, broken bottles, fast food containers, gutted cars. 70 years ago, the Lower East Side was a centre for poor immigrants and so it remains. Indeed, as the underground economy burgeons, sweatshops are returning to these streets.

The Lower East Side is poorly served by the subway system. In terms of the larger commercial economy of the city, it was and still is marginal. The immigrants who lived here were hardly sought-after employees and the transportation planners effectively isolated them. To this day the Lower East Side — with its countless small traders, its boarded-up synagogues, its streets choked with shoppers by day, and, over by the Bowery, a trickle of bums, alcoholics and junkies by night — seems oddly apart from the life of the city around it.

It's almost a matter of pride to be able to point to a Lower East Side ancestry, but it's also the neighbourhood from which, over the decades, families have thankfully escaped. Middle-class Jews still pour in on Sundays to shop for smoked fish, cut-price linen, and electrical appliances, but by evening they've driven back to Riverdale or Westchester. The resident Jewish population of 30,000 souls is overwhelmingly elderly.

Many streets still retain a Jewish presence. Orchard in particular is enjoying a peculiar renaissance, and on Sundays it's closed to traffic so as to accommodate peddlers and shoppers. Here you'll find the cheapest clothes in New York — and not just the mass-produced junk hawked on 14th Street. On Orchard a good number of shops sell Italian 'designer' clothes and shoes, usually for a third less than you'll pay for the same items in midtown stores and boutiques. There are the famous Jewish food shops too: Bernstein-on-Essex with its Kosher Chinese menu; the pickle shops on Essex which, cognoscenti affirm, are pickle heaven. Saperstein's on Rivington spaciously spreads its wares on either side of an old-fashioned shop, smoked fish to the right, and deep troughs of dried fruits and nuts to the left. At the better-known Russ and Daughters I bought some sable, a smoked fish related to cod, and took it home for my supper. If you like half-raw cold smoked fish, then you'll adore sable; after a few mouthfuls I gave up. Yonah Schimmel's sells the best knishes in town, and on Rivington is the surviving base of another ancient Jewish industry: Streit's Matzoth Company. On Grand Street, you can chew your way to toothache on a bialy (a ring of oniony dough with garlic in the middle) from Kossar's.

The surviving Jewish population inhabits a dense area south of Delancey. East Broadway, formerly the heart of the old East Side, is now Chinese as far as the Manhattan Bridge, which noisily carries traffic overhead to Brooklyn. Beyond the bridge the Chinese presence diminishes, and more Jewish shops and businesses appear. It's here, if anywhere, that the old life of the Lower East Side continues to limp along. At no. 175 is the old *Forward* building, constructed in 1912 to house the famous Yiddish daily. The paper survives, a weekly now, and the 12-storeyed building is no longer required by the paper, which moved to 33rd Street and sold its old headquarters to a Chinese church.

Just beyond it is the Educational Alliance Building, which is still in service, and it's here that I arranged to meet Rina, a worker at Project Ezra, a volunteer organization that provides care for the elderly. The Alliance was founded by German Jews in 1883 to help new immigrants to survive in their new environment. Its charitable activities continue, with an emphasis on helping the old and sick, if only because the old and sick make up the bulk of the local Jewish population.

It was crowded at lunchtime when I arrived. The old folks were just finishing their lunch and were talking excitedly about the film on Golda Meir they were about to be shown. It had been screened often before but was such a favourite that it was frequently repeated. I was introduced to ancient but lively crones. Toothlessly they chattered to me in Polish and Russian accents so sharp, after 50 years of failure to assimilate, you could cut diamonds with them. Occasionally their English, as limpid as borscht, drained away completely and they turned to Rina for assistance, letting her have it full throttle in Yiddish for her to translate.

In its heyday the Lower East Side sustained about 500 synagogues and religious institutions. Some of the old structures remain, though few are still in use. Some have become churches such as the Inglesia Pentecostal — a curious reversion, since many of the synagogues were themselves converted from churches — and others are boarded up. Elaborate façades, incorporating every extravagance known to architectural eclecticism, are crumbling or vandalized. Only the Bialystoker Synagogue maintains a large and thriving congregation.

A few doors away from the Alliance is the large but scruffy Yeshiva Ben Torah, where men of all ages still come throughout the day to engage in Talmudic disputation. Men only, let it be noted, and Rina nervously hovered in the hallway while I ventured into the study room. Around the walls was a library of texts, herds of antlered coat racks, and long tables, some which were leaned over by solemn but vivacious men, many bearded and bespectacled, arguing vociferously in Yiddish over the large old books spread before them. Orthodox Jews often wear a uniform (black Homburg hat and long heavy black coat, pulled down at the edge by pockets stuffed with learned commentaries and smoked fish in greaseproof paper) and because all the men in this yeshiva were costumed in this way, it seemed timeless. A yeshiva in the Pale of Settlement a hundred years ago would not have looked much different. I didn't linger; my head was uncovered and I was transparently a stranger. On leaving I saw tacked to the door a notice in Hebrew and English about the importance of saying 'o-main' (amen). Apparently certain worshippers in certain synagogues had become lax on this point, and some rabbinate or other had mustered its forces to warn the faithful against such departures from orthodoxy.

Walking west, we came to the magnificent façade of the Eldridge Street synagogue, Khal Adas Jeshurun with Anshe Lubz (the Community of the People of Israel with the People of Lubz — in Poland). The main synagogue has been closed for over 40 years but services are still held in the basement, and Rina led me down the steps. There we were met by Benjamin Marcowitz, the *shammos* — an office combining caretaker and warden. Although old and stooped and a bit unsteady on his feet, he was alert and wily. He was dressed at random: a large blue jacket many sizes too big for him (it might just have fitted Muhammad Ali), lighter blue trousers, a navy blue cardigan, an unknotted tie, and on his head an enormous cloth cap. His narrow eyes peered forward when he spoke, and I had a strong impression that, like a mole, he lived underground.

Marcowitz led us into a room separated from the main basement area by a balustraded screen. In this room, need I say it, the women sit while the men are conducting the services. Marcowitz hurried away to fetch a yarmulke (skullcap) to cover my bare head. In the main room five men, one or two of them quite young, were seated around a table while an elderly man with a white beard read aloud from a text, pausing to offer glosses. He spoke in Yiddish, and Rina told me the text was by the learned Rashi. At the far end of the room was the ark containing the Torah, the scrolls of the Law; most of the space was filled with pews and one or two long tables, such as the one at which the five men sat in disputation. A pile of dusty prayer books, unused, unneeded, lay in one corner, and propped against the pews was a stepladder used to change the naked bulbs that contributed glare rather than light. On the right wall, incongruously, an illuminated clock advertised Te Amo cigars.

Daily services are still held here, but they are sparsely attended. At 1.45 a few more men arrived, some nodding greetings to the men already gathered, others ignoring them; they were there for *mincha,* the afternoon service. Marcowitz came shuffling in to the room behind the screen, told Rina to stay put, and took me by the sleeve. He pulled me, unresisting, into the main room and thrust a prayer book into my hands, opening it at the right page. The white-bearded elder was leading the service from in front of the ark. Marcowitz was assuming (since the only people he ever meets are Jews) that I would at least be following the service if not actively participating. I was able to follow inter-mittently, but the orthodox service is hard to keep up with because large chunks of prayer are recited *sotto voce* at great speed, with every worshipper zipping along at his own individual high-velocity mumble. Some of the men were davening, bowing forward and back from the waist, a steady rhythm punctuated by the occasional heavy lunge when emphasis was to be given, vocally and physically, to a particular word or phrase in the babble of prayer, the chatter of supplication.

These practised hands could whip through the *mincha* at great speed, and it was all over in 10 or 15 minutes. A few more nods and handshakes, and the congregation wandered out. The service over, Marcowitz grabbed the stepladder, dragging it down the aisles to spots beneath defunct bulbs. I offered to help the old man, but he wouldn't hear of it and sent me back to purdah with Rina.

Before long he stumbled back in. 'Come,' he said, and led us to the table where the men had been arguing over their Rashi. A text lay on the table in front of where I sat, and I opened it: the title page carried the colophon 'Wien 1843' and the flyleaf was rubber-stamped 'This Book Stolen From Khal Adas' etc.

Marcowitz had a tome under his arm and pulled up a chair next to mine. He opened the book. It was a comparatively recent study of the synagogues of the Lower East Side, and he was particularly anxious for me to see that his synagogue was included. The reason for his eagerness became apparent when I saw peering out of one of the photographs the unmistakable features of a younger but only marginally less decrepit Mr Marcowitz.

'Oh,' I said on cue, 'that's your picture.'

'Yeh, yeh,' he said dismissively, pleased as punch. He turned to another section of the book. 'Here look.'

It showed another synagogue, with a middle-aged man standing in front of it. 'He was the rebbe, a fine man. Now he's dead. A young man, but he passed away on cancer. So young, but passed away on cancer.'

Rina was particularly enthralled by the book. She knew many of these old synagogues and it fascinated her to see them as they were before passing into their present desuetude. She said she'd like to buy a copy.

Marcowitz nodded. 'Yuh. I tell you what you do. The book, it costs' — 'castz' is the noise he actually made — 'almost 20 dollar. But you go to —' and he mentioned a small local bookshop. 'Go in, say you want this book, give him 12 dollar.'

'Is that all?'

'Sure. Just listen what I say. Don't ask about the price. Just give him 12 dollar.'

I asked whether I could see the upstairs synagogue, and Marcowitz happily obliged. To get from the basement to the ground floor we had to climb some rickety wooden stairs that led into the main vestibule, which was in a shambles. Marcowitz explained that the place was in better shape than it had been in a few years ago. Then the glass above the main entrance had been broken, so that the interior had been badly scratched by the long nails of a New York winter. Recently, however, the glass had been replaced, and he showed me a pile of the broken coloured glass that had originally filled the window. They were keeping it, nurturing the hope of eventual restoration.

The actual synagogue, erected in 1886, is a splendid room, with galleries for the women and a seating capacity of almost 600. There are rivals for the honour, but the Eldridge Street synagogue is said to have the finest interior of all the old Lower East Side houses of worship. The fittings were elaborate: a candelabrum, a menorah, and light fittings — all made of brass and originally intended for gas, though they had since been adapted to carry electricity. Since the 1930s the synagogue hadn't been used, but it has been left intact and, it seemed, despite the dust and the peeling walls, complete. I noticed some pews near the back with high partitioning, and asked Marcowitz what they were for. They were for the elderly, he said, but I was still puzzled.

Then, memorably, he explained: 'There can't get up high flies.'

Now I understood.

He showed me the ornate ark, which had been made in Italy. Then I looked down from the ark onto the front pew and noticed a row of a dozen identical — well, they looked like chamber pots. I asked Marcowitz to enlighten me.

'Spitenz,' he said.

'What?'

'Spitenz. You know, for spitenz in.'

'Ah, spittoons!'

'Yeh, spitenz. All original, all of them. All antics.'

It was stirring to see this proud, even lavish room, still undisturbed many decades after a sorrowful *shammos*, perhaps the same one bustling about now, had cleared up after a final service. Perhaps one day money would be raised to restore it, and tourists would come in droves to admire its magnificent fittings and its gleaming spittoons. Should that happen, the synagogue would have become a museum, which is certainly an improvement on a mausoleum, but at the cost of that frozen quality that gave it, under Marcowitz's stumbling solitary care, its poignancy.

When we returned to the main door, our leavetaking was elaborate, formal. Our repeated thanks were returned in the form of good wishes, back and forth. Finally, closing the door behind him Marcowitz leaned forward and shouted to me: 'I wish you all the luck in your future,' just as if I were some relative setting off from the shtetl to find fame and fortune elsewhere.

Walking up the steps I noticed a hand-lettered sign and paused to write down the text. The door opened again and Marcowitz — who else? — loomed towards me. He was chortling, happy that I'd spotted his handiwork. He told me he alone was responsible for the sentiment expressed, the wording, and the calligraphy. My transcription is exact:

> Any person that will bring anymols
> on this enterence stairway for cleaning.
> Note:
> If catched will pay a fine $1000.00 Dol.
> A year in Preson.

I was hungry, not having eaten all day, and Rina took me to the Garden Cafeteria. She explained that the food left much to be desired, but that no visit to the East Side would be complete without a cup of coffee at the Garden. It's on the corner of East Broadway and Rutgers, a large room with rows of plastic-covered tables on the right, and a long counter on the left. Behind the counter is the usual array of indigestible East European Jewish food: smoked fish, noodle pudding (which can also be used as ballast to keep hot-air balloons earthbound), blintzes, strudel, and what are probably the world's worst eclairs. I had a brick of strudel and coffee, and we sat down at one of the tables. Crotchety, noisy old women wearing woollen caps kept stumbling past carrying trays across which plates heaped with horribles slithered from side to side. Men may rule in the synagogue, but at the Garden they huddle fearfully in the corners. Legend has it that Trotsky used to eat at the Garden during his stay in New York. Well, if the hired assassin doesn't get you, the food will.

I walked Rina to her bus stop, then treated myself to a cab.

'You English?' grunted the driver. Suspicion? Admiration? Hostility?

'Yes.'

'Ever heard of Acker Bilk?'

Acker Bilk . . . Vague memories trickled back from my short-trouser days of listening to a record by a quasi-Trad clarinettist by name of — indeed, the very same Bilk!

'Certainly. Wasn't he a clarinettist who —'

'Got it in one. You like music?'

'Yes.'

'OK. Listen to this.' And he leaned over the empty seat next to his and pressed a button on a cassette recorder that lay there. Crackling clarinet bloopings emerged, the odd tunelet broken by scales and slides and swirls of an improvisatory nature. Unfortunately the lights were against us, and I was still imprisoned in the cab when the tape ended.

'So what d'you think?'

It was clear what the answer had to be. 'Very good. Impressive.'

'Any idea who that was playing?'

'It couldn't by any chance have been, not, could it have been — Acker Bilk?'

The driver turned to me with a look of triumph. 'Nah, that was me. I play the clarinet too. Not bad, huh?'

Having done my duty by Jehovah, it was fitting, the following Sunday, that I should give equal time to His immensely successful Son. Remember that in a city where everything has to be hyped, even God has a press agent, and his name is Norman Vincent Peale. He's been around for a long time, giving succour to the prosperous and advice to the successful. It was his church, the Marble Collegiate Reformed Protestant Dutch Church on Fifth Avenue at 29th Street, that Nixon used to attend when he was living in New York. Caveat emptor.

I decided to skip the 9.45 service (preacher: Dr Caliandro on *Gratitude: Your Happiness Key*) and get there early for Dr Peale's 11.15 show on *Your Built-In Miracle Power*.

On arriving I was greeted not by an usher but — as befits a church in the corporate capital of the world — by a member of the Board of Ushers and Greeters, no less, a team of men and women with big smiles, white carnations pinned to their lapels, names like Pam and Bruce, and a complete set of teeth. The church was packed, and sartorial standards were high, reaching a surreal apotheosis in the form of one or two Edna Everage creations that sat like bowls of fruit above imperious hair-dos. The odour was less of sanctity than of hair lacquer.

It was the usual arrangement of the deritualized church. No altar, no censers, no liturgical bric-à-brac, just a kind of boardroom on a podium furnished with thrones, and space for the choir well behind. The choir, 15 strong in red cassocks, filed in, followed by three ministers in black. Powerful lights flooded the stage, because the service was being transmitted on closed-circuit TV to an overflow congregation elsewhere. We were hushed. The service began with an invocation, followed by a trot through the Lord's Prayer, wherein we begged the Almighty to forgive us our 'debts' rather than our 'trespasses', which gives us more leeway when it comes to fornication and might assist our overdrafts.

Dr Peale, when he spoke, turned out to be an elderly man of medium build with the manner of a gruff but kindly self-made furniture manufacturer. He spun yarns, he waxed folksy, he made self-deprecatory allusions, jests about his wife ('much smarter than me'), asides about what a terrible profession preaching was. He jabbed his finger at us, he punched the air with his fist, injecting dramatic pauses into his sentences and varying the tone of his delivery from a rough snarl to a great roar. It was neatly calculated, discreetly oratorical.

The content was as benign as the form. The deity, Dr Peale told us, was 'a great friend', a comfort, and of course our salvation. God in His greatness had endowed each and every one of us with the capacity to do anything we wanted, he explained. 'You have the capacity,' proclaimed the wise doctor, 'to handle *anything* you'll ever be called upon to face.' But how so? Explain, Dr Peale. Well, 'God has created in you a resiliency, a come-back power, an enormous strength, a built-in miracle power!' Excuse me, that should of course read: A Built-In Miracle Power! — the theological equivalent of STP additive. We derive this power from God, and we all know about God and His associate Jesus: 'Jesus is really somebody, the greatest somebody who ever lived!' Men in trouble had told Dr Peale in person how in their perplexity they had turned to God in prayer and suddenly recovered their BIMP, so that the Lord Himself spake unto them: 'Listen, George, if you want to clinch that deal, you have the capacity to do it!'

The peroration began. 'Think miracles instead of limitations, think victories' — and the woman sitting next to me with rare acuity thrust her mind into his and completed for him: 'Instead of defeats.' Finally, Dr Peale blessed the congregation, even me, and said that he wanted 'every individual to go out of this church walking tall'.

After such spiritual nourishment, I asked the Almighty to recommend a good place for lunch. Gathering a couple of friends on the way, I headed for the Hee Seung Fung on the Bowery, and after queueing for 20 minutes we found ourselves seated. Dim sum — those succulent Chinese dumplings and noodle dishes — are wheeled slowly around the restaurant on trolleys and when something particularly appetizing passes by, you flag down the waiter and order from the trolley. I was taken by the quail egg Shiu Mie (steamed dumplings with pork, shrimps, and quail eggs), stuffed crab claws in batter, crabmeat shrimp dumplings, glutinous rice dumpling with ground anis, and beef Shiu Mie that resembles small meteorites but tastes much better. The trouble with dim sum is that one doesn't know when to stop. These small delicacies slide down the throat so effortlessly it comes as a shock to realize you've consumed about 20 of them. Such gross over-consumption at least induces that state of lassitude that's so appropriate to the Sabbath. I raised a glutinous finger to beckon a waiter, who rapidly cast his eye over the dozens of plates on our table and then decided what the bill ought to be. The afternoon's entertainment was cinematic: Paul Newman in the courtroom drama *The Verdict*.

A few nights later I was watching my favourite New York late-night chat show hosted by David Letterman. He introduced a segment which he calls Limited Perspectives, in which a popular film or book is reviewed by specialists. On this occasion the film for review was *The Verdict* and his guest critics were two energy management experts from a New York roofing and insulation company. Oh, they were hard on that movie.

'I hate to say it,' said one of the critics, 'but *The Verdict* shows no energy consciousness whatever.'

'Remember it's set in Boston in the middle of winter,' added the other.

'Yet nobody in that film even wears a hat.'

'That's a shocker in itself,' mused Letterman sympathetically. 'Say, any good things about *The Verdict*? Anything you guys liked?'

'Well, I'd have to say there was a good use of drapes.'

'I agree with that. But apart from that, it's a loser. In this movie Paul Newman plays a hard-drinking lawyer down on his luck. We thought about this and then we realized that the reason he drinks too much is because he's cold all the time.'

'Absolutely right.'

MAKING TRACKS

In the frightening film *The Taking of Pelham 123*, gunmen hijack a subway train. New Yorkers, so dependent and yet so fearful of their subway system, often speak as though this were a daily occurrence. They are eager to enlist visitors in their fantasy that to step inside a subway car is to risk assault and even death.

I used the subway daily, riding every line in Manhattan and a few in the boroughs, at dawn, during rush hours, in the middle of the day, and at two in the morning. It's dirty, noisy, shabby, confusing, but it's also efficient and inexpensive. If you obey a few simple rules — which can be summarized as Stick Together — you are unlikely to run into trouble.

There is, to be sure, something threatening about New York's subways, especially the older IRT Lines. Involuntarily I would step well back whenever an express leapt from the tunnel like a crazed jaguar and hurtled past while I was waiting for a local. Everything about the trains is metallic and raucous. They're embellished, smeared, daubed with graffiti in a ferocious beauty of violent swirling colour.

It can be unsettling to step through psychedelically painted doors into an interior that itself resembles a hallucination. In a half-full LL train late at night, observe your fellow passengers and you'll swiftly realize most of them are drunk, stoned, vagrant, babbling to themselves, dribbling, unconscious — or a winning combination of the above. A few souls simultaneously afflicted with homelessness and wanderlust try to sleep their way from one end to the other of the longest lines, such as the A, but their repose is likely to be disturbed by the ungentle proddings of nightsticks wielded by subway cops. For the subways never close. There is no such thing as the last train. Some subway entrances can't even be shut: they have no gates.

Keeping watch, every day and often half the night, over this ever wakeful network is a burly man called Hugh Dunne. He is the chief trouble-shooter of the Metropolitan Transportation Authority (MTA). When anything goes wrong — an accident or fire or breakdown — Hugh is likely to be first on the scene. A walking encyclopaedia, he probably knows as much as anyone in New York about the city's mass transit networks, their history and operations. His passion for his work is single-minded — and tireless, as I was to discover.

'Can you meet me early at the MTA offices on Madison?' he asked me when we spoke on the phone.

'Certainly. Nine? Nine-thirty?'

'How about five?'

I thought he was joking. He wasn't.

I arrived early and went off in search of coffee, which, of course, is no problem in New York at 4.30 a.m. I found a Burger King, or one of its clones, and ordered a Breakfast Special that consisted of drinkable coffee, and a gelatination of egg, molten cheese and a whisper of ham, flattened between the halves of what Americans fondly think of as a bun, although scientific analysis suggests it is in fact a papier-mâché construct.

Hugh arrived at the MTA building shortly after five and I climbed into the back of his car. He sat in front with the driver, and between them was a telephone; a walkie-talkie was slung around his waist.

'Nice to meet you, Stephen. Before we get going, we've got to go down to the Village to pick up one other person. Let's see, which one is Charles Street?'

'I can answer that,' I said surlily from the back. 'It's a block away from where I'm living.'

'No! Hey, if I'd known that we could have picked you up at the same time, and you needn't have come all the way up to Madison.'

'How true . . .' It wasn't his fault, though.

Our other passenger, Amy, was an MTA economist, who had decided it was time she got acquainted with the operations as well as the budget projections. She piled in, and Hugh directed the driver to take us to Grand Central.

'Here, you'll need these,' said Hugh as we got out, handing us flashlights and luminous yellow safety jackets. It was now 5.30 but the subway station at Grand Central was already busy. Going down a ramp, Hugh paused at a steel door, unlocked it with a key from a vast bunch attached to his belt, and we followed him down some grubby, blue-painted tunnels until we came to a subterranean hut labelled *Tower*.

Hugh greeted the men inside the signal box. The atmosphere was clammy, heavy with cigarette smoke and effortful heating. He explained that from the Tower all traffic on the Lexington Avenue line, which links the east side of Manhattan with the Bronx, can be controlled. A large illuminated board diagrammatically depicted the line, and green dots moving back and forth indicated the position of trains. By pressing certain switches on this board, points are automatically changed and trains can thus be routed as the traffic controller pleases.

'Right,' said Hugh, adopting the role of quizmaster. 'You've got a downtown express on its way from 33rd Street, and an uptown local at Chambers. How are you going to route the express? Amy? Stephen?'

'Mmm . . .' One of us eventually stumbled across the right answer.

'That's right!' said Hugh, beaming. 'Now do it.'

'Do what?'

'Route the train.'

And we did, pulling switches here and there and watching the little green bleeps trundling up and down Manhattan on our say-so. In the midst of this return to kindergarten Hugh's walkie-talkie went ape. He tuned in, had a hurried exchange with someone, then said, 'Let's go,' and we tore out of the Tower and back into the main ramps and passageways of the bustling station. Hugh started to run and we followed, catching him up at the top of some stairs.

'What's the problem?'

'Suspected armed passenger.' He whipped down the stairs and along a platform to the far end. The train had halted in the station and many of the passengers had stepped out to see what was going on. As the three of us, conspicuous in our yellow safety jackets, raced down the platform, we attracted a gratifying amount of attention. I could see the headlines in the *News* already: BRIT HERO DISARMS IRT GUNMAN. Unfortunately the MTA cops had got there first. A sad-looking man, heavily built but very subdued, was backed against a pillar by the steely arm of one cop, while another of New York's finest, aided by Hugh, frisked him. False alarm: he was carrying no weapon. The train was restocked with passengers, including the dejected object of our attention, and went on its way.

Hugh guided us back through the labyrinth towards the Tower. These complex midtown stations, where different lines converge and link arms, resemble Piranesi's *Carceri*. Most of the system dates back to the early years of this century; much of the rolling stock is 40 years old, and the stations considerably older. They aren't shiny and smart, like those in Paris, nor majestic, like the palatial vaults of Moscow. They are aged and tortuous and confusing. Although changes are promised, and cosmetic improvements planned, it will be years before any results are visible, and in the meantime the disgruntled citizenry must continue to reconcile itself to a harsh and often insalubrious system.

Hugh, about five eleven, a bit paunchy, rumpled, with a kindly squarish face and a pair of specs that gave him a slightly donnish look, was amiability itself. I asked about knavery on the subways.

He was dismissive. 'Not nearly as bad as people make out. We had only 13 murders last year, and rapes are *way* down.'

There are times when it seems that most of the patrons of the subway are uniformed cops. Over 3,000 MTA police patrol platforms and trains, and very reassuring they can be at three in the morning. Fortunately for the MTA, policing costs are borne by the city. There is no doubt that the subways are over-policed: about 3 per cent of all city crime occurs underground, while 15 per cent of the city's police force serves on the subway. This disproportion represents a response to a public perception rather than to a reality.

Hugh led us past the Tower and onto the tracks. 'We're at 40th Street, or thereabouts, and we're going to walk south.' With our flashlights pointing down onto the rails, we picked our way down the tunnel. The light was dim, just a few low-watted bulbs to pinprick the gloom, and in the distance a band of lights at 33rd Street station. We stepped over puddles and around small piles of rubbish, and through the usual grit and grime and cinders that garnish old track.

'Mind the third rail,' said Hugh, not for the last time, pointing to the live rail that carries enough voltage to cook you faster than a microwave.

'OK, we'd better step out of the way — train coming.'

It was as well Hugh had heard it. I hadn't. We leaned well back against the tunnel wall as the Lexington local thundered by, grinding its metallic teeth at us. Because we stood well below platform level, the perspective was unexpected, and I found myself looking up at the windows rather than straight at them as the train rattled by. Impassive, unseeing eyes gazed down at us.

'Look at this,' said Hugh in disgust, tugging at some loose cables strung in bunches along the wall. 'These are phone cables, and they haven't been touched since 1912. If one of these wires comes down or is cut, the whole system's in trouble. Now you see why we need to spend six billion, and soon.'

Over the next six years the MTA will spend $5.7 billion on new stock, maintenance facilities, new signals, and a few new lines. MTA and city officials insist that this huge sum is the minimum required just to keep the system functioning at a reasonable level. To restore the system to a state of 'good repair' would, estimates the MTA, cost eleven billion. Much of the plant is literally rotting away.

I asked to stop for a moment so as to listen to the sounds of the tunnels. We stood very still, and there was silence here, deep under the city. Irregular drips of water reverberated and I also picked out, far off, a faint hum. 'Fine, thanks,' I said, somewhat embarrassed at having asked for the poetry to be let in. Hugh hadn't minded, and I fancied that on his own solitary tramps through the tunnels he often did the same. I asked what the hum was.

'The compressor. I'll show you.' We tramped on another 50 yards and Hugh let us into the compressor room on the side of the tunnel. These machines pump air into the subway's drainage system, forcing water out of it; they extract millions of gallons each day. 'If the compressors break down, within eight hours the water levels in the tunnels would be so high we'd have to close down the system.' It was hot in there and I was being basted by the humidity.

We picked our way back to the Tower, pausing, routinely now, to let speeding trains pass by. There are legends in New York that when baby alligators, a popular pet in the 50s and 60s, were flushed down the lavatory by exasperated parents, the result was an infestation of giant alligators in the city's sewers and subways.

It was Amy who put the question. 'So where are these famous alligators and rats?'

Hugh snorted. 'A myth. In all these years I've never seen anything larger than a small mouse down here.' I suspect that's another myth.

If there was a single rat down here, Hugh would certainly have met it. There are 700 miles of subway track in New York and he told me that he'd walked along all of it, with the exception of six stops on the A line, and the two hundred yards between Seventh and Fifth Avenues on the E. 'I'm saving that for last. I want to come up onto the street at Fifth and know that I've walked the lot.'

When we surfaced at Grand Central and returned to the car, I was astonished to note that it was still only seven in the morning. I'd lost all sense of time in the tunnels. It was dawn and we drove north up Third Avenue. Hugh talked about the old 'El', the elevated railway that used to run along, and deface, some of the major thoroughfares. The last El on Manhattan, until its demolition in 1954, was up Third. 'Did you know,' began Hugh, and you can be sure I didn't, 'that when the city scrapped the El, it abandoned more mass transit than any other city in the States has today?' He paused, looked anxious. 'Perhaps Chicago. Not sure about that. Must check.' The walking encyclopaedia had dropped a footnote.

We stopped at the 100th Street bus depot in East Harlem, where 175 of the city's 4,000 buses are garaged. The depot was built in the days of horse-drawn carriages and the downstairs offices are converted stables. The structure is on two levels, but only one of the two ramps connecting them is serviceable; the other was condemned years ago. Quarters for the buses are so cramped that it requires 22 turns to move a bus from one level to the other, manoeuvres that discharge enough carbon monoxide to wipe out a dozen suicidal poets. Hugh took us into the storeroom.

'We had this place computerized three years ago. Before then, store managers had to phone around to other depots for spare parts and just pray that their opposite numbers knew what they had in stock. Reordering used to take up to 18 months. See that ceiling? It's new. The roof used to leak so bad that spares used to rust on the shelves.'

Even now the low-ceilinged building was damp and filled with noxious fumes, and I was glad to escape into the chill fresh air out on the street. I wasn't sure why Hugh had wanted us to see this showcase of obsolescence, though it increased my admiration for the reliability of the bus system.

We then set off for the Westchester Yards. In a far corner of the Bronx these yards are the main dormitories for the Lexington Avenue lines. Workmen were still putting the finishing touches to 15 foot-high double wire fences, with rolls of barbed wire on top.

'Is this heavy-duty fencing to keep grafitti writers out?' I asked.

'Not just them. It's also to protect the motormen who work here at night. Some sections of the yard were so bad that motormen would only go there in threes for fear of getting mugged or killed.'

Hugh showed us round the maintenance barns, where trains are overhauled around the clock. Bent double, we walked under a train to inspect its viscera. Want to know how a train works? Ask Hugh, not me. As we emerged from crawling around under tons of jagged steel, he looked up. 'Come on. Over here. Let's ride this diesel.'

And we jumped onto a small train — the kind called Puff in children's books — which was crossing to the other side of the yards about half a mile away. Two workmen, in addition to the driver, were also standing on the deck, staring intently at the track.

'See how everybody keeps their eye on the track?' said Hugh. 'That's because not only the driver but the whole crew is trained to watch the signals. They watch the signals and they read the iron. Because there's so much movement in these yards that sometimes the iron is changed just after a signal's been obeyed, and there have been the most godawful foul-ups.'

As we toured the yards, on foot and by diesel, Hugh would

pause to chat to a supervisor or a group of workmen. Some of them looked at him warily, as if he might be bearing some terrible edict from Management, but his banter soon put them at ease. It was apparent that Hugh either knew or was recognized by every single employee.

Back to the car. 'Where next, Hugh?' asked Amy.

'We're going to Bushwick.'

'Hugh? Any chance of breakfast? I'm starving.'

'Really? That's too bad. Well, we might just manage a cup of coffee in an hour or two.'

'I'm *really* hungry.'

10 minutes later we stopped, as Hugh had intended all along, at a café where he was evidently a regular, and he and Amy tucked into a substantial breakfast, while I abstemiously nibbled on a little toast, loath to confess I'd already breakfasted.

Back in the car the phone rang: a train was stuck at Eastern Parkway in Brooklyn. Detour. We ran — Hugh's natural mode of ambulation — up the steps to the Tower. Breathlessly Hugh asked what had happened to the stuck train.

'The 9.02?'

'Yeh.'

'It's OK.'

'You mean it's moving again?'

'Yes.'

'Oh, that's too bad. Shucks.' Hugh was genuinely disappointed that a problem had been solved without his intervention, that he'd been cheated out of a chance to shoot some trouble. To make up for it, he showed us round the lay-up yards behind the station. They were in dreadful condition. The hand-operated points freeze in cold weather, so smudge-pots filled with kerosene have to be lit and placed under them to keep them serviceable. Some of the ties under the rails were so rotten we were able to dislodge them with a light kick. Hugh shook his head. 'This place is a mess. Having it in such poor shape causes derailments, and we need to spend money on it. But with money tight, the first priority is to spend money on track that carries passengers rather than track in the yards.'

There's a complex of three stations at this point, and most of it is still part of the old El system. We walked along the tracks, with the street about 30 feet below. Crossing the tracks, I was admiring the view and failed to observe my leg disappearing through the wooden slats. Hugh heard me going down, and immediately turned and grabbed my arm. Not that I was in much danger, but it was unnerving to see part of me beginning a rapid descent onto the streets of Brooklyn.

'You OK?'

'Fine, fine. A tiny bit shaken. Otherwise just fine,' I said, feeling the blood slithering against the inside of my jeans.

'Good. We'll go more slowly.'

'That's all right. I can hobble fast.'

We visited another Tower and again played with some antiquated machinery. The place looked like a squat. It was ramshackle, the institutional green blinds over the windows hung in tatters, and the stuffed chairs in the room were decades old. But the signalmen had done their best to humanize it: there was a small Kew of plants at one end, and a rudimentary kitchen at the other. While Hugh was rerouting half of Brooklyn, Amy asked after my leg.

'I've decided to ignore it. If I roll up my jeans we'll all see something horrible.'

I crawled back to the car, where there was a message awaiting Hugh: another damned train stuck at Kosciusko. On our way we drove down Broadway in the Bushwick district. This part of Brooklyn had once been a prosperous suburb, as one could see from the number of churches, those markers of respectability. Some were stone Gothic-revival, others cheap storefronts, here today and gone tomorrow. But now the whole district was derelict, and on some blocks buildings had simply collapsed and had been left where they'd fallen, a mountain of timbers and roofing and rusting shop signs. Apart from churches there were countless bars, including the inappropriately named Utopian Lounge.

The Kosciusko problem solved, we drove back on a street parallel to Broadway, but a few blocks away. Here blight had made less headway: large wooden frame houses nested in large gardens, and all were well maintained. One block was guarded on each corner by tall blacks wearing white smocks and knitted white caps: these were black Muslims protecting their property and at the same time their neighbourhood.

At 11 we stopped at Kew Gardens in Queens so that Hugh could check the progress of track renewal operations, thus giving me the opportunity to lose the other leg through the slats of the El, and then drove on to Coney Island. We moved swiftly past tracts of meadow and landfill, and to the left shimmered Jamaica Bay and the Rockaways, a narrow spur that lies between Kennedy Airport and the ocean. Amy and Hugh were both catnapping (no stamina) but each time we passed a notable landmark or any MTA installation such as a bridge, some odd instinct would jolt Hugh awake: he'd point at the object of interest, offer a succinct identification, then drop off again for another 30 seconds. Amy gave up all pretence of staying awake, and announced she would be incommunicado for the rest of the drive. Three minutes later I had the pleasure of yelling in her ear: 'Wake up, Amy! We've arrived!'

Coney Island is famous for its run-down amusement park, but its true claim to fame is that it houses the largest subway yard in the world, three separate yards joined together to accommodate 1,000 cars. The immense base shop employs about 1,000 people to overhaul trains and parts. Hugh was full of praise for the men who run this place: 'They're amazing. If I asked these guys to build the Empire State Building, they'd nod, give it a job number, and get on with it.'

I thought we'd seen it all, but no, Hugh led us through a partition into an area at least as large as the one we'd just left. Here in the car shop, entire subway cars are overhauled, up to a hundred at a time. Huge overhead cranes on tracks can lift up and shift whole cars from one end of the shop to another.

On hot days the beach at Coney Island is jammed with supine bodies being worked on by the sun, and here a mile away was its mechanical counterpart, thickets of steel and aluminium pinned and helpless under the glare of blow-torches and welders.

By the time we emerged — Hugh had shown us each of 14 stages of axle repair — it was lunchtime, but it was clear that lunch was not on the agenda. 'Where do you guys want to go next?' asked Hugh.

To Amy's horror, I did have a request and voiced it. I wanted to see City Hall station, since I knew that Hugh was one of the few people in New York with access to it. The station, one of the first to be built, has been closed since 1945; its platform is far too short to serve the long IRT trains, and the nearby Brooklyn Bridge station has taken its place. The old station has been preserved, however, and for good reason. It was built in 1904 by the architects Heins and LaFarge, the same team responsible for the neo-Byzantine half of St John the Divine. Since the old station is completely sealed off, the only access is by train. The driver dropped us off at Brooklyn Bridge, which is the end of the line for Lexington Avenue locals. The trains, having discharged their passengers, then make a loop before returning uptown; that loop takes the empty trains through City Hall station. Hugh flagged down a local and we rode it the 100 yards or so into the sealed station, where we were dropped off.

We were worlds away from the large, harsh, noisy stations of the IRT lines. The platform is not only short, but curved, so that from any point on the platform you can view the whole station. The space is barrel-vaulted and tiled in green, white, and red-brown. From the roof hang simple chandeliers; a few bulbs give out a dim peaceful light. Three skylights used to contribute natural lighting, but only one still functions. The place recalled those scenes in Eisenstein's *Ivan the Terrible* where demented boyars scurry through vast underground passages in the Kremlin. In a city which is constantly devouring itself, it was oddly satisfying to be standing about in a place that had been deliberately entombed, yet preserved. It had the stillness and dignity of a crypt, and the three of us wandered slowly around, letting its anachronistic charm seep in.

POWER TO THE PEOPLE

Remember the Chicago Seven? Probably not; but for some it still has totemic significance that in 1969 a handful of assorted radicals and yippies were prosecuted by the government under the 1969 Anti-Riot Act. This made it a federal offence to cross state lines with the intention of inciting or participating in a riot, which was generously defined as a group of at least three people threatening to injure people or property. With laws like that on the statute book, you can prosecute anybody, but the Nixon law machine picked some stout opponents when it threw the book at Abbie Hoffman, Tom Hayden, and five others. These men were radicals of varying degrees of seriousness; those of a more frivolous bent had a gift for self-dramatization that was bound to turn the trial into a splendid media event. They were unwittingly aided and abetted by the judge, Julius Hoffman, who was ignorant and autocratic and insulting; Hoffman not only imposed jail sentences on all the defendants but also sentenced the defence lawyers to up to four years for contempt.

But, as the newspapers like to ask, where are they now? Well, Hayden's enmeshed in more conventional California politics, and Jerry Rubin (who, according to the prosecution, 'screamed and yelled for people to kill everybody') has now shaved off his beard and runs the Business Networking Salon.

I'd hate to put words into Jerry's mouth, so let him speak for himself (text taken from Rubin's essayette in the brochure *The Networking Concept*): 'Hi, I'm Jerry Rubin. You and the most interesting person you know are invited to The Business Networking Salon "Every Wednesday" at

139

Studio 54. From 5 to 10 pm the music is in the background and the lights are bright. Studio 54 becomes your living room. People wear business tags, and are encouraged by the environment to meet each other. You're *supposed* to ask people what they do, exchange business cards, and suggest lunch to your most interesting contacts.

'The people you meet may transform your business or personal life — or introduce you to someone else who does. Business Networking creates a support system for us to translate our financial and personal dreams into reality.'

This invitation induces hundreds of rising and falling careerists — indeed anyone with sufficient status to possess a business card — to queue up after a hard Wednesday at the office in order to spend an hour or three making business contacts. They may be 'invited' by Jerry Rubin, but as he thoughtfully adds in a footnote, 'Admission $8 with this Salon Card and your business card.'

Satisfied customers may progress to the day-long seminar *How to Network Successfully* for just $45. 'You will discover how you can promote yourself and participate in Business Networking — the best tool for a business person in the 1980s, a period Jerry Rubin calls "The Decade of Achievement".' He adds: 'Be sure to bring a handful of business cards. You will learn to turn every day into a Networking opportunity.'

Despite myself, I was keen to take a look at New York's answer to Emerald Cunard, so I phoned the Networking number. I explained that I was a British writer of an inquiring turn of mind.

'Sure, you really ought to go along and see for yourself. I'll tell you what I'll do. I'm going to put your name on our list.'

'Tremendous. How kind.'

'Come along to the Studio anytime after 5.30 and don't forget to bring your business card and eight dollars.'

'As I'm a reporter, don't you think I could be admitted without . . .'

'I'm sorry, we can't do that.'

'And I don't have a business card.'

'No problem. Look, you're going to have a wonderful time and you'll make all sorts of useful contacts.'

At 6.30 the following Wednesday I arrived at the Studio and

forked out. As for a business card, I always carry some defunct cards with me, like false passports. I dropped an old favourite into the bucket provided, from which, I assumed, it would be transformed into digits on a computerized mailing list. I consoled myself that Networking will waste more money on sending bumf that will never reach me than they would have lost by letting me in free. I was directed to a table where I had to inscribe my name and business on a lapel badge. At last I went in search of Rubin.

There he was, a stocky little fellow, perky, straight-backed, a red buttonhole erupting from his lapel. I introduced myself. He knew who I was, greeted me cheerily.

'Can I have a word with you?'

'Sure. Get rid of your coat and come and talk.'

I was puzzled. I am one of those rare creatures who can converse and hold a coat at the same time. I didn't see the point of queuing for 10 minutes at the cloakroom only to have to search afresh for Rubin, when we were already perfectly situated.

'Where will I find you?'

'On the floor. I'm around. I'm easy to find. You've found me already.' He smiled at his excursion into logic.

I walked off. This upstart wasn't going to tell me what to do with my sodding coat. I testily threw it into a dark corner, reflecting that it was OK for Rubin to be elusive, or for him to be effusive, but it was bad form to be both at the same time.

With lava in my veins, I glared round me, reading the lapel tags as they flitted by: photograper, financial services, calligrapher, producer at physicians' radio network, chiro-practor, financial reporting for Colgate-Palmolive. On tables stacks of business cards were laid out. Looking for a wild-life photographer? No problem, there are two or three over here, take their cards. What a service! Though you can get it for nothing by checking the Yellow Pages.

A tall gangly youth approached and peered at my badge. I peered back. His name was Gregory, he was a pianist and composer. We shook hands, and instantly we Networked, just like that, first time around, a piece of cake.

'A writer? Oh, that's great. I'm looking for a writer. Ever written a musical?'

'No.'

'That's too bad. I'm looking for someone to write the lyrics.'

'On what subject?'

'I don't know yet. It's kinda open.'

'I don't think I can help you much. Maybe a libretto some day, but I wouldn't be ideal for a musical.'

'That's too bad. Still, you don't know till you've tried.'

'Is this your first time?'

'Yup. It's hard for me to scrape up eight dollars —'

'Know what you mean,' I growled.

'— and I had to skip dinner, but I think it's just terrific.'

'You do? Wouldn't you rather have dinner than search a roomful of financial analysts and chiropractors for a songwriter?'

'No. I think it's great to be able to meet all these people like this. You can just walk up to anyone . . . All these contacts, it's fantastic. And all for eight dollars. Fantastic. You know something, to me it's worth eighty.'

I went in search of Rubin again. He was just sliding away from a small group of truss manufacturers. On seeing me, he slung a thick arm round my shoulder.

'Hi. Stephen. How you doing? Having a good time?'

'Wonderful. Can I take you aside for a couple of questions?'

He looked at me in horror. 'I can't do an interview *now*. I'm *working*.'

'So am I.'

'I'm sorry. It just isn't possible. Here's my card, though. Call me at my office any time tomorrow. I'll be there all day, happy to answer any questions you may have. This is my direct number.'

Overwhelmed at having his direct number, I slunk away. By now the floor of the Studio was crowded, perhaps 300 or so, many young women and rather older men, probably hoping to get laid rather than expecting a new career. A wan woman brushed by me and I glanced at the tag on her bosom: College Professor. Now what could she possibly be looking for at Studio 54? Students? But she had disappeared before I could ask her. Gregory too had vanished; perhaps he'd met the lyricist of his dreams and they'd gone back to his place in Queens to make sweet music. By the bar I heard a woman ask a thirtyish man: 'Are you married?'

My dislike deepened for the premise of the Salon: that what you do is more important than who you are. Moreover, the crowd here consisted almost entirely of Indians, with hardly a chief in sight. Only the hopeful were here; the movers and shakers were sensibly elsewhere.

Leaving, I phoned a friend and dragged her to the Pamir, where I found distraction in such Afghan delicacies as Bulanee Gandana and Sabei-Chalaw.

The next day I phoned my pal Jerry. Couldn't talk, too busy. Try again in five minutes, then he'd give me all the time I wanted. Busy again. And so on throughout the day. The next day I did get through, and he apologized for having been so tied up. I began with a few innocuous questions to warm him up, and received properly innocuous answers. He confirmed that Networking had begun as a scheme of private parties in his home to which he'd invited interesting people to meet each other.

I launched into the biggie. 'I'm going to ask you a question you're probably sick of hearing. But I'll ask it anyway. How come you've made this shift from opposing the capitalist system to devising an organization that in many respects bolsters that system?'

'You're right that I'm not happy with that question. To answer it properly would take hours, and I'm not about to have a philosophical discussion. Also, your question makes too many assumptions, both about what I'm doing now and what I was doing then.'

'I understand that. But I'm sure you understand that I could hardly fail to ask this question. Besides, I'm curious.'

'Yes, but your assumptions are all wrong —'

'Clarify them.'

'They're wrong, and it's not a question I'm going to answer.'

'OK. What are your plans? Where do you go from here?'

'I have no plans. I think at the moment I'm satisfying a need, and I'm sure something will develop from that eventually.'

'Would you go international?'

'Maybe. But I have no plans.'

'And I have no more questions. Thank you.'

Before the light faded I went for a walk and headed towards Sixth Avenue. The rush hour was building up. It was my favourite time of day, when immobilized cars buzz and growl across six lanes of avenue while pedestrians, free as air, thread between them. The liberty of the unmechanized is deliciously intensified by the sorrowful captivity of the motorized. About a million cars prowl around Manhattan each working day, and three-quarters of them leave the island every evening. Saturation point is frequently reached.

Red lights are now seen as street ornaments, a year-round extension of Christmas decorations, rather than as instruction. Even the Police Commissioner admits: 'Today it's a 50-50 toss-up as to whether people will stop for a red light.' Vehicles jumping the lights often block intersections, inspiring whole symphonies of honking and hooting from frustrated drivers facing a green light and obstructed crossings. As we say in New York, spillback causes gridlock.

In commercial districts, trucks don't simply double-park; they just stop and unload. If this happens to block the street for 15 minutes, that's too bad. Under Mayor Koch, the city has made efforts to keep the traffic moving and to take action against those who flout the rules. It's typical of Koch's style that on Wall Street I saw the sign: *Don't Even THINK of Parking Here* — and on Lexington Avenue the wisecracking injunction:

> No Parking
> No Standing
> No Stopping
> NO KIDDING

People who want to keep cars on Manhattan have a choice. They can park on the street, thus shortening the life expectancy of their car, and spend up to an hour a day shifting the beast to take account of regulations that specify that you may not park on one side of the street on certain days when the street is to be cleaned. Or they can park in a garage for a few hundred dollars a month. No wonder that most New Yorkers sensibly rely on a combination of subways and buses, the 16,000 or so city taxis, and their feet.

Inspecting, not without relish, the city's worsening traffic put me in the appropriate humour for the next morning's breakfast meeting of the ever hopeful Association for a Better New York. A few hundred of us assembled in the ballroom of the Waldorf Astoria to hear the youthful chancellor of City University, Joseph Murphy. The university's colleges instruct 173,000 students, making it the largest Catholic, black and Jewish university in the country. The problem exercising the city elders at 8.30 this morning was that, with 370,000 enrolled students, New York City is the largest college town in America, yet it has a declining 'market share'. After Murphy had spoken, someone stood up to ask the standard ABNY question: 'What else, apart from giving money, can the business community do to aid the universities?'

To which the suave and dapper Murphy replied: 'You mean there is something else?'

The Abe Beame doll was on display again, and had been joined on this occasion by another past mayor, John Linsday, and the present incumbent, Ed Koch. I was planning to sink my teeth into Koch on a later occasion, but now I wanted to corner Lindsay. Although he had been mayor for eight years from 1965 to 1973, he hasn't acquired the patina of an elder statesman. Of course the Kennedy-style promise of his early years was undermined by the dreadful problems that overtook the city in the 70s, and his reputation as an effective politician has been tarnished. His crusading spirit had rapidly run onto the sands of practicality. Nor did his ill-considered attempt to run for the presidency in 1972 do much to regain the respect of the citizenry. Disgruntled New Yorkers felt he should be trying to run their city more successfully instead of spending his time persuading the peculiar Florida mix of rednecks and retired matrons from the Bronx to vote for him in their Democratic primary. Perhaps the simple truth is that, politically, there isn't anywhere for an ex-mayor to go.

Yet I had a grudging admiration for Lindsay. In the 1960s he had been a breath of fresh air, leading an administration of gifted if inexperienced zealots, and it's unfortunate that he seems to be remembered more for his failures than for his successes. Even now, a decade after his departure, he still looked every bit as handsome and dashing as his campaign posters had made him out to be. The hair was greyer, the face slightly less lean, but he was still effortlessly patrician and ridiculously good-looking, a masterpiece of Wasp physiognomy. I followed him out of the ballroom and down into the lobby. When I caught him up I introduced myself. He nodded down at me from his considerable height.

'This place is full of Englishmen writing books about New York. You're the third I've met recently.'

'I'm distressed to hear it.'

'I'm off to London next month. One of my favourite cities. I'm going to write a book about London.' That was, I later realized, a joke, but it passed me by; his timing was poor. We twirled round the swing doors and out into the street. Lindsay clamped a tweed hat onto his head and buttoned his trench coat. I buttoned mine.

'I go to London quite often. Hmm. Seems that Maggie will be reelected if they have an election soon.'

'Sadly, yes. The opposition isn't organized.'

'That's right. My old friend Roy Jenkins seems to be standing still.'

'When he isn't lying down. It doesn't look too promising for the Alliance.'

'And my old friend Michael Foot — he can't seem to get his lot into shape. People need to realize' — ah, politicians, how good they are at knowing what people need — 'that most people want to stick near the centre. Left of centre, or right of centre, but not way out on the extremes.'

I asked him whether he had any regrets about his retirement from New York politics.

'Hell, no. I'm back with my old law firm, I get to travel a lot, spend weekends in the country again, don't have reporters following me every minute — and I need to rebuild the pocketbook. You've no idea how expensive it is to be in public life.'

I had no idea the wealthy Lindsay had ever been seriously strapped for cash. Nor should politicians keep reminding the public of the sacrifice they make by holding office.

'May I be indiscreet and ask how you think the present mayor's doing?'

'I won't comment on that.' He turned to me as we walked; he walked very fast, but that's what long legs are good for. I scampered to keep up. 'I made a policy decision some time ago not to express my opinion.'

My, a policy decision. I tried to envisage the Lindsay circle debating the pros and cons in smoke-filled back rooms in the Hamptons.

'OK, let me put it differently. How's the city's economy doing?'

'Manhattan's in reasonably good shape, the boroughs less so. And the main reason Manhattan's doing well is because of foreign money. Our friend Lew Rudin puts up his building on Park Avenue and half the tenants are foreign. Every overseas business wants a presence in New York. We're becoming the Hong Kong of America.'

Lindsay was heading for Rockefeller Center. He said a cheerful goodbye as he loped into the RCA Building. I couldn't complain. Lindsay had been rather pompous but he hadn't refused to talk, and even in retirement he must, as he implied, get awfully tired of being asked the same questions over and over.

I was heading for Manhattan's homage to Houston, Sixth Avenue, but also turned into Rockefeller Center. I had to make some phone calls and I knew there were banks of phones inside the complex. I hate to pay tribute to monopoly capitalism but I have nothing but admiration for the New York telephone system. Banks don't work — it can often take 20 minutes to cash a cheque — but the phones do. I made hundreds of calls and on not a single occasion did I get a wrong number or crossed line; and I hardly ever encountered a public phone booth that didn't work. Moreover, in the busier parts of the city almost every intersection has one or more public phones, as do most restaurants, office building lobbies, and many shops. The subways too are sprinkled with them, though the noise down there often prevents one from using them.

In addition I award a prize, for poetry, to the Manhattan telephone directory, which tells us how to contact Thalia Stitch, Iancu Posmantir, Albino Ong, Chidilim Onyiagha, Richard Ooms, Siegmund Kiwi, Brain T. Kivlan, Fleurin Eshghi, Ida Ipp, Oy Turoa, and Babington A. Quame.

COLD TURKEY

Thanksgiving Day — always the fourth Thursday in November — is that national holiday when all true Americans devour a turkey and give thanks for 'divine goodness', whatever that may be. But it's a cue for food and drink and that's good enough for me.

In New York Thanksgiving Day begins with an annual parade, organized by the giant department store Macy's, a procession so splendid that it is televised well beyond the borders of the city. Its distinguishing feature is the size of the immense balloons, depicting favourite cartoon characters, that slowly move down the broad streets of the city from the Upper West Side to 34th Street. This year the women's movement had made another stride forward: the Olive Oyl balloon would be the first ever female balloon in the parade.

A sub-tradition has grown up over the years. The night before the parade, the floats have to be driven from the storerooms in New Jersey through the Lincoln Tunnel to Manhattan. Once they are in place, the balloons have to be inflated in readiness for the start of the parade at nine the next morning. In company with hundreds of New Yorkers of all ages, I made my way at eleven at night to West 77th Street to watch the great inflation.

West 77th is one of the most attractive Upper West Side streets, especially the block that runs from Central Park to Columbus Avenue. The large windows of the slender neo-Gothic facade at number 44, as well as most of the other windows on this block of apartment buildings, were lit, and inhabitants peered down onto the curious sight on the street below, where Olive Oyl, the Red Baron and Donald Duck lay flat on their backs, waiting for canisters of helium to bring them to life.

The street itself was cordoned off, but as its north side contains the southernmost blocks of the cavernous Museum of Natural History, it was a simple matter to hop over the railings and stroll through the museum gardens until a gap in the crowd facing the street allowed me to view the proceedings. Huge arc lights hitched to trees helped the crew to see what they were doing. Lorries loaded with helium canisters were parked nearby and large hoses pumped the gas into the slack rubber bodies. When I arrived, Donald Duck was almost inflated but one arm rested inert by his side. As I watched, innumerable cubic feet of helium were injected until, with great improbable twitchings, Donald's hand flexed and slowly rose into the air. From the crowd, someone yelled: 'Let it go! Let him be free!' It wasn't to be: since an inflated balloon is liable to float away, the monsters are bound with netting to keep them earthbound for the night.

It was cold. Walking up Columbus, one hand clutching an ice cream cone and the other thrust into my coat pocket, I hadn't felt bothered by the icy wind, but standing about in the museum gardens I began to freeze over. I began jumping on the spot to chase some warmth into my chilled limbs. Now that Donald's arm was triumphantly raised, the helium-bearing lorry slowly reversed down the street intending to line up with another rubberoid awaiting resuscitation. It bumped into one of the trees on which an arc light was slung, knocking off the light which crashed to the ground. At last, some excitement, and more cheers. For a few minutes irritated Macymen scrabbled around in the dark. Next to me, leaning against the railings, was a teenage girl with a friend of similar classification. She turned to her and said with considerable disgust: 'Let's go. I don't want to hang about all night watching them pick up lamp pieces.'

My sentiments entirely, and two minutes later I was hurdling the railing onto Columbus and heading for the nearest bar.

And the Parade itself? I skipped it. I'm sorry, but it was cold and breezy, not the weather for hanging about on street corners waiting for Snoopy.

So I stayed in bed and watched it on TV.

Macy's don't organize this extravaganza purely for the love of it. The final float is of dear Santa, and his presence inaugurates the Christmas season. Everybody accepts that this should be so, though I have searched holy writ in vain for scriptural authority. Commerce has reared its friendly head, and once Thanksgiving is out of the way, the gloves are off and the department stores and retailers are at liberty to chase the consumer with every weapon at their disposal. I've no objection. As my former father-in-law, a retailer, used to say: 'It's time we got the Christ out of Christmas.'

But back to the Parade. Or rather, back to bed after a quick excursion to the fridge for a glass of Alsace Riesling. On the screen I see the *Sesame Street* float arrive, a brownstone occupied by all the familiar creatures from another channel. It's fitting to watch TV heroes of our time on TV. The wind's picked up and the little children look frozen. The residents of *Sesame Street* are lending their talents to a maudlin number called 'Keep Christmas With You' (even though we won't get it for another month), which has the refrain: 'Christmas means a spirit of giving/Peace and Joy to you.'

I reach for my lorgnette when, in a delirium of titillation, in strides the Chrysler High School Trojan Marching Band from New Castle, Indiana, led by scores of long-legged nymphets cast as drum majorettes, twirling their batons and raising their heavenly thighs and slender calves high into the air. It's clear to me that at least half of these perfectly formed majorettes have just rushed away from the set of the forthcoming porn movie *Twirly to Bed, Twirly to Rise*. Should this kind of thing be displayed in the streets, and be beamed by television into millions of open-plan living rooms? Trojan, I may add, is the brand name of America's best-known condom.

Calm is restored to the frenzied streets as the band is followed by an antique car full of Muppets, followed in turn by a Kermit balloon that is six storeys tall and dragged by dozens of acolytes. Next comes Mickey Mouse, 57 feet tall, and a showboat (sponsored by York Peppermint Patties) carrying an accomplished children's chorus, who use sign language — not, presumably, for the benefit of the handful of deaf kids on the street, but for the thousands watching at home. My guilt at watching the Parade from the comfort of my bed vanishes. The children on the street seem to be dying of exposure.

There's a great cheer from the feminist separatist collectives lining Broadway as Olive Oyl comes by, followed by Felix the Cat. There are more floats to come, more balloons, more tiny tots succumbing to frostbite, there's at least another hour's worth, but I've had as much as I can take.

Parades are all very well, but the point of Thanksgiving is to eat vast quantities of food in the company of family and/or friends. James and Anna Atlas had kindly invited me to join them for lunch. James has always combined diffidence with ambition, a combination I find curiously disarming. Whenever either of us crosses the Atlantic we arrange to meet and exchange literary gossip. Jim always dresses so conservatively, usually in jacket and tie, that it suggests scant effort goes into sartorial matters, and that he prefers to devote his energies to swinging his machete through the literary jungle. Seated across a table over dinner, we would unpack our axes and grind them for all we were worth. Shortly after he became an editor of the *New York Times Book Review* (he has since moved on), I commented that he was now in an enviable position, able to assign reviews to writers he favoured. 'Yes,' he murmured happily, 'I can devote the rest of my life to settling scores.'

Not that James is vindictive. Indeed he often seems surprised that a writer should take violent exception to some critical opinion he's expressed in a review. James regards himself as the victim rather than the perpetrator of literary malice. One day I casually mentioned that a writer I'd been talking to had been somewhat unkind about him.

'What did he say about me?'

'I wouldn't want to hurt your feelings, Jim.'

'Don't worry about that. Just tell me what he said.'

'No, I don't think I should.'

'Come on, you bastard, tell me. It's unfair to hint at these calumnies if you're not prepared to say what they were.'

'OK. Just don't hit me, that's all. I assure you I defended you vigorously against this slander.'

'So? Get on with it. What did he say?'

'He said you were stupid.'

James roared with laughter. 'Oh, is that all?' I stared at him in disbelief. 'That doesn't bother me at all. I have many faults, but I *know* I'm not stupid.'

Like many men of letters, James is a good cook, and masterminded a traditional Thanksgiving meal: turkey with turnips and cranberries and stuffing, with apple and mince pies to follow. A couple of cases of Beaujolais were tucked in the corner. Quaffing wine, they call it. We quaffed.

Nine or ten of us sat down to lunch, including a foreign correspondent from Italy, James's brother Steve and his wife, and a woman who'd achieved notoriety a decade earlier by blowing up her father's house in Greenwich Village while manufacturing bombs for some violent radical escapade. She'd gone underground for many years but had since surfaced, spent some time in jail, and was now at liberty. We sat next to each other at lunch, but I'd gathered that polite chitchat about her explosive past would not be welcome and the word 'bomb' never passed my lips.

There were too many writers present for comfort. An unguarded word might find its way into one of Mario's despatches or into James's autobiography and into my own narrative. James, late in the afternoon, began to reminisce about his childhood in Chicago and called on his brother to confirm his memories, to supply the details that had faded from his own mind. But Steve was wary. 'This is stuff I haven't thought about in 30 years. Of course, I know why you're asking me all this —'

'No, no —' protested Jim.

'Yes, it's all going into your book. Everybody else here thinks you're making tender conversation about our infant days, but I know it's really research. Whatever it is, I deny it all. Speak to my lawyer in the morning.'

By 7.30 lunch was drawing to a close. Almost all the Beaujolais was gone, and we all rose to leave. I said goodbye to host and hostess, goodbye to various indistinguishable children, goodbye to the bomber, good night, good night, just point me in the direction of the bus stop.

While anchored to our chairs by repletion, some of us chez Atlas had suggested that it would not come amiss to spend part of the next day restoring our bloated bodies to their former prime condition by taking a spot of exercise. This was the opportunity I'd been waiting for. Weeks earlier I'd complacently observed the joggers in Washington Square, and now I had a chance to share the experience. It was agreed that a select group of us would set off at two the following day.

Never having jogged in my life, I lacked most essential equipment, but Carol, a friend who lived near the Atlases, offered to lend me some indispensable items. So I turned up at 1.30 on a crisp Friday afternoon, wearing a selection of my shabbiest clothes. Carol lent me a sportif T-shirt, and the one object that would transform me into a bona fide Manhattan jogger: a Sony Walkman. It took me a while to get wired up, to find a suitably raucous rock station on FM, to adjust the headset so that it neither deafened me nor slipped off as I strode vigorously along. I jogged spryly from her front door to the lift in just over four seconds. Then we walked, not ran, to the Atlases', where James was waiting for us. Anna was hovering in the background.

'What a delightful surprise! Anna will be joining us?'

'Certainly not,' declared James. 'She's on her way to bed with a pile of magazines. She's no fool.'

The three of us jogged up the road that runs through the west side of Central Park towards the Reservoir. On weekends this road is closed to traffic and restricted to joggers, cyclists, skateboarders, and other freaks. We trotted past the dells and glens and sudden views that constantly surprise one in this superb park. On this late autumn day it was not looking at its best, but seemed bedraggled and forlorn. The Reservoir fills the ten blocks between 86th and 96th Streets and spans the width of the park. It is probably the most popular, and most chic, joggers' circuit in the city. The setting is tranquil, the views lovely, and there are always enough people limping around to ensure one's safety, even in some of the more remote northern stretches of the circuit.

We waited at the southwestern corner of the Reservoir for James's brother Steve. He was late.

'They stayed last night in the Village,' James explained, 'and he was going to drive up here at lunchtime. I guess what's happened is that he's driving around looking for a parking place. You know, ever since Steve moved away to Boston he's lost his New York hysteria.' He shook his head sadly as he spoke of this terrible decline. 'Steve just doesn't have the necessary edge any longer. I've noticed that he doesn't cross red lights and he's even forgotten how to cheat other drivers out of parking spaces.'

10 minutes later Steve arrived. James's surmise was correct. Steve confessed all: 'Yes, it's true. I just don't have those old parking rhythms any longer.'

We set off, the two Atlases at a fair clip, Carol and I trotting behind them, steadily but a bit more slowly. So this was jogging! It reminded me of running for the bus, except that it was slower and less exciting. Without stopping, we admired the towers along Central Park West rising above the treeline: the Majestic, the San Remo, and the Kenilworth to the south, and closer to us the Beresford and the Eldorado. Nearing the top of the Reservoir we could look down to the needles of Central Park South a few miles away. What makes Central Park so attractive and so beloved is not just its diversity and size, but an element of wildness. In some of the glades and lawns it's possible to feel you're in the country rather than a landscaped park, and then you look up and see the towers and skyscrapers of the city only a mile or two away. Circling the Reservoir we were always looking across water, which made everything seem even more remote.

Carol, I sensed, was feeling annoyed. I could tell from her mouth movements that she was talking to me, but naturally, with Marvin Gaye and Laura Branigan pouring decibels through my Walkman headset, I couldn't hear a word. I smiled a lot, to let her know she wasn't forgotten, but I couldn't speak. Finally, on a lonely stretch of path at the top end, she tapped my arm and signalled that she was going to pause. I was surprised, as I was cantering along quite happily and had no need to stop. I unplugged.

'How are you doing? How are your legs?' roared Carol.

'No need to shout, my dear. You're only two feet away.'

'Oh, thank God you've turned that machine off.'

'I love it, Carol, I love it. Nature all around me, music in my ears, the steady rhythms of my sturdy legs —'

'Enjoying yourself OK?'

'Wonderfully. I feel part of history. To think that part of *Annie Hall* was set right here, and do you remember that scene in *Marathon Man*? That was shot at the Reservoir. And now: me. Hey, what are we stopping for? No slacking now. On, on.'

When we completed the circuit, we found the brothers

waiting at our starting point, panting gently. James was curious to know whether I'd survived. 'Do your legs hurt?'

'No, why should they? My knee hurts but that's because some hoods tried to push me through the subway tracks in Brooklyn the other day. Anyway, we've only run 1.6 miles, hardly an epic journey.'

'2.6, including the run from the apartment.'

'I dare say. OK, everybody ready for the next lap?'

Groans from the Atlas. Carol shook her head. 'I've had it.' 'So have I.'

'What? You keep-fit fanatics pooped after two and a half miles? Just a joke, I know. OK! Let's go!' I hopped from foot to foot.

'Not me.' 'I need a shower.' 'I have to write an article.'

After showering, I ventured out onto the streets again with Carol, for this was a special day in the history of gluttony. With 9,000 ethnic groups clinging to their identities, it's not surprising that a vast range of edible madness is available all over the city. If Manhattan is the mecca of consumerism, then Columbus Avenue is its Ka'ba. On a single block, between 73rd and 74th Streets, you'll find Il Cantone, a restaurant with a basement wine bar where opera is sung for your entertainment; The Last Wound-Up, which sells nothing but wind-up toys (the owner sprinkles his busy little shop with hateful signs that read 'I Hate People Who Don't Smile' and 'Toys Reflect a Spirit Not an Age'); a pizza parlour; then Cones (more preposterous homilies: 'Our customers get more than just another ice cream cone. We provide the highest quality product available, unique unto itself, in a surrounding that completely engages the senses'); then a folk art gallery and a sweater shop; next, The Cultured Seed: Theatre of Flowers (a florist's, in case you're wondering); and the trendy clothes shop Design Observations.

On the other side of the Avenue is the bizarre but charming Only Hearts, which sells a variety of objects — cake pans, crockery, jewellery, ballet shoes, stationery, clothes — with one common factor: they are either shaped like a heart or decorated with a red heart. New York shop owners compete for cute shop names, and my prize goes to the pet shop Fish and Cheeps. James complains that

Columbus Avenue is now so trendy that shopkeepers who provide essential services have been driven out. 'If I need a tube of toothpaste I have to put on my backpack and head downtown.'

Carol and I made our way further up Columbus to the official opening of the DDL Foodshow. Dino De Laurentiis has had the unnecessary idea of opening yet another food emporium in Manhattan. With a staff of a hundred, the Foodshow advertises itself as 'a gastronomic treasure wonderland' and the shop is as vulgar as the prose. The lofty plastic vaults and the displays are beautiful enough, but the atmosphere is truly Roman in its gluttonous excess. DDL stocks, it claims, 340 cheeses and 40 pâtés, out-of-season vegetables, and wild boar roasting slowly on immense spits. Boar was off on opening day. The first thing I saw as we pushed our way into the crowded shop — 31,000 of us looked in that day — was a pile of tomato-flavoured pasta, bearing out DDL's claim to stock just about everything — however disgusting. The chocolates, and I'm an authority on this, looked poor, but the prepared foods were beautifully presented, and had prices to match. Impressive too was the bakery, which stocks what one wit called Designer Bread.

Rapidly sated, we soon left and headed towards Broadway and an older temple of food: Zabar's. It's here that late on Saturday night greybeards totter in with their shopping bags to buy bagels and lox for Sunday breakfast. On Saturday afternoons, 10,000 customers pass through Zabar's, and on a typical weekend a whole ton of smoked fish will be sold. Densely crowded with both people and food, Zabar's is Manhattan to DDL's Los Angeles: it's busy, raucous, good-humoured. The theatricality of DDL makes for a more dramatic and stylish presentation, but the conventional wisdom in New York is that you go to the Foodshow to look and on to Zabar's to buy — which is exactly what we did, trying to choose between the three varieties of prepared duck, the curried chicken, the brie en brioche (I think not), the chicken in pesto. No interior designer has ever been near Zabar's; it's not hi tech, it's not beautiful, but it satisfies most appetites without charging excessively. When De Laurentiis tried to hire Zabar's manager Murray Klein, he replied: 'Buy Zabar's and you can have me.'

Carol had sweetly invited me to dinner on condition that I cooked the meal, so later in the evening I returned to the Upper West Side and worked my magic over her stove and fed the hordes she'd rounded up. We finished eating just in time to see the David Letterman Show. Tonight he was introducing an item called Stupid Pet Tricks, in which dogs, egged on by their owners, attempt to do ridiculous things. Dog Milton checks out books from the library. And dog Sam was supposed to be able to catch a ball, but conspicuously failed.

Then Letterman showed a videotape, allegedly shot in his studio when it was empty, of an immense bald fat man stealing valuables from Letterman's desk. Trying to show how our eyes can sometimes deceive us, Letterman produced a line-up of people, including the mountainous bald man, who was promptly identified by the studio audience as the culprit. Letterman moralized that we were 'too quick to condemn, and just because he's an elderly man, and not our kind . . .' He then replayed the videotape in which the identical scene was repeated, except that the thief was shown to be a little old lady. Which goes to show.

I was delighted, too, by an ad, in which a heavy-set man was telling New York about the great deals to be had at his Bay Ridge Toyota dealership. So thick was his Italian-American accent that they ran subtitles as he was speaking. That had a zany charm, but a prize for crisp ingenuity should have been awarded to a Brooklyn shoe shop that put the following sign in its window just before Christmas:

> Pierre Cardin Shoes
> Buy One
> Get One Free

UP YOURS

The gay presence in New York isn't nearly as formidable as in San Francisco, where support for gay rights is almost a minimal requirement for electoral popularity. There, old neighbourhoods have been transformed as the gays moved in, buying up and prettifying wooden houses and installing boutiques and restaurants where dry cleaners had formerly flourished. Organized homosexual communities have become economically powerful, if only because they don't need to fritter away their hard-earned money on such costly pursuits as raising a family. Instead, the loot can be exchanged directly for the latest icons of consumerism, be they clothing, food, a smartly furnished loft, a subscription to the ballet, or supplies of cocaine.

The West Village is the heart of New York's homosexual life, and Christopher Street is its principal artery. In this neighbourhood five out of every four men are gay. Tourists come to gawp at the windows of leather shops and gay bars and squeeze fearfully past black leather boys parading down the street. At night, though, the leather crowd swamps Christopher, which begins to emanate not exactly hostility so much as a kind of overloaded macho bravura that amplifies the predominant gay style in these parts.

Gays are not solely responsible for the wave of gentrification and consumerism that is washing over more and more of Manhattan, but they are certainly at its crest. As neighbourhoods such as Chelsea and TriBeCa are reclaimed first by artists and then by real estate developers, it is often the gay population that keeps the economic motors humming. So it wasn't surprising to see, on picking up the 50-page programme to the annual Gay Market, that the event had been endorsed by the Mayor with an official proclamation of these two days as 'Gay Market Weekend'. There's no clearer indication that gays form a constituency that no city politician can afford to dismiss. The president of the borough of Manhattan was even more enthusiastic; the Market, he declared, 'affords us the opportunity to applaud and celebrate the enormous business achievements and gains of our gay women and men'.

What surprised me about the Market itself was the extent to which the most conventional businesses advertise themselves as gay-owned and operated. I'd expected bookstalls and posters and jewellery makers, but not gay insurance companies, opticians, and photocopiers. Spur Productions makes gay cable TV shows; Front Runners is a gay running group; Patway Enterprises wholesales gay erotic sculpture. Various associations were represented: the Gay Teachers ('closet rights are respected'); Parents of Lesbians and Gay Men, Inc.; and SAGE, an organization 'addressing the needs of older lesbians and gay men'. Then there were the representatives of gay hotels, clinics specializing in sexually related diseases, real estate brokers offering weekend cottages. Culture was represented by the New York City Gay Men's Chorus, which gave its annual concert in Carnegie Hall a month later, and the Lesbian and Gay Marching Band.

Browsing round the crowded friendly market was fun, but visiting the bars was another matter. The anonymity of the baths made inspection easy, but bars are by their nature gregarious places. I dislike hanging out on my own in bars of any description, but I did want to see the famous back-room bars of the Village. I was in need of a Virgil to take me round. A friend put me in touch with a young economist at a distinguished university who was willing to show me round. He seemed quite amused by the assignment, told me the places he could take me to in exchange for my footing the bill. It was a deal.

Larry rang my doorbell on a Saturday midnight as arranged. Short, slight, and humorous, he looked like a competent version of Woody Allen.

'I'm a bit early, but I'd like a cup of coffee before we set off. Not much point hitting the bars before one or so. They looked pretty quiet as I walked over. One thing I ought to tell you right away: you can't go out looking like *that*.'

I don't recall what I was wearing: probably corduroy trousers and a bright green sweater. We discussed the ideal outfit for the tour, and the constraints of my wardrobe, and while he sipped his coffee I changed into a blue denim shirt and jeans and grubby running shoes.

'That's better,' said Larry approvingly. 'The shoes are just about grimy enough. Your leather jacket is too elegant, though. Where we're going you won't need it, and even on the street it's still warm.'

We walked over to a Greenwich Avenue bar I'd often passed without realizing it was a gay bar. Uncle Charley's Downtown was huge and so packed with T-shirted bodies that I never grasped the layout of the place; I just tagged along as Larry pushed his way through to what he hoped was a quieter corner. Quiet it was not, but it was possible to stand without being jostled. We had a beer and looked round. Charley's wasn't much different from a gay bar or pub anywhere in the world. There was very little leather. The body beautiful was on display here, and the place resembled a conference of swimming instructors.

'OK,' said Larry, 'I've broken you in gently. Let's head down to Christopher Street. It's been a while since I was down this way, so I think I ought to make some inquiries.'

'How do you propose to do that?'

'Oh, we'll just check out a couple of bars and I'll ask around. Let's try Boots and Saddle.'

As we clattered through that bar's saloon doors I began to laugh. Here in Manhattan were a hundred or so men in leather or lumberjack shirts or other varieties of Western gear, though for a certainty no more than one or two had so much as laid eyes on a cow, let alone rounded one up. A shiny saddle hung from the centre of the ceiling and across the middle of the bar a rustic wooden fence had been constructed, the kind of fence Dale Evans sits on while she watches Roy Rogers breaking in a four-legged friend. A few tightly jeaned men in check shirts and bristling moustaches sat on this fence, and there was a little manly smooching going on.

Larry approached a small droopy man standing on his own with a can of beer in his hand. 'Been a while since I was in the Village,' began Larry cheerfully. 'Could you tell me where J's is?'

J's is near 14th Street. We retraced our steps. Like Charley's, it's a bar I'd often walked past on my way home without ever being aware that it was a bar at all, let alone a fairly rough gay one. A solid black doorway, which had always been blankly closed by day, was open now. Inside, the crowd was white, mostly over 30. I bought two Budweisers.

'Mostly B&T,' murmured Larry disdainfully.

'B&T?'

'Bridge and tunnel. They come into the city from Jersey or Westchester or Long Island. Especially on Saturday nights. Let's take a look at the back room.'

'Good. Never seen one of those before.'

J's was far darker than Charley's and at the far end of the bar the gloom was even thicker, though features were perfectly visible once the eyes had adjusted to the low wattage. The so-called back room was little more than a vague hinterland divided off from the rest of the bar by what looked like a communion rail. There was no need to enter the back room area, since most of the activity could be surveyed from the bar. The difference between the bar and the back room was not so much that the former was decorous and the latter orgiastic, but rather that the back room was darker and more tightly packed. Some heavy groping was going on in the deeper recesses of the crowd, and there was a constant flow of traffic in and out.

'When you see a guy coming out with a smile on his face,' explained Larry sagely, 'you know there's no point cruising him. It's a sad thing, a guy with a smile. Had enough?'

'Yes. Where next?'

'Let's try the Mineshaft, if I can find it. It's not far from here.'

The Mineshaft is in the heart of the meat-packing district, an eerie and fascinating corner of the city sandwiched between Greenwich Street and the Hudson, a strip of warehouses that only comes to life at night, as at most wholesale markets. The pavements are narrow here, as half the area next to the warehouses is raised to form a loading dock, so that when the huge trucks back towards the warehouse entrances, it's easy to send the carcases swinging off the trucks and into the storage area. These loading docks are sheltered by rusty iron canopies. Metal rails are suspended from the canopies, and to them are attached evil-looking hooks from which dangle immense sides of beef that then rattle their way into the arctic depths of the ware-houses.

The streetlighting is dim but illumination is provided by the warm glow beaming out of the warehouses, and by flaring fires lit in oil drums by the bums sleeping under the disused canopies — for even though the weather was unseasonably warm, a chill set in if one remained motion-less for too long. The roughly paved streets are full of potholes; almost the only traffic here is that of heavy, multi-axled trucks that churn up the paving with their huge tyres. Rows of trucks were parked along the streets, their powerful engines and refrigeration units throbbing away.

This is the meeting place of meat. I'd visited the Truck Stop; here was the real thing.

'Wouldn't mind climbing into *his* cab,' sighed Larry, as we passed a burly driver unloading a bleeding carcase and wiping his scarlet hands on a dingy apron. We stepped gingerly to avoid the blood and grease underfoot; the smell rising from stacked garbage bags awaiting collection was rancid and sharp, pricking the nostrils. And then at the end of the journey, more meat, hunky men in leather and rough denim, their bodies taut with sexual anticipation.

Larry turned a corner and we saw ahead of us a narrow doorway, its yellow welcome surprisingly warm against the blank walls of the deserted warehouses. We moved briskly up the steps and I enrolled us both as 'probationary members'. By the entrance was a notice specifying the dress code. Larry hadn't been joking when he'd given me exact instructions about what to wear. The code is as follows:

>No Cologne or Perfume
>No Suits or Ties
>No LaCoste or Rugby Shirts
>No (Designer) Sweaters
>No 'Disco' or Other Drag
>No Sandles or Guccis
>No Ruffled Shirts
>All attire subject to inspection
>Please open your coat
>We welcome jock straps, T-shirts, and sweat

If you're on your way to the Mineshaft don't dine first at the ultra-respectable New York Athletic Club, which also has a dress code:

>Main Dining Room: Suit or Sports Jacket and Tie at all times.
>Athletic Facilities only: Sports Shirt, Turtleneck with Slacks acceptable. Jacket preferred but optional.
>Dungarees, overalls, work clothes & boots, running shoes, warm-up clothes, etc. NEVER ACCEPTABLE!

How hard must be the life of a rich New York banker with a penchant for rough sex! So many rules to master, so many outfits to buy.

In we went and found in the first room a bar, at which I bought more Budweiser. There was little choice. Larry leaned towards me and whispered: 'It's up to you, but perhaps you should take off your glasses.'

'Yes, of course, you're quite right.' I noticed he'd done

the same. Unfortunately neither of us could see far without them, and since the whole point of the exercise was for me to watch the hacking at the sexual rockfaces of the Mineshaft, we both shrugged and put them back on.

'There's something to be said for looking out of place. At least nobody is likely to bother us.'

I nodded.

'Too bad,' Larry added. Indeed, it did worry me that I might be cramping his style, but he seemed content.

'Hey, look at this,' I said, beckoning him over to a glass-fronted wall display cabinet behind which were dozens of colour snaps of frolickings at the Club, rather like souvenir pictures pinned up after a ball on the QE2 or after the wizard social that followed the cricket match on the green. Only I doubt that the Second Eleven usually gets up to the kind of antics shown in these photographs.

'What the hell is this?' I pointed to a photograph showing what I can only describe as a double catheter being inserted into someone's penis. 'Major surgery or sex?'

'Major sex.'

We sauntered into the back room. Near the entrance was a cloakroom where you can check your clothes, some or all, and here in the back and down in the basement there were quite a few men naked or wearing jockstraps. It was much darker back here and it took a while for my eyes to adjust. Cubicles lined the rear wall; they didn't have doors, but they did surround occupants with three low walls so that their exertions wouldn't be in full view of the entire room. Slings and straps hung from the ceiling, but weren't in use. The night was still young. As we strolled through, a slender young man with a moustache bumped into Larry. 'I'm sorry. Excuse me.' It was the first snatch of ordinary conversation we'd heard, apart from our own and brief dialogue at the bar.

'Not at all.'

'My,' said the youth, shaking his head, 'this is some place. I've never been here before. You know your way around?'

'It's four years since I was last here.'

'Wow. This is my first time. My name's Danny.'

'Larry.'

'Larry. Nice to meet you.' He turned to me.

'Stephen.'

'Steve.' We shook hands. 'Well, been nice meeting you guys. See you around.'

'Sure. Bye now.'

Danny dived into the crowd and Larry and I leaned against a partition from which we had a good view of the room. Next to me was a man in black leather, in his 40s, heavy set. Facing him stood another piano mover, a bit younger, wearing a grubby white T-shirt (but then it's hard to keep your clothes whiter than white down the Mineshaft). They were tweaking each other's nipples and absent-mindedly groping each other as they talked. The younger man was trying to date Mr Leather. Why they didn't head for a cubicle and have it off, I didn't know, and they were talking so quietly that I couldn't catch all the subclauses of their negotiation. But I did notice that every sentence uttered by the younger man ended with 'sir': 'Can I call you tomorrow, sir?' 'I would like that very much, sir.' Voluntary enslavement before my very eyes.

My attention was diverted by some activity on a curious wooden construction in front of us. It was not unlike an easel: two ladders at 45 degrees met at the top to form an apex, and two men were about to demonstrate its uses. A naked man leaned face down against the ladder, so that the length of his body was within easy reach. Behind him stood a Nazi. I use that term as shorthand for a standardized brute wearing jacket, trousers, boots, and a peaked cap, all in black leather; optional extras include studded gauntlets, bikers' insignia, and a chain or two. This Nazi was wielding a crop with which he was slowly whacking the buttocks before him. The slow beating went on for some time, after which the naked man heaved himself off the wooden frame. His place was taken by the Nazi.

'Shall we check out the downstairs rooms?' suggested Larry. I nodded. We crossed the room, where there was a good deal of coming and going, coming and blowing, and descended a rickety staircase to what felt like a basement, but was in fact the street level. Down there were three or four rooms and passageways. I found it hard to keep my bearings. The smell hit me first: dampness, the sharp whiff of amyl nitrate, and the equally pungent aroma of piss. Sanitary facilities at the baths and bars leave much to be desired, and in the Mineshaft, or at least down at the coal-face, bodily functions too are tendered as sexual coinage.

Here in this dank hole there were fewer clothes than upstairs, partly because of the warmth of the fetid atmosphere and partly because the sexual activity was in full spate. There were more cubicles, more slings, more leather thongs hanging on chains from the roof, and from dark corners came the sounds of slurping and the thwack of callused palm or leather strap coming down hard on undulating buttocks.

I had to sidestep deftly to avoid another Nazi going at it hammer and tongs. This thug was stocky and orange-bearded, and his jacket seemed to be delightfully decorated with ball bearings he'd probably split with his teeth. He was standing over a younger man, similarly attired, and with teeth clenched and head thrown back the Nazi was, Larry informed me, masturbating. So that's how it's done!

This, however, was harmless fun compared to what was going on in the next room. The smell alerted me, as did the slipperiness of the concrete floor. The room contained two deep metal bathtubs. In one of them crouched a plump and sodden man. Encircled by other men who were pissing on him, he kept shifting his position to catch the full steamy force of these arcs of urine. To my astonishment he was clothed, and his wringing wet T-shirt, by now blotchy yellow in colour, was kneaded and pressed by many eager hands. So, never shake hands with anyone at the Mineshaft; you never know where they've been. Later on we passed the bathtub again and this time there were two men in it sharing the golden shower. Piss and sweat, piss and sweat.

We went up and had another beer.

Danny came by. 'Hi Larry. Hi Steve.'

'Hi.'

'Good to see you guys again. You lovers?'

'No, friends.'

'Yeh, I don't have a lover now. I did a year ago. But I don't think I will again. I wasn't comfortable, you know, not

just with this one guy. He was good to me, though, Ishmael
was —'

'Ishmael?'

'That's what I called him. But his real name was Nestor.'

'Oh.'

'But like I said to him, I have more love to give. The way I
see it is that each of us is holding a cup of love.' He mimed
holding a cup, lest we'd failed to understand.

'Yeh.'

'And this cup, we all hold it, and it just flows and overflows
with love. Isn't that right?'

'Absolutely,' I said to the twerp, who then gripped my arm
and squeezed it warmly.

'It's love that makes the world go round, Steve.'

'Sure is.'

'Well, it's been great seeing you guys again. Say, can I hug
you?'

So Danny hugged Larry and then he hugged me, and
all the while I was praying he hadn't been anywhere near
that bathtub. He drifted away, a ludicrous but appealing
figure.

Larry nudged me. 'I could see that you didn't hug him with
a real man's ardour.'

'Oh, I don't know. I thought I did quite well.'

'I think Danny was trying to cruise me, actually.'

'Funny. I thought he was trying to cruise *me*.'

Larry tapped me on the arm. 'Would you feel abandoned
if I — er — went off for five or ten minutes?'

'Heavens no. Please feel free. I'll wait here.' I didn't want
to prevent Larry enjoying some sexual scrounging of his
own.

'I won't be long. It's just that since I'm here, I may as well,
you know, investigate . . .'

Larry returned, shaking his head. 'I've come back without
having had an opportunity to catch an incurable disease.
Shall we go?'

Everybody in New York jokes about sexually transmitted
diseases, men and women. When a friend told me a mutual
acquaintance had contracted herpes, she did so not as a

warning but in the spirit of 'There but for the grace of God . . .' The gay community worries about herpes too, but another far more disturbing seam of horrors is stitched into their minds: AIDS, the immune deficiency syndrome that lays people open to a number of diseases, especially a form of cancer that is invariably fatal. AIDS is not restricted to gays; other socially cohesive groups, such as Haitians, are prone to it. It was felling an alarming number of people and there was fear in the air, since homosexual promiscuity did seem to be a factor in its transmission.

It was four in the morning by the time we stepped out onto the pavement. I'd expected the street to be deserted here in the belly of the night, but not a bit of it: there was a queue of cabs waiting by the kerb. It was odd to think of those sweaty, pissy, fucked-out men in uniform stumbling out of the Mineshaft in the wee hours and falling into waiting cabs that would take them back home.

'I thought we'd try the Spike,' said my counsellor, and so we headed up Eleventh Avenue along the river's edge. The street was full of men, some just walking to and fro, others plainly hustling as they leaned against parked cars or stood in doorways. A small group of what could have been mistaken for Hell's Angels without their bikes loitered outside the Spike. It had just closed. Larry clapped his hand to his head: 'Of course, I forgot, the bars have to close at four. That was dumb of me. We should have come here first. Let's head back.' So we walked back down Eleventh and then down West Street as far as The Ramrod, probably the most notorious of the Village leather bars, since it was here that some years ago a trigger-happy goon who hated gays opened fire on a crowd similar to the one now gathered outside its door. Most of these men, it appeared, were simply hanging about nurturing the hope of finding a body and a bed for the night.

Larry seemed apologetic, as if he'd short-changed me. 'There's a bookshop on one of these streets that's open all night. We could take a look.'

It was 5.15 by the time he found it. Like a number of similar establishments in the West Village, it has a back room. As we walked in to the shop I could hear a sound I had learned to recognize: leather against flesh, followed by the groans of the happy whackee. But I no longer wanted to look at more bodies in sexual travail. I wasn't tired, but I had decidedly had enough, and said so. Larry wasn't sorry.

'It's been a pleasure,' he said, shaking my hand. 'Any time you want a tour of the bushes on my campus, just let me know. In the meantime I hope you won't reveal my identity to your readers. After all, discretion is the better part of squalor.'

After a busy Saturday night of S&M, it's good to purge the soul and rest the body by attending holy worship at the Metropolitan Community Church on Seventh Avenue. Arriving late, I slipped into a pew near the back. Many of the worshippers were on their own, though a few men in lumberjack shirts and women in dungarees were in the company of their primary other. The service opened with a Singspiration and we droned through a number called *Spirit of the Living God*. The performance picked up when we all bellowed out the carol *Deck the hall* which includes the line: 'Don we now our gay apparel.' My enthusiasm dwindled when the Kiss of Peace was announced. I demurely shook hands with a few other solitary figures near the back of the church, but further up in front entire pewloads headed for the aisles and cruised up and down, hugging and kissing en route. I don't care for niceness and goodwill dispensed at random. You can dislodge a grope at the Mineshaft but it seems churlish to decline a Kiss of Peace. I decided to slip away, and not a moment too soon, for as I kicked open the swing doors I heard the now familiar strains of *Spirit of the Living God* starting up again.

For my money, the gay church of the year is the Eucharistic Catholic Church on West 14th Street. It's a tiny cave that reeks of incense. Derivative icons line the walls and rows of candles nod and flicker in front of them. The altar is umbrella'd by a baldacchino from which red ribbons dangle. Over the pulpit is a checkered conical canopy in green and purple. Vestments were lavish, and there was more genuflection than in a month of Sundays at All Saints, Margaret Street. I preferred the instruction I'd seen in the Grace Gratitude Buddhist Temple in Chinatown: PROSTRATE SINCERELY. NOISELESS PLEASE. The clergy numbered four: an archbishop, bishop, and two priests. One of the priests read from the Gospel while an acolyte dressed fetchingly in white held up the holy texts. Reading wasn't the priest's strong point; he was scarcely literate, but he had a lovely shock of black hair, ideal for growing mustard and cress. The archbishop gave the sermon to the dozy congregation of 30, and as the theme was fund-raising I once again made a quick getaway from this curious place, with its Byzantine and crypto-Catholic liturgy. East is East and West is West but ne'er the twee shall meet.

SEEING JUSTICE DONE

Sandwiched between the municipal office buildings and the indistinct borders of Chinatown is a ribbon of courthouses: state courts, federal courts, the family court, the city courts, the court where you go to explain why you haven't paid your 412 parking tickets. The New York City Supreme Court is housed in a formidable pile at 100 Center Street, adjoining the notorious Tombs prison, which until its closure for rebuilding incarcerated prisoners awaiting trial next door.

The actual courtrooms are spacious but dingy, with half-hearted wood panelling. One enters through double swing doors to find eight rows of seats for family, reporters, bums keeping warm, and other onlookers; the front row is reserved for lawyers, a numerous tribe. A rail divides this public area from the judicial area, where sit the prosecutors, the clerks, the stenographer, a clutch of gum-chewing armed guards with pot bellies, and the Judge, who was expecting me and waved me up to the bench. On his left sat his clerk, looking bored, so the Judge put me on his right.

I was in a calendar court, not a trial court. After arrest and formal indictment, the accused is brought here. If the accused agrees to plead guilty, the judge will dispose of the case and sentence the prisoner. More likely, motions will be filed by the lawyers and all the judge can do is assign a date for a hearing at which these motions will be heard. If the defendant persists in pleading not guilty, and no further legal stratagems are devised by the lawyers to protract the proceedings, the judge will set a date for trial. So the calendar court is like a junction box. The roster is deliberately overloaded with cases and the judge, often operating at lightning speed, disposes of as many cases as he

171

can and assigns hearing or trial dates for the rest.

Criminal cases are brought before the courts by the Manhattan District Attorney's office. In addition to the DA himself, there are almost 300 assistant district attorneys. That's just Manhattan. In Brooklyn the DA's office has an even larger staff. In this court I peered down on three ADAs. Defence counsel were thin on the ground, because Legal Aid, which usually represents most of the defendants, was on strike. Once or twice proceedings ground to a halt because no counsel was present. A Legal Aid supervisor acted as counsel in most cases, and it appeared that he hadn't even seen the defendant's file till five minutes before the hearing began.

Backs of envelopes play a large part in the pursuit of justice. The attorneys, when asked for information by the Judge, would rummage through the files until they found the right scrap of paper. The Judge himself would peer at the scrawl he'd scratched onto his calendar or onto index cards weeks before, when this case had last come up. There was a faint but constant note of exasperation. The pressure was on, it never relented, and delays, especially on trivial grounds, frayed tempers. A number of cases had to be adjourned. One defendant couldn't appear because he'd just been re-arrested while out on parole; another hearing was postponed because a police report was not yet available. Prisoners were often driven the 10 miles from Rikers Island only to discover that their hearing was being adjourned.

During a brief respite while Fishman, a plump curly-haired young ADA with the expression of a child dragged to one birthday party too many, made a phone call in an attempt to retrieve a mislaid file, the Judge talked to me about the pressure. 'There are 8,000 indictments coming through the Supreme Court each year. There's no way we can try more than 1,500. If every case came to trial the system would come to a halt. So it's part of my job to dispose of as many cases as I can. That's where plea bargaining comes in. If I can arrange a deal between the DA and the defendant whereby in exchange for a guilty plea he gets a negotiated sentence, then we save all the trouble of a trial.'

The Judge implied that such deals were struck only when the DA is reasonably confident that the outcome would be the same if the case did go to trial, and if counsel suspected that the prosecution's case was strong. Later, an ADA I spoke to admitted that defendants often got off fairly lightly, 'but on the other hand, there's always the possibility that the defendant could be acquitted, sometimes on a technicality. If we plea-bargain, at least we're sure of getting a conviction. And in New York a first conviction often means a mandatory sentence if the offence is committed again. So it's in our interest to secure those convictions, even if the sentence agreed upon is rather less than we feel the defendant deserves. Remember that often a plea bargain simply isn't acceptable either to the DA or to the defendant and his counsel. Or the Judge will say no.'

The Judge strongly defended the system. 'Sure, there are people opposed to plea-bargaining. Not me. I have 650 cases in this court. I can't send them all to trial.'

Events moved so fast in the courtroom that I often had no idea what was going on, even though I was in the privileged position of sitting on the bench. I soon realized that often nobody else had any idea either.

Judge: 'Is Jose Ribera here?'

Fishman: 'I don't think he's on this indictment.'

Judge: 'Well, he's on my calendar. You haven't got him down?'

Court clerk: 'He's definitely not here. Not unless he's also known as Tony Burns.'

Judge: 'Are we all on the same case? Does anyone know what's going on?'

It's a choice tactic of certain experienced criminals to give false names or even to swap identities with another frequently indicted criminal. This invariably generates exquisite confusion.

The first bout of plea-bargaining was about to begin. The defendant's counsel was the overworked Rizzo, the Legal Aid supervisor. The ADA handling the case was the delectable Miss Sacher, a copybook blonde with, any expert could tell, a heart of stone, yet all was redeemed by unimprovable features that could have sprung from a Crivelli painting. Anyhow, that's my legal opinion. During the tedious intervals when lawyer or judge was searching for a crucial envelope, I would cup my chin in my hands and gaze with art historical ardour at the vision below me. She displayed a complete indifference, but I shall always carry a torte for Miss Sacher.

The Judge waved Rizzo and Miss Sacher up to the bench. These whispered discussions are off the record, so the bargaining can be conducted unofficially with only the agreed-upon outcome going into the official record.

Judge: 'What's the defendant's first name?'

Rizzo: 'Julio.'

Miss Sacher: 'No, it's Joseph.'

Rizzo (poor, beleaguered man): 'Er, that's correct. It's Joseph.'

Judge: 'I'm going to offer two to four years.'

Rizzo looked unhappy. 'He's looking for one and a half to three.'

Judge: 'With *his* record? No. Two to four.'

Rizzo (suddenly recalling that the defendant is charged with two separate offences): 'Make it one and a half to three and you'll get rid of two cases.' He's appealing to the Judge's self-interest. 'I *know* he'll take one and a half to three.'

Judge: 'Of course he will. He'll also take whitewall tyres for his car when he gets out of prison.'

Rizzo (despairingly): 'He won't take two to four.'

Judge: 'Well, that's too bad. I'll send him for trial. He can't dictate the terms to me.'

The Judge turned to me. 'He's been spoiled. The defendant's read about soft judges and thinks he'll get off lightly if he goes to trial. My hunch is he's wrong. For what he's done he could find himself inside for up to 10 years.'

The next round of plea-bargaining was successfully negotiated. The Judge then had to take the defendant through a formal allocution hearing. The defendant changed his plea from not guilty to guilty of second-degree robbery. The Judge recited the litany, but in such a way that it was clear he wanted to be certain that the prisoner understood what was happening.

'Do you understand that you are pleading guilty, which is the same in law as conviction after trial?'

'Yes.'

'Did you discuss this with your lawyer?' The ubiquitous Rizzo.

'Yes.'

'Were you intimidated in any way?'

'No.'

'Were you threatened in any way?'

'No.'

'Did anyone, including your lawyer, try to talk you into this?'

'No.'

'OK. Now describe what happened when you were arrested.'

'The officer —'

'No, tell me what *you* did.'

'?'

'When you were arrested you were discovered with a knife in your hand and a large sum of money in your pocket. You have pleaded guilty to robbery. So explain what happened.'

He had, said the defendant, been in Central Park at 4 a.m. A man approached, grinned, and reached for the defendant's penis. He reacted by whipping out a knife, and then relieved the other man of his watch, at which point he was apprehended.

When the story, which seemed to beg a few interesting questions, was concluded, the Judge resumed. 'By pleading guilty, you have forfeited certain rights.' He listed them. 'You understand this?'

'Yes.'

'You have pleaded guilty to a violent felony. If you are convicted again within the next 10 years, you must by law go to prison for at least half the term for which you are sentenced before you are eligible for parole or release. Understand?'

'Yes.'

'Bearing in mind that these are the first serious crimes you have committed, the DA has agreed to defer your sentence. You will be on probation for six to eight months. If during that time you are arrested on another charge involving violence, I shall sentence you for both crimes consecutively. Do you understand? If there's anything you don't understand, just ask. OK?'

'Yes.'

The Judge turned to me and said confidentially: 'That's called sticking your neck out.' He smiled, then shrugged. 'But it's worth a shot.'

The next guilty plea is offered by a stocky bald Hispanic

man with a black beard. He speaks no English and an interpreter has to help him through the allocution hearing. This lovable character is accused of stabbing someone with an ice pick on the Bowery; but he was, in mitigation, drunk at the time, since he's an alcoholic who's drunk all the time. The Judge summons a bench conference to check on the details of the plea bargain.

Judge: 'Before deciding, I want to be clear about his intent.'

Fishman, murmuring as he turns to look out of the window: 'I can't look into his mind, since he doesn't have one.'

Until now all the defendants had been black or Hispanic, but now attention was focused on two young white men, well-dressed, well-groomed, with their hair slicked back. Give them spats and they could have been extras from *Gatsby*. They were rich kids who had become involved in drug smuggling. (According to the city's special narcotics prosecutor, the illegal drug trade generates gross revenues of $45 billion a year, almost twice the revenues of the city's retail trade. Drug dealing is not only a big business in New York, but arguably the biggest of them all.)

The appearance of these two youths in court prompted a complete change of cast. Rizzo was replaced by a team of three lawyers, and the beautiful but uncommunicative Miss Sacher and the pouting Fishman were bounced by a more senior ADA, who had come into court to argue against the defence motions. The ADA was implying that these motions were simply delaying tactics which the Judge should handle as rapidly as possible. The Judge assured him he would do so and keep the proceedings on schedule. The ADA didn't appear convinced. The Judge adjourned the case. He stretched back in his chair and turned towards me. 'In this case I'm in a power struggle with the DA, and he's gonna beat my ass. He won't negotiate a plea. I think it's outrageous.' He paused, then laughed. 'But maybe I'll find a way . . .'

The next case clearly engaged the Judge's interest. Maria Felix was the daughter of a successful Hispanic business-woman. A prostitute from the age of 14, she had recently emerged from a drug detoxification centre. I assumed she was before the court on a drug-dealing charge. She was accompanied by a social worker, a remarkable man who'd been a junkie with innumerable robbery convictions. He was tall and dark with an engaging smile. Her boyfriend, a bearded black man, sat sullenly at the back of the court.

The Judge waved the lawyers and the social worker up to the bench. 'I have to tell you, I have my doubts that Miss Felix is going to abandon a lifestyle that's suicidal to her, and dangerous — but not very dangerous — to the community. It's that boyfriend of hers who worries me. He's got a record and he's a bad influence on her. He's a pimp, isn't he?'

The social worker shrugged. The Judge radiated the earnestness of an uncle concerned for a favourite niece who'd gone astray. 'Well, whether he is or he isn't, he's not doing her any good, and if she can be kept away from him, she'd be better off. If I send her to jail, at least he won't be able to get at her so easily.'

The social worker shook his head. 'No, it won't help. The boyfriend will still have access. There isn't a prison in the country that you can't get drugs into if you want them.'

The Judge leaned forward eagerly. 'I want to do things for her. She has a certain quality. I'd like to save her —' it was strange seeing the Judge transformed into a Victorian reformer, a man who could haul whores from the gutter — 'but if not — well, we'll lose her, I guess. It can't be helped.' The gap between good intent and the realities of a harsh world yawned open again; even authentic concern had to bow before a sense of limitations.

Miss Felix was replaced by Omar Brown, a heavy bearded man accused of attempted second-degree murder, having shot a man in the leg in the course of a robbery. This was his first arrest. Bench conference!

Rizzo, back on the job, was clearly puzzled by the whole case. Brown appeared to have failed to rob the victim, only to have shot him. 'Why did he shoot? Usually you get the robbery under way before you start shooting.'

Fishman, who can't be surprised by anything any longer, shrugged and gave a wan smile: 'Usually.'

The next case was grand larceny: the theft of a van. The defendant had 16 previous arrests. At the bench Rizzo negotiated with the Judge. They both seemed to dither: one and a half to three? two to four?

'Try two to four,' said the Judge. 'He's from New Jersey,

isn't he?' Rizzo peered at the file and nodded. 'Perhaps we should let them take care of him. I'm only bothered if he hangs out in New York and commits crimes here. Why don't I let New Jersey send him to jail instead? Let them pay 20,000 bucks a year to keep him.' He adjourned the case. The Judge saw me scribbling away. 'Hey, don't write down that stuff about New Jersey. I was only kidding.' The Judge was only kidding.

After a string of routine crimes, it was refreshing to hear a case which involved a cunning scheme to melt the names off stolen credit cards and substitute fictitious ones. The defendants were two women and one man, and the case was complicated by the fact that one of the women had accepted a plea bargain, the other had refused. Furthermore, the man's lawyer wasn't present ('He never is,' grumbled the Judge) and a second lawyer had to substitute. He came up to the bench.

Judge: 'I'm offering him one and a half to three.'

Counsel: 'He won't accept it.'

Judge: 'He's crazy. He'll come before a trial judge and they're sensitive to charges like this. Either they've had their credit cards stolen or their wife has. They're not going to have any sympathy with a scam like this. Your client should accept.'

Counsel (shaking his head): 'He won't. Frankly, I agree with you, but what can I do?'

Judge: 'Educate your client.'

Counsel shrugged. 'I've tried, but he won't budge.'

Judge: 'Well, I've tried too. It's the Christmas spirit.' He set the date for trial.

Finally, a small-time pusher is brought before the court charged with selling $20 worth of cocaine. It's two o'clock and nobody is keen to prolong the proceedings. Miss Sacher, who may be lovely but also has cruelly thin lips, indicates at the bench that she's amenable to a deal.

Judge: 'What's his record?'

Miss Sacher (green eyes looking down at her file): 'Couple of sheets of minor stuff.'

Judge (rummaging through his file): 'Here. Let me see. Mmm. Doesn't pay his subway fare, I see. One of Mayor Koch's lepers. Oh, he's a junkie burglar too. Well, let me think. 60 days plus five years' probation?'

Miss Sacher, heartlessly chewing gum, nods. The Judge claps his hands. All cases have been dealt with, except for the defendants on bail who haven't turned up. He orders their bail forfeited, then tells the clerk to adjourn the court. Followed by his lugubrious clerk and myself, the Judge lopes to his disrobing room, flings off his black robes, shakes my hand, says goodbye and speeds away.

CLAIRBUOYANT

New Yorkers are caught up in a swirling environment that is changing faster than they can absorb the transformations of architecture, fashion, new restaurants, new news. They must keep up with this shifting world, and they must also keep up with themselves, pursuing their careers, as if a career were something sprinting out there ahead of them, to be followed and overtaken and brought to heel. They live intensely in the present but always with a cold eye on the future, which is guarded by the city's many fortune tellers. They alone predict the unpredictable, and offer the minimal certainty that there will be a future of sorts in which you will play a part. Their *modus operandi* is much the same throughout the city: a shopfront with a neon sign announcing TAROT READ HERE or SPIRITUAL ADVISER or some such rubric. In the window are symbols of the ancient science: cards, a diagrammatic model of a hand, incense sticks, cheap busts of Egyptian deities. A small front room is divided by a curtain or partition from a parlour where there may be some armchairs, a standard lamp with a tasselled fringe, perhaps a TV set in the corner so that the fortune teller can catch the soaps when business is slow.

These unenticing temples of clairvoyance are not just situated in the poorer parts of the city, inhabited by the gullible and the desperate. They are found all over town, on Madison as well as on 125th Street. A sandwich board on a pavement just two blocks from where I was living advertised readings of all varieties: palm, Tarot, leaves. It was on Bleeker Street, just doors away from Pierre Deux and Bleeker-on-Perry and other ultra-smart shops.

I walked in. An unprepossessing woman wearing a

vaguely gypsy get-up — perhaps she belonged to the genuine gypsy family that lives on nearby Leroy Street — waddled up. I asked Ms Ray (first name? last name?) what her rates were.

'It's 15 dollars for Tarot, 10 for half Tarot, 10 for two palms, 5 for one.'

'I see.'

'I'll tell you your past, your present, your future. I'll tell you about your love life, all you want to know.'

A grand offer. I thought about it. 'I already know about the past, though.'

Ms Ray grew indignant. 'You need to know about the past in order to understand the future.'

'Yes, of course.' Silly of me to have forgotten all the clichés.

Her tone softened. 'I'll do you a nice palm reading for five.'

'Another time.'

Ms Ray was an undeniably crude specimen but New Yorkers of all types and classes are prone to the same anxieties, and there were a few clairvoyants in the city who attracted a fashionable and devoted following. I'd already met Beatrice Rich briefly at the restaurant opening, and I had friends who swore by her. I phoned for an appointment. Beatrice never answers the phone; instead I left a message in response to a recorded message that bore the signature of her manager John Newhouse. John and I spent a merry week leaving messages on each other's machines, a minor sport in New York, but eventually we spoke, voice to voice. Beatrice, he explained, was fully booked for six months, but as a special favour, pleaded for by mutual acquaintances, he would put me on stand-by.

A month later the phone rang. It was John. There'd been a cancellation. Could I see Beatrice at 6.30 that evening? I had an appointment at the Athletic Club at six, so I felt I had to say no.

'That's too bad,' said John reproachfully. 'I've had to cancel a large number of appointments recently because Beatrice has been ill this last month. I'm not even accepting any more bookings for her at the moment, and many of these people are never going to get to see her. I'm offering you this cancellation because I know you'll be leaving —'

'I'll be there.'

'6.30 at Bondini's.'

I lied my way out of my original appointment.

I walked promptly into Bondini's and waited by the bar in the front. When I heard Beatrice quietly saying my name, I turned to greet her. A small staircase leads up from near the cloakroom and I followed her up it to a balcony overlooking the main restaurant. There were a few diners below but we had the balcony to ourselves. Beatrice operates from a small round table in a corner. On the tablecloth stood a lamp, a jug of water, a glass, and a pack of cards.

Beatrice, who had struck me on first meeting as very shy, was entirely in command. Slender and erect, so that she appeared to be taller than she actually was, she was dressed expensively in a jacket, skirt and bulky turtleneck. Frail and bony, her face framed large eyes that look directly at me, serene and unblinking. Her lips were remarkably wide and set in a gentle smile that gave her expression a sweetness and calm that inspired trust.

She used ordinary playing cards and asked me for an object that had belonged to me alone for many years. I gave her my watch. 'I can tell you about your love life or your work or some other aspect of your life. Love and work are the most popular categories. Or I can give you a general reading, which may include those two but may be about something quite different.'

She agreed to split the session between love and work.

'I see six months into the past and six months into the future. It isn't always clear which. I may be telling you about something that has just happened or it may be about to happen in the next few months. There may be bad or unpleasant news, but I needn't tell you if you'd rather not know.'

'Tell me anything you like.'

'All right.' She explained that, while concentrating hard on my work and career, especially any problems that I might be having, I was to shuffle the cards very carefully and cut them. I did so, and she then laid them out in a kind of U with a tail. She stared at them for a few moments, while fondling my watch in her left hand, and began to speak. Much of what she told me — about my personality, my defects — was true enough, but any highly perceptive person finely tuned in to all the signals that other human beings emit could have reached similar conclusions. What was more startling was that she told me things about my family that she could not have known previously or discerned.

Beatrice not only predicts the recent past and immediate future, but feels free to tell you what to do about it. She laid her long bony finger on the flaws in my character, and urged me to deal with them. There was no trace of fatalism in her attitude; she was simply using her psychic gift for my benefit. Again and again I would blush and nod my head in mournful confirmation as she identified yet another trooper in my battalion of inadequacies, and then she'd tell me to shape up, to push out of my way the blocks that I, more than anyone else, had strewn in my own path. With her head high, her eyes firmly set in my direction, and always the most gentle expression on her knowing lips, she read me the riot act.

After 40 minutes my session was over. Feeling distinctly shaken I walked up Fifth Avenue to Maria's loft. I brooded as I went. I hadn't realized that psychics give advice; I thought they only gave information. It had thrown me. The next day I phoned James to report.

'So tell me, what did she say?'

'All sorts of terrible things.'

'Anything about your book?'

'Yes!' I wailed. 'She told me I'd have difficulty writing it, difficulty finishing it, quarrels with my publisher!'

James snorted with derision. 'I could have told you *that*! You don't need to spend 35 dollars for that information!'

Emerging from the lift directly into Maria's loft, I was met as usual by a committee of Astro and Cosmo the cats, Rebus the dog, and the Siamese twin kittens Lapis and Lazuli. Maria had disappeared to answer the phone. Two minutes later she returned.

'I've just had to cancel my morning appointment at the Tranquility Tanks. That's too bad — I'll have to wait two months for another, but I've just had my hair permed and the salt would wreck it. Hey, that's an idea! Stephen, why don't you —'

'No. Certainly not.'

'You really ought to. Go on. Take my place.'

'Sweet of you, but floating in Epsom salts for an hour isn't my idea of fun.'

'It's wonderful, it really is.'

'It's hardly a New York thing to do. It sounds Californian to me, like jacuzis and growing muscles and taking your clothes off for Jesus.'

Just after I'd given in, our mutual friend Katy arrived and the three of us set off to sample *cuisine tibétaine*.

Let me say a few words about Tibetan food: don't eat it.

The Tibetan Kitchen is on Third Avenue: a justly modest exterior leads into a small dingy dining room. It was full when we arrived, and we were asked to wait downstairs in a gloomy windowless basement room with a non-functioning bar in one corner, two tables with cheap tablecloths, and along one wall banks of slats with rugs thrown on top, which looked suspiciously like a make-shift bed. Tattered Christmas decorations adorned the walls, including a single orange balloon. Katy and I went out to stock up with beer (the restaurant had no licence) and when we returned found Maria happily settled in front of the TV set in the corner. Like many people who don't possess a television ('on principle'), she's devoted to watching other people's. A large genial waiter came down the stairs and proceeded to lay the table.

We resigned ourselves to eating in this crypt. Maria was delighted, as she could entertain us by watching television. The waiter came downstairs again with a spray can and, parting a curtain, went through into another room. Squirting sounds followed. He emerged and returned upstairs. We crept into that other room, a store room with freezers and cartons of noodles, but were overwhelmed by swirling mists of Glade Early Spring. We speculated: was he covering up the smell of the dead rats or the rotting food? We did not stay for an answer, but went upstairs and insisted on eating in the main room. The food was awful.

The next morning I walked up Fifth to 21st Street and presented myself at the reception desk at the Tranquility Tanks at nine. The tanks are discreetly housed on the eighth floor of a commercial building, as part of a holistic health centre that provides acupressure and other body therapies. The tanks are kept in two small rooms. While Tod, small, kindly, bearded, prepared a room for me, he gave me the instructions to read, and asked me to sign a form saying I was in good health.

The tank itself, the size of a large sentry box laid on its side, filled about a quarter of the room. The end was beveled to provide a hatch for entry. It looked like a horizontal Citicorp Building. In a corner was a shower, and the rest of the room, with its slatted wooden floor, contained a dressing table, and space for one's clothes. Tod reminded me of some of the procedures specified in the instructions, answered a few questions, then left me, closing the door behind him. I undressed and showered. I dried my face and inserted wax earplugs to deter invasions of saline solution once I was in the tank. Vaseline was provided for smearing on sore spots that might smart in contact with the salt. I peered through the hatch at 160 gallons of Dead Sea. I still felt dubious about the whole exercise; I *like* my nervous energy, I feel good when all my systems are buzzing, and I wasn't sure I wanted to switch them all off for an hour. The only sound was a soft mechanical hum; above me gentle light was being projected through a revolving prism, throwing soft rainbows round the room. Excellent conditions for Nirvana. Grabbing the inflatable pillow which Maria had recommended I use to support my head, I put one foot into the tank and slowly slid my whole body in. I was floating.

These tanks were invented in 1954 by John Lily to aid his investigation of altered states of consciousness. The water is only 10 inches deep but contains 800 pounds of Epsom salts in solution, filtered and kept fresh, giving such a high degree of buoyancy that there is no possibility of sinking. By pressing down hard with my foot or arm I could indeed touch the bottom, but I had to thrust hard. The water is maintained at body temperature, so as to minimize any awareness of its accquosity and break down the tactile divisions of body, air, and water.

I closed the hatch and found myself in total darkness. To keep claustrophobia at bay, the hatch closes only with its own weight; there is no latch or lock. To escape, you lightly push it open. I felt around me. I could touch the sides with my arms and legs, but I soon settled down and kept my arms beside me in the centre of the tank. Whether I opened my eyes or kept them closed made no difference in this Stygian blackness. Floating in the sea requires some effort, but in the tank there was no other option. All the senses are invited to take a rest since there is nothing for them to exercise on. I wasn't even aware of being hot or cold since everything around me was the same temperature as my body. Oddest of all, no demands were made on my muscles; there was no need to worry about defying gravity by staying on one's feet and moving about.

Nevertheless I didn't relax. My body remained tense and my brain was busily taking in and analysing the peculiar circumstances I found myself in. Part of the experience was alluring, especially the silence. In New York there is no such thing as silence, but here in this black tank the only sound that was registering was the thump of my heartbeat. Yet my mind was turning over at its usual rate of rpm's. Beatrice's prognostications had disturbed me, given me a restless night, and instead of escaping from them in this tank of tranquillity, I was dwelling on them all the more obsessively — until I came to with a start and realized my mind had wandered, so that what had begun as a rational train of thought had imperceptibly been derailed. It was similar to the state just before falling asleep, when one is dimly aware, as if from afar, that one is still conscious but one no longer has rigid control over the direction and contents of one's thoughts, which, now their keeper's vigilance is slipping, loosen the bolts to admit the fripperies and arabesques of fantasy. Odd images would dart into my mind and dart out again, thoughts would shuffle past then turn somersaults and vanish.

Drifting in this half-stupefied state, I was jarred by a soft tapping sound. I was puzzled. Then I recalled that Tod had told me he'd let me know when my time was up by tapping on the side of the tank. I felt worlds away. He tapped again, and I roused myself to a single-noted 'Yes'. It was some minutes, though, before I could bring myself to open the hatch. Had I been asleep or had my mind simply been wandering? In any event, I didn't feel rested, I wanted to stay in there for a bit longer. Eventually I dragged myself out, removed the earplugs, showered thoroughly (shampoo and conditioner were provided). On the dressing table were deodorants and other unguents; a hair dryer too. I dressed and emerged. Tod asked me how I'd liked the tank, but I couldn't give a clear answer yet. My face felt heavy and drawn, as if the forces of gravity, with which I was once again in contact, were tugging me down, keeping me earthbound in defiance of my newfound floating powers.

Experienced floaters report that after a session in the tank their sensations are heightened: birds sing with a new sweetness, the scent of lilac becomes more piercing and lovely than ever before. For me it was otherwise. I felt my contact with the world about me was loosened, as if some wires had been pulled out; there was a sense in which I was still floating, still remote from the bustle and racket of the city. In short, I felt spacey. Half an hour later I was talking, by appointment, to a newspaper executive. I'd prepared my questions, but when he answered them evasively, I found it difficult to whip back with a follow-up; my probing mechanisms, my inquisitorial techniques had atrophied. I felt doltish. Later in the day I phoned the Tanks to ask whether this response was typical.

'I find that I'm simply not functioning as well as usual. I'm less alert, less snappy, less agile with my brain.'

'Perhaps you're saying you're more relaxed. It may not be such a bad thing not to operate on your nervous energy, but to relax and be in tune with the natural rhythms.'

'I'm sure that's true. But it's not helping me function. I'm so relaxed I'm no longer effective. Well, I suppose, given what I do, that relaxation isn't an asset.'

'I guess not.'

Perhaps this is why New York is so appealing to me. I'm a city boy, always have been. I too relish the poetry of kerbstones, the music of the street. If I wake in the morning and hear a bird singing, I know something's wrong. New York is inhospitable to nature: its fields are concrete and tarmac, its forests are 100 storeys high, its gardens perch on rooftops. To function in such an environment you must be alert — and paradoxically, given that the city is brazenly Against Nature, you must be fully alive in order to survive. In New York, the tanks strip you of your armour and shower you with gifts that are of no use.

By noon my spaciness was wearing off, but only to be replaced by hunger, which has overlapping symptoms. So it was good to be walking into the sober entrance of the Four

Seasons on East 52nd Street knowing that at least a decent lunch would be awaiting me. If there is a more beautiful modern restaurant anywhere than the Four Seasons, I do not know it. Its two palatial rooms, each three storeys high, are magisterially elegant, with barely a trace of the vulgarity that comes naturally to so much American design. Located on the edge of Mies van der Rohe's refined Seagram Building, the restaurant was designed in 1959 by Philip Johnson, the architect responsible for much of Manhattan's most noteworthy and controversial building.

The restaurant's gimmick is well known: as each season passes, the menu, the uniforms, and the immense plants that decorate the rooms are changed. As one comes up the stairs, the bar is on the right and the Pool Room to the left. Both rooms are walnut-veneered, and tall stately windows rise to the full height of the rooms. In the bar these windows are curtained not with cloth but with swashes of thin chains that glide and rustle quietly as they are touched by currents of air. Such extravagance, such restraint! The effect would be too dazzling if it called attention to itself, but it's in tune with those tall dark walls. Above the square bar is a vertical sculpture by Richard Lippold that consists of shimmering brass rods pointing down, suspended from wires; it is both fragile and immense, like the copper curtains which form its backdrop. The other great backdrop at the Four Seasons is the Picasso tapestry for *Le Tricorne* that hangs in the lobby.

I was a few minutes early so I strolled around. In the bar some tables were laid for lunch and a few early parties were tucking in, while around the bar itself a few morose businessmen twirled the olives in their martinis. At the reception desk in the lobby stood a grave official, surrounded by no fewer than six waiters and pages ready to show arriving guests to their table. I asked whether Mrs Lewit had arrived, and rather to my surprise was told she had. A flunkey asked me to follow him and we marched smartly down the short corridor that leads into the Pool Room.

Here the shape of the stately white marble pool in the centre determines the layout of the tables, which are arranged in squares, three or four rows of them. It's like a theatre in the round, with the pool as stage, and gently ascending banks of tables on all sides. Because the pool makes it impossible to cross the room, one must walk round it, and the flunkey took me to the furthest corner. Eyes were discreetly raised as people wondered who I might be, an instinctive response to each new arrival. I was reciprocating the inquisitiveness and scarcely noticed when the page came to a halt at a large corner table. Seated there were six or seven elderly people, but there was one spare seat which he invited me to occupy.

I smiled at the perplexed woman who acted as if she were the hostess for this lunch. 'This looks like a most delightful party, but I have to confess I am not a member of it.'

The page looked startled. 'Didn't you say you were with Mrs Uris?'

'No. Mrs Lewit.'

Blushes, apologies, bowings, smiles. And dignified retreat. Two minutes later the swift unmistakable figure of Julie came smartly up the stairs. For a second time, but now properly accredited, I trekked round the pool.

'Not bad, not bad,' said Julie professionally, whisking open her napkin. 'The table, I mean. You see, this whole place is a power game. The closer you are to the pool, the more important you are. People in the back row by the wall are as far off as Siberia.'

We were in the second row. Those in the first could actually lean their elbows on the white marble of the quietly bubbling pool.

At all too many restaurants, the tables are so close that one's elbow is often in the soup plate on the next table. In New York space is money — and I dare say some entrepreneur has already tried to buy the air rights over the Pool Room — but here space was handled with a lavishness that was exhilarating and elegant. The proportions had been calculated, as had everything else, down to the last detail: the off-white linen, the deeply comfortable banquettes, the ornate silver platters on each table. Service was punctilious. Unwilling, but legally required, to employ waitresses as well as waiters, the Four Seasons had retaliated by dressing its few waitresses in drag, like military cadets or escaped trouser-role singers from operetta.

And the food? I couldn't quarrel with the impeccably braised fillet of striped bass stuffed with lobster and lightly coated with shredded leeks and a delicate white sauce. We drank a good Sancerre, and a glass or two gave me a third dose of spaciness to add to the two I already had: I surrendered by leaning back and talking nonstop for an hour and a half.

As Julie was hocking her diamonds to pay the bill, I noticed a man seated by the pool speaking into a telephone.

'He's always there,' said Julie dismissively. 'I don't know who he is. Ostentatious, don't you think, keeping a phone by the pool?'

'Absolutely. If I were as grand as he'd like me to think *he* is, I wouldn't *know* anybody who could be reached by phone in the middle of the day.'

ENEMIES

New York's tradition of fierce liberalism was nourished in large part by the presence of a vigorous Jewish community. Its earnest, intellectualizing strain may have derived from the German Jews who settled in the city in the nineteenth century, while a more radical and politicized strain emerged from the waves of generally far poorer Russian and Polish immigrants who arrived at the turn of the century. Whatever the intellectual archaeology of Jewish liberalism, no one would deny that from the 1930s until the 1960s the majority of New York Jews would have identified themselves, politically and culturally, with progressive ideas and policies. The Trillings had thought hard and deeply about liberalism and politics in their relation to the literary culture in which they were steeped; left-wing journals such as the *Partisan Review* argued the case for radical change; Paul Goodman was not unhappy to be labelled an anarchist, an identification that might have earned him a lynching elsewhere. New Yorkers ardently supported the nascent civil rights activists in the early 1960s, and although New York Jews had no monopoly on the growing opposition to the Vietnam War, there were few East Coast liberal Jews who wholeheartedly endorsed the war.

Yet now in the early 1980s all that seemed to have changed. Lionel Trilling, Hannah Arendt, Paul Goodman — they were all dead, and the survivors of that spirited clerisy — Diana Trilling, Irving Howe, and others — were disenchanted in varying ways. It wasn't merely that an intellectual movement and tradition had run its course, but that there was a marked shift to the Right; former liberals were now proclaiming themselves to be 'neo-conservatives', despising the liberal establishment that had bred them and openly supporting policies that would have been anathema to them 10 or 15 years before. Most of the old journals of what Americans like to think of as the Left were still around, but some of them, such as *The New Republic,* had distanced themselves from the liberal, occasionally radical, views they had once espoused; while others, such as *The Nation,* had kept their edge but not their influence.

What had happened? That liberalism had, in some sense, 'failed' was, arguably, more apparent in New York than elsewhere. The humanity and generosity of the city's social policies, liberalism in action, had contributed to the near bankruptcy of the city in 1975. This disaster rightly provoked harsh and heretical questions, but what seemed to be happening was not so much a rethinking as a defenestration of the very premises of New York liberalism. The intellectuals were now leaping into bed with some of the most reactionary elements in American society.

There was a mystery here. A great city is more than the sum of its buildings or bodies. Less tangible, but central to its cultural identity, are the intellectual ferments that bubble away in its universities and coffee houses and bars and journals. It was evident not only that a great intellectual tradition was in decay, but that little had arisen to take its place apart from defections to the Right. In the face of a reactionary government in Washington I had imagined that there would be a fierce counter-reaction, however restricted. Yet the established opposition, the Democratic Party, appeared to have caved in to such a degree that its sole response was to offer mildly less radical policies than the Administration, without seriously questioning the political and ideological foundations of that Administration's programme.

These are mighty issues, though scarcely exclusive to New York, and I carried them with me when I went to see Diana Trilling. Ten years had gone by since my last visit to her comfortable flat on Claremont Avenue, a street of ornate apartment houses close to Columbia University. In those days her son James had been a friend of my ex-wife's and the three of us would put in an appearance at the Trillings' on our occasional visits to New York. I've forgotten Lionel Trilling's conversation but distinctly remember Diana

Trilling refusing to let us drive back to Harvard until she'd prepared a mountain of sandwiches for the journey, a task she set to with, I imagined, the same determination and passion with which she'd produce some of her more polemical writings.

After ten years the flat looked much the same — with its well-groomed and spacious beige living-room densely occupied by desks and armchairs and sofas and tables laden with books. As before, she prepared tea and cucumber sandwiches and pound cake, which she brought in on a silver tray. Very civilized, very British. I felt out of place. We chatted for a while and discussed urban decay. Then Mrs Trilling said: 'I'm sure that's not why you wanted to see me.'

She was seated at the other end of the sofa, and as I looked at her I realized how little she had changed. With her sturdy build and prominent round eyes, she remained a formidable presence, but she struck me as bending ever so slightly under the weight both of personal sorrow and a disenchantment, felt as well as analysed, with the spirit of the age.

'That's true,' I said. 'What I wanted to ask you is this. Can you disabuse me of the impression that New York's creative energies are no longer channelled into intellectual pursuits so much as into food?' She laughed, acknowledging a frivolous statement of a fairly serious topic. On the other hand, food is a serious topic too, and it sparked her off. 'It's clear to me that people of your generation can't know what food tastes like. I've compared notes with other people of *my* generation, and we all agree that food used to taste entirely different and much better. Nothing has any flavour anymore.'

I looked doubtful.

'No, it really is so. I made a fruit salad the other day for some dinner guests. The apples were mushy. The oranges — well, the oranges had no flavour. The pears seemed to have been bred to be edible billiard balls. And the bananas — nowadays they're green one day and overripe the next. Maybe they inject them the way they do chickens, for fast growth.'

We both pulled up short. We'd met to have a serious talk about intellectual matters, and here instead —

She poured me more tea. 'Getting back to the reason why

I came to see you . . .' She nodded. 'When I was in New York ten years ago, one knew of and read Irving Howe, you and your husband, Hannah Arendt, Dwight Macdonald, Susan Sontag . . . Now in 1983 I hear the same names, though of course some have died. Where are the young thinkers and writers, the people of my generation with a broad interest in the life of the mind, to put it pompously?'

'I suppose it may have to do with the decline of the universities. If you accept the fact that there's a close link between literary criticism and the intellectual life, you must see that there are bound to be fewer people devoted to serious criticism than there used to be. Of course there are plenty of people who *call* themselves literary critics, and nowadays there are endless varieties of criticism to choose from. But that's not what I mean by criticism. You may not be aware of this, but over 40 years ago, when Lionel, his generation, his friends, started to write, there was almost no literary criticism in this country. Very little, at any rate. Lionel and his Columbia generation all but invented American criticism. When in the 1940s I became the fiction critic of *The Nation,* it was a notable thing to be. All of us who wrote criticism in the literary journals were considered important figures in the culture. We were known by name, read, talked about. Nowadays nobody cares who writes criticism in *The Nation* or anywhere. Literary criticism is no longer a major profession.'

'Perhaps that's no bad thing. It means we take a literate culture for granted today. A book review is no longer a special event.'

'Maybe. But I still think intellectual life has lost its excitement. There's much activity, but no excitement.'

'Where are the *young* intellectuals? Whether philosophers or historians or critics?'

She thought for a while. 'I don't know. It's a good question. There are people like —' and she named a prominent young literary journalist. 'People speak highly of him. But he's not too smart.'

'Whatever you think of his abilities, you have to agree that he's not particularly interested in politics. What's happened to the people who used to call themselves liberals, or even the liberal Left?'

'It hardly exists any longer. It may exist in terms of

individuals but not of a group. A great many journals have been recently taken over by the new conservatives: *The American Scholar, Commentary, The New Criterion,* the *Wall Street Journal,* of course. That's the trouble, they've got the field to themselves. These neo-conservative organs, these New Right journals, are lively enough, but it's a vigour of polemic, not of ideas. I don't think they have any new ideas, either in politics or culture.'

'Is there any one person, or possibly more, on the New Right for whom you have a modicum of grudging respect?'

She didn't hesitate. 'I hate most of them. Their personal attacks are vicious. But I have respect for a few individuals, like Irving Kristol and Gertrude Himmelfarb. I wish Kristol weren't so flippant. But they are serious historians, both of them. And I suppose I think almost fondly of that established right-wing journal *The National Review.* William Buckley can be very beguiling. But for the most part these people comport themselves like Stalinists of the Right. They think they invented anti-Communism. Lionel and I were anti-Communists for over 40 years. But anti-Communist liberals. Of course, liberalism does seem to have lost its content. Those of us who consider ourselves liberals no longer know what it can accomplish. I think I'd now have to call myself a Centrist rather than a liberal.'

(In the preface to his memoir *Breaking Ranks,* the neo-conservative ideologue Norman Podhoretz also identifies himself as a Centrist. Yet it was hard to imagine Diana Trilling and the Pod so much as shaking hands.)

'Is the prominence of the New Right simply a matter of fashion? Ebb and flow? Will they fade away in time?'

'I don't know. At the moment conservatism certainly has things much its own way.'

She told me about a man she'd liked and encouraged in his career. He became a successful critic, but also, by way of his fanatical anti-Communism, joined the neo-conservatives. Yet he had remained a friend of hers, until Podhoretz, in *Breaking Ranks,* 'wrote as he did — all those wonderful inventions of his — about Lionel,' and she'd asked her friend to dissociate himself from those statements. He refused, even though it meant that their friendship terminated. 'He told me this was one of the saddest days of his life, but he wouldn't change his mind. Apparently his political solidarity with Podhoretz was more important to him than either truth or our friendship.'

How intricately these debates curl around the egos and personalities of the disputants! There seemed — and I heard it later from all sides — so much bitterness, so much anger. On the one hand there was championing, and on the other betrayal. A disagreement, 10 or 20 years old, between two New York intellectuals could take on the character of a mythic struggle. What was really at issue? Ideas, or far less tangible notions of discipleship and self-assertion? Lionel Trilling, it seemed to me, still resided in his widow's memories as a hero of their culture. That was easy to understand; they had fought their battles jointly for 40 years. Yet how much significance did those battles have beyond the academic and journalistic circles within which they were fought?

We rummaged around for the names of some representatives of the Left, and did manage to come up with a handful. When I mentioned Susan Sontag, Mrs Trilling was withering: 'She's just learnt that Russia isn't a good country. She just learnt it this year. Somebody just told her that they suppress freedom there. They even jail people.'

Gloomily we stared into our tea cups under the lamplight. She shrugged. 'I guess this is just a lousy culture. You've been prodding me and I've been trying to come up with some redeeming features in our intellectual life, but I can't find any.'

'Things aren't quite that bad,' I said consolingly. I felt I'd unintentionally imposed the entire burden of the liberal conscience on her shoulders — though an element of self-dramatization in her may have relished it. For the intellectual climate had changed, and hardly for the better. In part it reflected the intellectual failure of her generation, which she looked back on as pioneering and humane. She herself seemed to have little fresh to offer in the place of liberalism: Centrism sounded like an evasion rather than a declaration.

It was getting late. The cosiness of teatime was giving way to the solemnity of a winter evening. As I rose to leave, Mrs Trilling said: 'The trouble with taking a centrist position is that you don't please either extreme, Right or Left. You're attacked from both sides. If you're short of enemies, let me know, and I'll send you a couple of mine.'

ACID RAIN

It would be illuminating, I thought, to track down some of the champions of the New Right that Diana Trilling had mentioned to me. I felt it wise to keep some distance between myself and Norman Podhoretz. I hadn't liked his books, and I suspected I wouldn't like him either. Instead I contacted Irving Kristol, editor of the scholarly journal *The Public Interest,* and Samuel Lipman, concert pianist and music critic and publisher of *The New Criterion.* Both men kindly invited me, on separate occasions, to their respective clubs.

The New Criterion, modelled, as its name implies, on T. S. Eliot's famous journal, first appeared in late 1982, reasserting the values of high culture in an uncompromising way. Despite its advocacy of a free-market economy, *The New Criterion,* handsomely produced but with a modest circulation of 4000, survives only with the financial support of four well-heeled foundations. The journal does print articles that don't endorse its publishers' philosophy, but as Lipman candidly put it, 'the debate is run under our auspices and on our terms'. The first issue set the tone with these fighting words: 'We are still living in the aftermath of the insidious assault on the mind that was one of the most repulsive features of the radical movement of the Sixties. The cultural consequences of this leftward turn in our political life has been far graver than is commonly supposed . . . The effect on the life of culture has been ongoing and catastrophic.'

Lipman said to me, 'A piece in the *Washington Post* described us as the verbal equivalent of acid rain.' He looked at me with mock astonishment. 'But we never aimed that high.'

He took me to lunch at the Harmonie Club on East 60th Street. The Harmonie was, and still appears to be, patronized almost exclusively by New Yorkers of German-Jewish descent. The smartest New York clubs were, and apart from a little tokenism still are, 'restricted' — a code word which means, quite simply, no Jews, no blacks, Aryans preferred — and consequently prominent, and rich, New York Jews opened their own club. The menu still includes some Jewish favourites, such as the chicken livers (reheated) that accompanied my omelette, and the cheese cake that followed. I met Irving Kristol at the far grander New York Athletic Club, which does admit Jews, though perhaps not with open arms.

Lipman is a short, rotund man who exudes bonhomie: over lunch he lolled, he chewed, he gave himself no airs. He was easy to be with and easy to talk to, and it was generous of him to entertain a stranger and an alien. If Lipman was an open book, Kristol lurked behind his binding. A small man with greying hair and twinkling eyes, he was more guarded. He talked freely and without bringing self-censoring mechanisms into play, and he did so with considerable charm, but there was a knowingness verging on cynicism that made me uneasy. I could never be sure that Kristol wasn't overstating his position so as to have the pleasure of watching my growing dismay. Lipman's portliness was the consequence, I imagined, of a hearty appetite, while Kristol had a very middle-European embonpoint that suggested placid prosperity rather than voracious consumption. It didn't take me long to realize that Kristol, though far from lovable, was no fool, whereas with the more cuddly Lipman that question could not be so easily resolved.

I asked the two men what had caused them, and so many other New York liberals, to take that long trek to the Right from their earlier political positions. Lipman specified a number of issues that were now 15 years old: Hannah Arendt's book *Eichmann in Jerusalem*; the 1967 teachers' strike (a row about 'decentralization' of schools in black neighbourhoods, which arose when 'community-controlled' school boards dismissed white teachers; the outcome was bare-knuckled confrontation between white, often Jewish and liberal, teachers, and black militants); and the disturbances at Columbia in 1968. In *Breaking Ranks*,

Podhoretz gives a similar list. Kristol was more expansive.

'First, there was the 1967 Arab-Israeli war. At least for Jews here that was a crucial dividing line. It came down to this: do you support Israel or the Third World? There were certain persistent characteristics of Third World countries that began to make an impact on us: the spread of Marxism, totalitarianism, anti-Americanism, and hostility to Israel. Secondly, there were the student rebellions of the late 60s. Liberalism encouraged that rebellion and thus demonstrated its own failure. The title of Midge Decter's book [she is, as it happens, the wife of Norman Podhoretz] says it all: *Liberal Parents, Radical Children.*

'Then there were the problems with Johnson's Great Society programmes. I and a number of other writers and scholars were sceptical about its policies and that's why we founded *Public Interest* in 1965 as a revisionist journal. By revisionist I mean that all of us associated with *Public Interest* still considered ourselves Democrats, but we were increasingly sceptical about the means employed by the Great Society architects. We were unhappy about the structure of the programme. We came to see liberalism as a kind of disguised romanticism, and neo-conservatism is a reaction against that kind of political romanticism. And here in New York the school decentralization strike was crucial. Jewish teachers were thrown to the wolves for no educational purpose, but on ideological grounds. The movement for black control of their schools was an attempt to acquire black patronage.

'And too there was Vietnam. Many of us thought the war was stupid, perhaps immoral, but we were anti-Hanoi. This isolated the revisionists among us from, say, the *New York Review of Books* and other leftist groups who were not anti-Hanoi.'

'At what point did you actually join the Republican Party?'

'In 1973, though I supported Nixon in 1972.'

'Doesn't it worry you that that's put you politically between the sheets with such characters as Jerry Falwell of the Moral Majority? I can't imagine the two of you have much in common.'

'Yes, there may be some bedfellows in the Republican Party I wouldn't have chosen, but that's a condition of politics. Look, so far as I was concerned, the key question was: who would listen to you? In a Democratic Party controlled by men like George McGovern, no one was much interested in listening any longer to the likes of me. And remember that not all Republicans are hostile to notions of a welfare state. Some of us' — and he smiled — 'are trying to reconcile traditional Republican business values with the welfare state.'

Lipman, in discussing what had prompted some liberals' journey to the Right, had paid tribute to Kristol. 'In the 1950s conservative thinkers had been grouped around Buckley's *National Review*. It was a mix of social, economic and religious conservatives. The link between that crowd and the East Coast Jewish intelligentsia was Irving Kristol.'

He frowned on my suggestion that conservatives weren't known for great sophistication of thought, the kind of sophistication that would appeal to an urban intelligentsia. 'I can cite major thinkers like Hayek and Popper. Listen, there was another factor too. For those intellectuals disillusioned, as so many of us were, by the events of the late 60s, where else was there to go? You either moved to the Right or you joined the Children's Crusade.' He leaned back in his chair to let that derisive remark reverberate.

I contented myself, as I stared speechlessly at the tablecloth, with contemplating how much pleasure it would give me to pick up my starched white napkin and beat him over the head with it.

'You could say we're not racked by self-doubt, nor are we given to over-cautiousness.' He smiled. I smiled back. 'We think we know. I'm not saying we do know, but I am saying that we think we know.'

I laughed politely. 'Well, it's nice to have confidence. But how influential do you think the neo-conservatives are?'

'In numbers we're small. But we're noisy. The three principal journals together publish 120,000 words a month, though not all the articles take our line. But we have no political power as a group, no vote force. That may change if we can strengthen the ties between the Old and the New Right. But at the moment we have to accept that our effect on national politics is very marginal. We have a long way to go. There are many battles still to be won.'

'That sounds oddly combative to me. Reagan's in the

White House, and yet you're talking in terms of battles. Right now you appear to have won.'

'Would you say that Carter's victory was a victory for liberalism?'

'No, there were too many other factors involved.'

'Quite. Wouldn't you say the same is true in the case of Reagan's victory? That he won doesn't necessarily mean that the conservatives are completely in the ascendant. The intelligentsia is still overwhelmingly liberal, I'd say nine to one. And there are still the Stalinist forces to be reckoned with.'

'Hang on. Stalin's been dead for 30 years.'

Lipman smiled, wiping his mouth with his napkin. 'Do you read *The Nation*? No? Well, I'd say it was not immune from Stalinism. Or try reading Alexander Cockburn in the *Village Voice*. You know who his father was?'

'Indeed.'

'Well then, you can see why I say the battle is not over.'

Actually, I couldn't. Claud Cockburn, I hoped, would smile to know that even from the grave his name strikes terror into the hearts (if they have any) of American conservatives.

Kristol also felt that neo-conservative influence remained small. 'In book publishing in New York, almost none, and nationally, nothing fundamental. Some of the traditionally liberal journals are touched more and more by neo-conservative ideas. The *New Republic* and *Harper's,* for instance.' *Harper's* had just printed a maddening piece by the prolific Pod 'claiming' George Orwell as a proto-neoconservative.

'Do you think it's possible that New York liberals were chastened by the near bankruptcy of their city?'

'No,' Kristol replied with a chuckle. 'Liberals are never chastened.'

I asked Lipman to define some neo-conservative ideas. 'There's the economic argument,' he explained. 'Socialist economies are characterized by deficit, which suggests they simply don't work. We're not ashamed of our devotion to the idea of private property. And we question the liberal assumption that public is necessarily better than private, that it's better, for example, for pictures to be in museums rather than in private collections. Perhaps, we'd argue, it's better for books to be owned and cherished by individuals rather than deposited in public libraries?'

Perhaps, but I was astonished with what ease Samuel Lipman was enshrining self-gratification as political principle.

With Kristol, on the other hand, I wanted to discuss specifically how a neo-conservative would view and resolve New York's more dire problems. He was happy to answer. His objection to the welfare state, he told me, was that it was a hindrance to assimilation. 'It diminishes the importance of the family unit. I don't begrudge deprived people the money, but the money corrupts them by making them dependent on the state. The city has a large black and Hispanic population that is now imprisoned, yes imprisoned, in low-income housing. Why should they move? There's no incentive.'

How would he deal with poverty in the city? 'Give them money.' He smiled, to let me know he was only half frivolous. 'But of course the only real solution is to get the economy moving again. Until that happens I suppose you have to apply Band-Aids. Look, I've no objection to public works as a temporary measure. I don't care if the government spends money in order to put some people back to work. I'm not hung up on balancing the budget.'

That struck me as a deviation from neo-conservative ideology, and certainly differed from what Lipman had been saying.

'There are two school systems in the city, one for the rich and one for the poor. Does that bother you?'

'Well, it's an example of what I've been talking about. It was liberal ideology that wrecked our public schools. They endorsed students' rights and it became impossible to impose any discipline in the schools. Black activism too helped to destroy education in the city. But if you ask me whether having two systems bothers me, let me remind you that no one *wants* to send their children to private schools. They're very expensive.'

The municipal institutions, the hospitals and universities, Kristol dismissed as 'an absurdity' which should have been absorbed into larger state and federal systems. 'But the city's problem is larger than an economic or administrative one. It's also a question of family structure. Some of the new immigrant groups — the Koreans and Greeks, for example — are prospering. That's because those communities stick to a strong family structure and believe in education for their children. The black community, on the other hand, is riddled with problems that arise from a breakdown of the family. Everybody knows that.'

'But what can be done about it?'

Kristol leaned forward, folding his hands and gently shaking his head. 'I have no idea. We need a black John Wesley to do something, but there doesn't seem to be one on the horizon. Blacks need to get themselves out of their rut. After all, blacks do well enough when they enter the middle classes and join bourgeois society. Still, there are some specific things we could do which might help, such as changing or abolishing the minimum wage. There's nothing wrong with a 50-dollar wage for simple work in a depressed economy. And we could also lower the school-leaving age.'

'How far?'

'I don't know. 12? As long as leavers have an option to return. You can't force people to learn. If you don't *compel* kids to stay in school, you'd be surprised how many would stay.'

I looked around the panelled bar of the comfortable club, at the suited businessmen relaxing over cocktails, at the smartly outfitted barman, at the dwindling Glenlivet in my hand. And I thought of those benevolent businessmen out there in the city employing illiterate 12-year-olds to do the shittiest jobs for 50 bucks a week.

MIRO, MIRO,
ON THE WALL

'I know you haven't done this in a long while, but . . .'

A groan rose up from the occupants of 40 leotards who were lying panting on the floor. The speaker could have been a black football player, American style: he was at least six foot four, massively built with legs like pillar boxes, his gleaming skin catching the light as taut tendons and muscle undulated beneath its surface. There was no trace of fat anywhere on his immense body.

Wilton was conducting an advanced callisthenics class at the New York Health & Racquet Club, and Julie, tiring of my sneers at keep-fit fanatics, had suggested I come along to the class she regularly attends there. So there I was, touching my toes in company with a few dozen sweaty men and women in the bare mirror-lined classroom. Wilton was Mr Cool. He never smiled, never joked, and drove his charges without mercy or respite. They loved it. The more they protested, the more Wilton made them work. Julie, together with other Wilton worshippers, was in the front row, while I cowered at the back, though there was no hiding from Wilton. Fortunately he'd been tipped off, told I wasn't a regular student and had never done a day's exercise in my life. If he had enforced the 50 press-ups and other exercises he prescribed in multiples of 20, they'd have had to take me out on a stretcher.

There were two kinds of body being worked on by their owners. There was the slender well-knit body, evidently in excellent shape — and so I couldn't see the point of giving up precious lunch hours to punishing it. And then there was the body flaccid, paunchy and wrinkled, made lumpish by pouches of fat and tissue — so clearly all that exercise wasn't doing much good. In addition there was the body ravishing, as represented by Wilton and myself. The work-out was strenuous indeed. After about 30 minutes of doing funny things with your head, your arms, your legs, stretching now this limb, now that, quite a few of my classmates had more or less given up and simply lay gasping on the floor while I cast scornful looks at them. I myself had no difficulty finishing any of the arduous exercises, though it's true that I may have been dilatory in starting them. As my mates began dropping like flies, Wilton said loudly, 'Don't even *consider* stopping,' and gradually limbs started to flap once more. As the self-flagellants performed a rite in which they lay on their backs while keeping their feet up in the air at uncomfortable angles, Wilton drawled: 'Get *your* feet off *my* floor . . .' Some weak creature complained that her bum was getting sore, but Wilton was unmoved: 'It's not hurting *my* butt.' And indeed I doubt that even a hand grenade would have made any impression on his steel-muscled butt.

'OK!' roared Wilton. 'All over for another day!'

I looked round. My strangely fatigued classmates were panting and groaning as they stood in pools of their own sweat, clutching their sides and wiping their sodden brows. I strolled to the front to see whether Julie was still alive. She still looked vaguely human, considering what she'd just been doing to herself, and she had enough energy left to show me round the other torture chambers. The Nautilus machines fascinated me most: a large room contained two sets of 16 machines, which consisted of different combinations of straps and weights and metal shafts, rather like a mad dentist's chair. Julie encouraged me to try a machine that requires the victim to raise a bar with his toes, an exercise of increasing degrees of effort and pain according to the weights you attach — or that your personalized instruction programme attaches — to the spring mechanism. The design director of the Mineshaft ought to come here and pick up a few ideas.

In the warm-up room, elderly gentlemen were seated on cycling machines reading the *New York Times* as they pedalled away. In another corner was the treadmill, or jogging machines as they call them, and participants were tantalized by running on the spot on a revolving track. It's important to realize that this hellish place is not regarded as a penance but as a fashionable spot at which to waste a lunch hour or an evening after work. The Health & Racquet Club has five branches on Manhattan with exercise and pool facilities, not to mention yoga, karate, aerobic dancing, and hydro-callisthenics (doing silly things in the water). Membership costs about $500 a year, though many companies throw in membership as a perk. The grimly named Cardio-Fitness Center offers close supervision and a complete diet programme as well as the usual run of machines. The most chic health club in town is the Vertical Club, which attracts Upper East Side debs and matrons who like to limber up before committing adultery.

As a 'treat' Julie kindly gave me lunch at the small restaurant on the ground floor. It was, of course, health food: leaves with grated things on top and a creamy dressing curdling over it like liquid fertilizer. Julie wanted my honest opinion. I gave it.

'I still think it's a good thing to do,' she perversely insisted. 'Of course some people overdo it. There's one woman who takes three advanced classes a day and runs every night.'

'So she has a terrific body — and no time left in which to allow others to enjoy it. What a waste of her youth, when she could be eating spaghetti and screwing instead.'

'That's the point. New Yorkers love to eat and they love to screw, and they don't want to give up either, so they have to exercise like crazy to keep in reasonable shape while pursuing their pleasures.'

'Could be. I prefer to have my cake and eat it. Which reminds me, I don't suppose they have any chocolate cake in this place?'

'No, but why not try the carrot cake?'

'Forget it. Let me tell you a story that's told about Rab Butler. Butler, who was the flabbiest man I ever met yet lived to a ripe old age, once declared that the only exercise he ever got was climbing the stairs of hospitals to visit friends who'd been injured in skiing accidents. What can I add?'

That afternoon, however, I chose not to walk up the 67 flights to the office of the executive director of the Port Authority of New York and New Jersey. The Authority is a special agency that controls the docks along 750 miles of waterfront, the four New York area airports, six bridges and tunnels, a truck terminal, and the famous Port Authority Bus Terminal. It has over $5 billion in assets, is establishing a Bank, no less, of Regional Development, and, incidentally, financed the building of the immense twin towers of the World Trade Center that now brutally dominate downtown Manhattan.

However stark these 110-storey towers appear from the ground, they do at least offer splendid views from the haven of their interior. From Peter Goldmark's office I had the dubious pleasure of overlooking miles of New Jersey coastline on the other side of the Hudson. Goldmark, though in his early 40s, looks far too young to be running an operation as powerful as this; but since he was budget director of all New York State when he was in his mid-30s, I suppose he's qualified for the job. I watched him review some documents with his staff. He explained to me what it was all about, but I was lost: my brain was still tying up its shoelaces by the time his had completed the first lap.

His office was an executive analogue to the Four Seasons, decorated in a lovely blue-grey, with a complex of sofas that can seat eight moguls, or perhaps ten mortals. He deposited me in a deeply comfortable leather chair while he took an important call from an official who was worried about some impending legislation. It was a hurried conversation since the official was speaking from a pay phone in the jail where he was serving time and he only had one dime.

Goldmark was enthusiastic about the future of the city — at least about Manhattan and the Jersey shore, which he felt was ripe for both residential and commercial development. When I talked again to the Banker about this, he was less sure: 'These guys think you can just will economic development into existence, and I'm not so sure. I believe you're more likely to end up with inflated costs for construction and a swollen bureaucracy. But it's too early to say. The jury's still out.' A view shared by Roger Starr, who writes leaders for the *New York Times*: 'When it comes to redevelopment schemes, everybody's on board except the manufacturers.'

Goldmark's secretaries were tidying their desks and the telephone switchboard had calmed down. He'd persuaded me, without difficulty, to survey his bailiwick from a helicopter the following week, and now he offered me a rapid tour of his fast emptying offices. We rose to our feet. We crossed his office, which is larger than my entire London flat, and passed through a wooden door into another spacious room equipped with a long table and chairs.

'This was built as a private dining-room. Not bad. The only thing is, I've never used it. Perhaps on my last day as director I'll give a party in there . . .' We slipped out into the lofty corridor, which was lined with large tapestries by Miro, Calder, Le Corbusier.

'They brighten up the place nicely,' I said appreciatively.

'Too nicely. I don't think public money should be spent on art in offices, so I put a stop to any further purchases after I came here.'

We turned into a large room with an immense table and I expressed appropriate awe. Goldmark laughed. 'You may think this is the board-room. It's not. This is where we have discussions before board meetings. The room's equipped with movie screens and sliding walls — the works. And the board-room's in here.' Through more doors.

At its head was a shallow curve of desks for the members of the board, and facing them rows of desks for the Authority executives. 'There used to be a lectern here,' Goldmark explained, 'but I had it removed. It was an unusual object. It contained a TV set and you may be wondering why.' He took me over to one of the desks. 'This is the executive director's desk, where I sit. You'll notice that it too is equipped with what looks like a TV screen. Now, let's assume that one of my officials is addressing the board from the lectern. I wish to communicate with him while he speaks. So I take a piece of paper and write a message on it and slide it in here. The message is then transmitted onto his screen. So if one of my people is off on the wrong track, the director can rapidly tell him — and no one else — "Shut up, asshole, the traffic in that tunnel goes the opposite way."

'Here's another device I've had disconnected. Originally the press were not admitted to meetings. Can you imagine it? A public body and the press excluded? Well, they were allowed to sit in the adjoining room and the sound was radioed in. Let's assume somebody is saying something that the director doesn't particularly want the press to hear.

Well, I push this button here' — and he pointed to a small button beneath his desk — 'and the transmission to the press room cuts out. Tells you quite a lot about the mentality of the people who used to run this place.'

On my way home I was stopped in the subway by a foreigner asking for directions. I was happy to oblige.

'It's quite simple,' I explained. 'What you want is the IRT, except no one here actually refers to it as the IRT for fear of confusing it with the other IRT lines on the East Side. The train you want is also known as the number 1 train, to distinguish it from the 2 and 3 which cover much of the same route. You've got to be careful, because 2 and 3 are expresses, whereas number 1 is a local, which is what you want. Most people refer to that line as the Broadway Local. You're quite safe doing that here in midtown, but you've got to be careful elsewhere in the city because the RR line is also known as the Broadway Local.'

'Thank you, monsieur. Do I stand on the right platform?'

'Oh no. You'll have to take the staircase at the other end and look for the aforementioned signs for the Broadway Local or IRT or number 1. This platform serves the A, the AA, and the E. I would also advise you to look carefully at the numbering on the train before you step in. Here's a train coming in now. You'll see that the identifying letter is lit up above the front of the train.'

'I do not see it.'

'No, you're quite right. Neither do I. Well, sometimes it isn't there, so look instead on the side of each car where the line will be identified.'

'I do not see it.'

'No, that's true. This train has no markings of any kind, it appears. In such instances, I advise you to peer in and look at the map displayed on the inside. That is an infallible guide. For instance, in this car here we have the map for the RR.'

'But you told me this platform only receives the A, AA, and E.'

'And so it does. Which means that this cannot possibly be the RR.'

'And in the next car I see the map for the B line.'

'You are observant, monsieur, and will have realized by

now that which train you end up on is often a matter of pure chance. That is, you will agree, one of the pleasures of travel, the delight of the unexpected. May I offer you a final piece of advice?'

'You are too kind.'

'Prenez un taxi.'

CORRECTIONAL

Set Rikers Island adrift and New York's crime problem would sharply diminish. On this flat, bleak 600 acres of marsh and landfill off the Queens coast across the water from a distant corner of the Bronx, the city houses 8,000 of its prisoners. A new jail is being built close to the downtown courthouses, despite noisy protests from nearby Chinatown, but in recent years prisoners attending hearings or trials have had to be bused in from Rikers every day. Its sprawling, featureless buildings contain six prisons: for men, for women, for adolescents, and the mental health unit. Most of the prisoners on Rikers are in custody and have not been sentenced, and those who have been are only inside for short terms of up to two years. Prisoners serving longer terms spend their days in grimmer fortresses upstate such as Attica and Sing Sing. Rikers might be regarded as a well-run modern prison were it not for appalling overcrowding.

The bus that goes from East 59th Street, where the Queensboro Bridge spans the East River, directly to the island was crowded with men and women of all ages, mostly black and Hispanic, on their way to visit relatives or smuggle dope to their loved ones. I was to meet a Captain Duvalier at the first control point at ten, but I was half an hour early. The bus hadn't stopped at the control point on the mainland side of the causeway that leads to the island but had driven straight over, discharging its passengers at the main Control Building on the island. There were already about 50 people sitting about in the large waiting room when the busload piled in. The receptionist asked me to stay put till 10, so I went to join the others.

The Control Building, like most of the facilities on the

island, was built fairly recently and has at least the merit of being light and airy. Rows of metal chairs were lined up, and in an aisle between there were large blue oil drums functioning as garbage cans. Many visitors were clearly expecting a long wait, and they'd come equipped with thermos flasks and baskets of food. Vending machines served those who hadn't come prepared. This waiting area was separated from the rest of the building by a high glass partition, and guarded turnstiles divided the two areas. Near the turnstiles notices reminded the visitors that it was illegal to take contraband into the prison. A young blonde girl with striking white eye make-up told me she was visiting her 17-year-old boyfriend, who was doing six months. My sympathy dissolved after she went on to say that this was her first visit to him, though he'd already been in for two months.

At 10 I returned to the reception area. At the adjacent window people were queuing up either to pay their bail or fine or to collect their property after release. A small wiry man, on my side of the counter, was signing a receipt for his property and saying, 'You want me to sign my *real* name?'

A few minutes later, my guide, Captain Duvalier, walked briskly in. A sturdy, handsome man, he was dressed in a well-cut three-piece suit. He was also pissed off, since he'd been waiting since 9.30 by the mainland control post, and had only just discovered that I'd been sitting happily for half an hour in the main Control Building. His problems weren't over. There was some confusion about authorization, and the reception guards weren't sure why I should be admitted to the prison. Duvalier denied that he'd been asked to show me round, but it was clear that nobody else had been sent along to take care of me. It was time, therefore, for the name-drop, and I tipped a few out of my hat and let them resound in the officials' ears. Duvalier confirmed that I did have permission, and somehow, despite the absence of forms in triplicate, it was agreed that I could be admitted. Poor Duvalier, who surely had better things to do with his time, had to spend the entire morning with me. He wasn't too happy, and it showed.

He took me to the Correctional Institution for Women, which houses 475 women, plus 300 males who have been put there because of overcrowding elsewhere. First I had to snip my way through layers of security precautions. I was asked to empty my pockets before being electronically frisked; my camera was locked up; my hand was stamped; I had to sign a visitors' book and then a sheet of paper in invisible ink. Duvalier took me through an electronic door which led into what looked like a decompression chamber. Only when the door had slid shut behind us did the door on the far side open to admit us into the corridor of the prison itself. There we were met by a CIFW captain, a hefty bollard of a woman, tough but amiable, who would be showing me around.

First we visited a 'housing area' — cells, in other words. The structure was a V-shape, each of its two wings accommodating 30 male prisoners on remand. In the day room a television sprouted, but nobody was watching; a few tall blacks were sitting at a table playing cards. I walked slowly down a corridor with cells on either side, each measuring six by nine and containing a sink, a toilet, a desk, a bed. They were institutional, with drab green paint and basic furnishings, but there were no bars on the windows (just a strong mesh in the glass) and the cells were light and crisp on this bright wintry day.

Some prisoners like to spend more time than required in their cells. 'Remember you've got 30 tough guys in here who don't like each other,' growled Duvalier. One or two cells had been decorated by their occupants; one displayed a huge collection of comic covers tacked neatly to the walls. I was surprised that a prisoner awaiting trial should take so much trouble to settle in, until I recalled that it's not unusual to wait over two months for your trial, so you may as well make yourself comfortable.

I passed an open door and looked in. There was a Chinese boy, about five foot ten, loose-limbed; he smiled shyly when he saw me. He was wringing out his underwear and hanging it on the radiator to dry.

'Go on in,' said Duvalier, and when I hesitated at invading this boy's meagre patch of privacy, Duvalier pushed past me and I followed him in. 'Not too bad, huh? Plenty of light. No bars.' He turned to the boy, who was standing quietly watching the swaggering captain. 'What are you in for?'

'Murder.'

'Anything to do with them barroom killings in Chinatown last week?'

The boy shook his head. He looked at me. I'd been

smiling, out of embarrassment more than the pleasure of the moment, and now found myself stupidly grinning at this youthful alleged murderer.

Duvalier turned to me. He wasn't embarrassed at all. 'Don't get too many Chinese in here for murder. Guess their family structure is starting to break down too.' He turned sharply to the boy. 'You didn't do it, did you.' It was a statement, with a derisory edge to it, rather than a question.

Again the boy shook his head, looked away.

'No, you never do, do you.' Duvalier's tone was harsh. Since American law assumes innocence until guilt has been proved, the boy was hardly going to say that he'd done whatever he'd been accused of. Duvalier's sneer was gratuitous, though I dare say his scepticism was justified. Prisoners end up in Rikers because their bail has been set at such a high rate that they can't pay it, and the judge usually has good reason for doing so. In another cell we talked to a black kid. Duvalier this time didn't ask what he was in for, but he did ask him what his bail was. 'Five thousand,' said the boy, and Duvalier shook his head as we left the cell. 'Must be pretty serious,' said the captain. 'A kid doesn't have his bail set at five thousand for stealing candy.'

Because of overcrowding, the Corrections Department has constructed 'modules': prefabs built in the grounds adjoining the main building and attached to it by a corridor. The noise level was appalling: radio and television blared out all day long. There were no partitions, just a small locker behind each bed. Inmates were watched by each other; there was as much privacy as in an anthill. All 50 men in this module were awaiting trial; they had not been convicted of any crime, although they had been charged, most of them, with felonies. Duvalier said: 'We don't put very aggressive prisoners in here. We stick 'em in the cells.' The implication was that it was worse to be locked into a cell than herded into a single room with 50 other men. I wasn't so sure.

On our way to the women's section, we passed the workroom, where female prisoners make clothing and mattress covers, and the commissary, where they were queuing up to shop. They're allowed to spend up to $40 a week, with the one restriction that they can't buy more than two packs of cigarettes a week; this is an anti-barter precaution. We made another detour to look at the school, run, like any other, by the Board of Education. All school-age prisoners must attend. The principal, an imposing black woman with white hair, wore a florid long dress and looked more like a night club hostess than a headmistress in a prison. I peered into what the principal called the 'libery'.

We arrived at the women's dorm, which resembled the module. The area is controlled from a glass booth, which, as in the men's housing areas, operates all locks electronically. We went into the booth to get clearance. The guard spoke through the loudspeaker: 'Male visitors arriving. Male visitors arriving. Please make sure you're properly dressed.' The prisoners appeared to pay no attention. Buttons were pressed and doors opened, and we walked in. It differed from the male prisoners' module in one crucial respect: there were partitions, four feet high, dividing the beds and thus forming small cubicles. A few women were sitting on their beds, others were wandering about, talking. Why, I asked Duvalier, did women have partitions and men not?

'It's because women are more sensitive about showing parts of their bodies. Guys don't care so much who sees them when they're getting undressed — fact is, some of them are quite proud of their bodies. With women it's different.'

We drove over to the Anna M. Kross Center, which, in spite of its cosy name that conjures up a community hall where OAPs gather in the evening for square-dancing, is an immense complex of buildings that incarcerates 2,000 prisoners, all pre-trial except for a handful of sentenced prisoners who are there to help service the prison. The complex includes a three-acre athletic field, which prisoners use every day, weather permitting. Within the Center are 700 custodial officers, plus 72 civilian employees. Like the CIFW, the AMKC is overcrowded; areas designed to hold 50 beds now hold 58.

Once again I had to make my way through the security net. Duvalier took me to the receiving room, where new prisoners are brought from the courts. After they arrive, there is paperwork to be completed, then the prisoner is photographed, searched, showered, taken to the clinic for a medical examination, and then housed. The civilian in charge of housing was a cheerful young woman. 'We get 60 new inmates every day, and we have to find them a bed within 24 hours, which means this office operates round the clock too. It's not as easy as you may suppose, because there are specific problems with certain prisoners. Diseased inmates, homosexuals, mental observation patients — they all need special treatment. I can't just put them in an ordinary housing area. My job is like running a giant hotel, except we don't take credit cards.'

We took a long walk down a seemingly endless corridor, past clusters of guards and groups of prisoners shuffling along in single file. We turned a corner and passed through some doors and into another glass control booth. 'This is the detoxification dorm,' Duvalier explained. 'Prisoners do seven days in here if they're on dope, fourteen if they're on methadone.' As in the CIFW module, the dorm was airy and open-plan, with rows of beds. Guards stood about uneasily. The atmosphere in here was more charged than in the cell-block I'd visited. These were men in varying states of withdrawal and their misery and resentment were plain to see. It was late morning, but some men were still in bed, while others lay sprawled face down and motionless on top of the rough blankets. There were two men of terrible obesity, as if every foul substance they'd ever ingested had simply remained inside their bloated bodies. As in the other housing areas, there was a day room, painted as ugly a green as you can devise, with a TV set high on the wall showing closed-circuit movies. A guard took me into the communal bathroom, which was spotlessly clean. A man stood in the shower, very still as the hot water pounded down and the steam wrapped around him. The guard said, with a kind of pride, 'The men can shower any time they want. Many, like this guy, like to steam themselves half to death. It's a luxury for them.'

'Any questions?' said Duvalier brusquely to me.

I looked around me at the miserable scene: a few shuffling figures, but most of the men idle or inert or asleep, some of their faces registering indifference, others undisguised hostility.

'Yes. Apart from taking a shower, there's no way of getting any privacy here. No way of spending a few minutes quietly, without interruption, without being watched. That would get me down more than anything.'

Duvalier dismissed this view, which he probably regarded as sentimental. 'If they're all in together, they can bolster each other.' I didn't see much bolstering or camaraderie in front of me. 'And there's no possibility of suicide.' Ah, so that was it.

'And what's that?' I pointed at the belt of the guard standing next to us. Attached to it was a small black box with a red plunger.

'That's a personal alarm system,' said Duvalier. 'Every officer here carries one. If he finds himself in trouble, he presses down on that plunger and a signal goes out to the other guards. The system allows them to locate him exactly. They know an officer's in trouble and they know where to find him. Press that plunger and in 30 seconds this whole area would be swarming with officers.'

Duvalier took me to the grievance office. A few months earlier the Corrections Department had introduced a scheme whereby prisoners with a gripe could bring their complaint before a jury of peers, the Grievance Resolution Committee, made up of two guards and two elected inmates. There was a complex system of hearings and appeals so as to give the prisoner and the committee every opportunity to resolve the problem. I talked to one of the officers on the committee who insisted on giving extremely detailed answers to my general questions, and this exasperated me, almost as much as it infuriated the long-suffering but visibly impatient Duvalier.

By now the corridors were teeming with prisoners on their way to lunch. They are counted when they leave the housing area, counted again on entering the mess hall, and yet again on leaving it. They are allowed up to 20 minutes to eat. The officer in charge was proud of his mess. 'We got a unique type of feed here — the blind feed.' Until recently prisoners were served by other prisoners who stood behind the stainless steel counters dishing out the food. But disputes would arise along the lines of 'he got more than me' and so the prison authorities built a screen with hatches so that it was no longer possible for inmates to see who was serving them — and vice versa.

'How's the food?' I asked. 'Is there much choice?'

'The choice,' replied Duvalier, 'is either you eat it or you don't.' Then recalling that his function was to act as a sort of

PR man for the jail, he added: 'It's a balanced diet, checked by dieticians, and kosher food's available too.'

'Mind if I take a look round?'

'Go ahead.'

I walked in. A typical tray, fresh from the hatches, contained soup, hard-boiled eggs, a baked potato, a dish of beans, a pile of bread, fruit juice. Not haute cuisine, but moderately nutritious and certainly plentiful. After they've finished, the prisoners, as in any cafeteria, empty their trays and return them, but they hang on to their spoons and forks (no knives are issued for obvious reasons) which have to be handed in to an officer on duty before they leave the hall.

We returned to the receiving area and I noticed by the door large cells, brick on three sides and with a large grille facing the corridor. They were filled with prisoners, perhaps 20 in each, some standing, some sitting. 'Bull pens,' murmured Duvalier. 'That's where prisoners wait to be taken to the courts.'

The now familiar security procedures had to be gone through and then I was out in the car park with Duvalier, who drove me back to the Control Building. It was packed. There had been 50 or so visitors when I'd arrived four hours earlier, but now there were hundreds. I didn't have to wait long for a bus and soon it was rumbling over the causeway, and the tall wire fences and rows of prison blocks and wings were receding. As they say of Capri, it was goodbye but not farewell.

On reaching Manhattan I changed to another bus and headed downtown. A huge man lumbered on and clomped towards the back where he sat down heavily.

'How come I can't hit a cab round here?' he said loudly to no one in particular. 'It's no problem in Brooklyn. Always get a cab there. But here, Jesus, they seem so stuck up they won't stop for me. Hey, I seen lots of empty cabs going by. Not one stopped.' He ruminated. 'What's the matter with these guys? Maybe it's because I'm big and black.' He roared with laughter. 'Yup. I'm big and black and I'm stayin' that way.'

I got off at 14th Street and started to walk east. This is not as easy as it sounds, because here, as on many other streets, you have to run a gauntlet of street vendors, peddling every conceivable form of merchandise; pretzels, watches, umbrellas, jewellery, ET spin-offs, fake LaCoste shirts, radios. Peddling is legal down here, but it's against the law in midtown streets. You wouldn't know it, since day in, day out, Fifth and Madison are crowded with peddlers selling the same bewildering variety of cut-rate goods. Peddlers, of course, pay no rent, no real estate taxes, and they don't accept returns either, for the simple reason that you are unlikely to find again the person who sold you the malfunctioning watch in the first place.

Although the city claims to lose $24 million each year on unpaid sales tax, Roger Starr believes most peddlers do pay their taxes. 'It's illegal to trade on certain streets, and it's illegal to evade sales tax. But you can't go to jail for peddling on the wrong street, and you can go to jail for tax evasion.' There are an estimated 5,000 food vendors, mostly Greek, on the city streets every day, and 3,000 peddlers, many of them Middle Eastern. From time to time the police will swoop on unlicenced peddlers in the midtown area and it's a common entertainment to watch scruffy young men hurriedly throwing their wares into cardboard suitcases and making a run for it. If they are caught, their goods may be confiscated, but the cost of retrieving impounded merchandise is regarded by peddlers as a standard overhead.

I turned the corner and walked down Hudson Street into the West Village. Two or three buses were lined up on the corner, waiting to begin their uptown journey.

The first bus was flashing on its electronic indicator above the front window the discouraging words NOT IN SERVICE followed immediately by HAVE A GOOD DAY.

HUDDLED MASSES

'Come along now, put a little pep in your step!' shouted the crew as they herded a polyglot boatload of tourists off the ferry at the Statue of Liberty. 50 years ago and more, millions of eager but bewildered immigrants had steamed past the statue on their way to Castle Garden or Ellis Island, where up to 2,000 arrivals were processed each day. It's still easy to imagine how stirring must have been that first sight of the immovable green goddess holding aloft the great welcoming torch.

The statue is still a potent symbol, though one that's been corroded by American devotion to profit rather than liberty. Immigrants still flood into the country, but few pass by the Statue of Liberty. Great numbers enter illegally, hoping to pass unnoticed by blending into the melting-pot like pepper in the national stew. Nobody knows how many illegal immigrants there are today in the United States: guesses range from 6 to 12 million. According to Byrne, there must be more than 200,000 in New York alone. Byrne is an immigration lawyer and we spent a long lunch-hour talking. His office was typically decorated with framed diplomas that testified to his ascent up the academic foothills. At least he didn't stack his golf trophies on a sideboard.

'How do you know there are 200,000 in the city?'

'I don't. I'm guessing. But look. There are 250 immigration lawyers in this city alone. Between us we're handling about 75,000 clients, and those are just the people that want a green card, that want to acquire legal status so they can stay here and work. There are plenty of others who don't bother. They enter the country just to live off welfare.'

'How do they get in?'

'Well, the wetbacks come in from Mexico over the Rio Grande or by boat to Southern California. Canada has a huge unmanned border, and there are teams of people known as Coyotes who, for a fat fee, take immigrants over. Others come in legally on visitors' visas, but then stay on indefinitely. And a very few jump ship.'

'So your job is to devise ways by which people can get to stay in this country after their visas expire?'

'Sure, these people are after a green card, but it can take about two years and it's almost impossible to work through the process without a good lawyer. That's where people like me come in. I handle their labour certifications — they state that the immigrant won't be depriving a US citizen of a job — and help to bring in relatives. It's true that the system, the way it's set up, invites abuse, but some lawyers abuse it for good and some for ill. I'll give you an example. In many neighbourhoods here you'll find marriage mills, since getting married is a popular way to get a green card. These marriage mills churn out fraudulent marriages, and immigration officials tell me they think 80 per cent of all applications for residence based on marriage are phony. There are women in this city who get married about 20 times. Clients pay between two and five thousand bucks to get married. I won't touch that kind of thing.'

'Is there much overt corruption, money in unmarked envelopes?'

'It happens, but not often. It's so risky that I don't believe much of it goes on. Some of my clients, though, can't understand this. Last week I had a millionaire from Rio in your chair. He said he'd give me $10,000 if I could get him a green card pronto. I said it couldn't be done. He offered me $20,000. It took a long time to persuade him that things don't work that way here.

'Middle Eastern people are the same. Just after the Iranian revolution there was a consular official in Washington who said he could get green cards for Iranian exiles at $10,000 a shot. He claimed to be in league with an immigration official. Nobody knows how much money that guy collected from those desperate Iranians, but the guess is somewhere around five million. He's underground now. He's cheated so many powerful people that if he ever surfaces they'll kill him.'

Byrne leaned back in his chair and laughed. He was a sleek man, expensively dressed, with black hair that had been sculpted by some classy salon, and smooth cheeks grown puffy with prosperity. I guessed that he was skilful and successful. The skill resided in a whiff of the raffish that suggested he knew his way around. In a profession that demands that lawyers be manipulative and brazen, though not necessarily dishonest, he held those qualities in reserve, as extra notes that could be played when required.

'Most of your clients are rich rather than poor?'

'Yes. Lots of Israelis, South Africans — who are terrible about paying their bills, incidentally — and people from Sweden, France, Italy, Hong Kong. The French are afraid that Mitterrand's going to take away all their money. Hong Kong millionaires are convinced that the Chinese will take over when that treaty expires. Most of these rich guys don't want green cards for themselves, but for their families. Possessors of green cards have to pay US taxes, and that's the last thing they want to do. So the men will come over for long visits on regular visas, while it's their wives and children who apply for the green cards.'

'How about Arabs?'

'Not many. Remember, this is a Jewish city and Arabs don't feel too welcome here. It's uncomfortable for them. They are given the cold shoulder, they can't get into co-op buildings because the tenants vote against them.'

We were interrupted by his secretary Sharon, a voluptuous, blasé, black-haired girl dressed in loose silk. Her teeth, white and strong, pounded on some gum as she handed Byrne a sheaf of letters to sign. He introduced me. She nodded. As he duplicated his signature I reflected on the strange mixture of people — Brazilian millionaires, dirt-poor Latin Americans, Haitian refugees, ambitious Koreans, nervous French bankers — that immigration lawyers were stealthily easing into the already tumultuous city. Did the city benefit?

'Yes. New York's an amazingly flexible city. For decades it's benefited by absorbing immigrants and it still does. Much of the immigration — especially the Asians — is middle-class. These people work very hard and as a result the quality of life in the city improves — for them, for everybody. And as the rich flee from the rest of the world and settle here, they invest millions in real estate and services, and bring prosperity to the whole city.'

There was a touch of supply-side fantasy in envisaging the influx of Italian millionaires having an effect on the urban poor in the city, but it was undeniable that New York thrived on its diversity, that waves of new immigration, far from being a threat to the community, stimulate it and enrich the already polyglot culture. We started to talk about London — it turned out we knew and despised some people in common — and I was looking out of the window as I spoke. I stopped. My jaw slowly fell.

'Yeh. Amazing sight, isn't it?' Byrne laughed.

'Does this go on all the time?'

'Every day. Here, I'll open the window for you, so you can get a better look.'

'She's not wearing a stitch. Nothing. What's going on?' I was gazing rapt through plate glass that was framing the exemplary body of a woman slowly turning to admire herself in a mirror while another woman, clothed, fiddled with her hair.

'It's the bridal department at Bergdorf Goodman. You're looking at brides having fittings for their wedding dresses.'

'You mean they're not just any old naked women. Those are rich young virgins.'

'You bet. Hey! Sharon! Come in here a second. I want you to see something.'

'Yeh, I know,' chanted a languid voice, 'it's the naked women again . . .' She stayed put.

'You won't believe this, but I had a client in here once — a Chinese guy — and he spotted the brides over the street just as you did. He got so excited he offered me $4000 a year just to rent this one room.'

It was 1.30 but Byrne was in no hurry for me to leave. We talked about the city and its night life; he recommended places I ought to visit.

'Sharon! Come in here a second. Mr Brook needs your advice.'

I did? Sharon slouched in. Byrne explained: 'Sharon goes out with all these rich older guys, businessmen from Italy, so she knows all the latest places. Don't you?'

She shrugged. Byrne mentioned some clubs. Laboriously raising her eyes, she would indicate whether or not they passed the test.

'How about Club A? Didn't you say that was great?'

'Yeh, that was pretty good. Very fancy.'

'OK, that's where you've got to go. Write it down for Mr Brook. Say, you going to be around for a while longer?'

'Yes.'

'Let's go out one evening. I'd like that. I'll check with my wife and you can call me tomorrow.'

We never did manage to go out, but I did visit Club A.

I recruited Julie. She'd never heard of it, and neither had her team of trend-setting advisers, but she was game, and a few nights later we made our way to the East River wearing our party clothes. East 60th Street is a curious place to locate a night club, as the front door looks onto the fretwork girders of the Queensboro Bridge. There were three heavies at the door. For some obscure reason patrons of night clubs and discos like to feel these places are almost impenetrable, though as far as I could tell all you needed to do was pay up $20 a head to be readily admitted. I whispered magic words at one of the bruisers and we were admitted gratis. We left our cloaks at the cloakroom and made our way up the swirling staircase to the main room. Julie was looking at me oddly.

'Yes, I know what you're thinking. But let's give the place a chance.'

It was as though I had been dropped onto the set of *Dr Who* and was being ushered into the lavish private suite of the Leader of the Gurks or some other evil tribe of metalheads. In the centre was a sunken area for dancing, and on two rising tiers were rings of tables where for a fistful of dollars you could enjoy a rum and Coke and watch the gyrations below. Above the dance floor was a mirrored ceiling, smoky-glassed so that one only received a hint of dervishing from up above rather than a reproduction only distinguishable from the original by being upside down. The walls, between soft cloth wainscotting and the low ceiling, were lined with another mirror-like substance and divided into what might have been small video screens, each section lapped by drapes pulled up on either side, sarabandes of velveteen caressing the walls and descending to uneven lengths at random. Utterly bizarre were stalactites of some white styrofoamoid substance; the Leader of the Gurks was a weird dude. Light emanated from half-concealed orange tubes. The circus ring around the dance floor was broken at three points to admit elegantly attired couples; each gap was monitored by a pair of bronze statuettes of naked women kneeling and leaning backwards, so that their pointed breasts protruded like the noses of Boeings.

'Come on,' said Julie, impatiently. 'We can't just stand here. Let's find a table.' We did so. 'Your friend *recommended* this place?'

'Actually, it was his voluptuous secretary, who goes out with middle-aged camel dealers.'

'Figures.'

On the dance floor the men were in expensive suits, the women in long shiny dresses with plunging backs that revealed flesh smooth as linoleum all the way down to the waist. There wasn't a man under 40, and scarcely a woman over it. A few women were sitting on their own in couples at small tables. Why? They didn't look like hookers, even though the whole place was carefully decorated in glittering Contemporary Bordello. The music, quintessential Easy Listening, featured swooning string orchestras of a thousand violins with falsetto choruses softly moaning in postcoital languor.

'OK, Julie, tell me about this place.'

'Well, first it's heavily B&T.'

'No question about that. There was a sign advertising valet parking outside, even a couple of limos already double-parked before midnight.'

'This is the place where you bring your secretary when your wife is visiting her sister in Denver or is in Mount Sinai for cosmetic surgery. A few couples have driven in specially from Queens because they like to dance to Mantovani and spend money. They're wealthy, the Solid Gold Rolex crowd.'

'And this must be where UN diplomats come after dinner. They're too plump and swarthy to feel comfortable at Xenon, but they're at ease here. That couple there — they may not pour Venezuelan oil on their cornflakes, but I bet they're diplomats.'

I was focusing on a tall blond man, with the kind of firm features bas-reliefed on coinage; in his perfectly judged grip glissandoed the equally disciplined and trim body of a woman slightly his junior, her hair still permed in the fluffy, curled style that survives all the sharp corners of fashion. He was, I felt sure, the Norwegian cultural attaché and she his wife Gertrud. They never smiled, they didn't look at each other, they concentrated like lasers on the activity at hand: their harmony was as close as a melody in thirds, and they were undoubtedly married and happily so. They came to Club A because it was one of the few places where they could quickstep and foxtrot until even their sweatless Nordic feet grew weary.

Not far from Wotan and Fricka was another very tall man, about 45, in a dark suit; from his breast pocket flared a scarlet hanky. In his arms he held a long-haired woman in a toga-like dress, all folds and romanesque pleats, enclosing a body whose pivotal balance was determined by two self-proclaiming breasts. Her prince had a permanent smile on his routinely handsome face; when he looked at her, peering down beyond his jaw, it never altered, since he was smiling at himself and not at her. Only his eyes changed, and as he crushed her downy body against his or flung her from him to the full length of his slender arms in the calculated abandon of a tango, he would close his eyes, still smiling, as if to work up the ecstasy appropriate to the moment. She aided and abetted, and in the comfort of his embrace would fling wide her arms, so that the only thing preventing her from a painful tumble was his hairy hand around the whiteness of her waist. They never faltered.

'Let's dance.' Julie was tapping her foot half in time to the music, half in irritation.

'That's absurd. Last time I waltzed I was 10.'

'You don't have to waltz. Just shuffle. That's what most of them are doing.'

'Not Ronald Colman and Wotan. They're pros. I hate to be shown up.'

'Stop making excuses. Come.' She took my hand and tugged.

So we shuffled around, while Henry Mancini and his orchestra whiffled and sighed from discreet loudspeakers. I collided with Ronald Colman, but failed to throw him off his slippery stride. When the tape ended, I returned to our table to recover my dignity. Julie's restless eye fell on the next table, now occupied by two tall women of identical build, with deceiving eyelashes and fire-engine lips, and nails as long as a mouse's tail. They were both wearing full-length fur coats, and had before them tough drinks, probably bourbon.

'Hookers,' I whispered to Julie.

'I don't know,' she said, with an expertise derived from years of observation in her neighbourhood. 'Let's find out . . .' She unleashed a smile that could warn ships away from rocky coasts and turned to the ladies. I was wrong. They were, unbelievably, mother and daughter from Las Vegas.

'We went to Regine's last time we were in New York, but this time we wanted to try Club A because we heard it's the latest place in town.'

'How d'you like it?'

'It's a nice place, we like it OK, but we like Regine's better. Regine's is very expensive, though.'

The three ladies discussed the night life of Las Vegas while I sat by, speculating on what it would be like to roll my dice up the long limbs of the swish daughter, all curly hair and smooth fox. After all the conversational ore had been extracted, I suggested to Julie that we move on to a less geriatric pleasure dome, such as the Red Parrot, and we raced for the door.

EBONY AND IVORY

> Down here we're too ignorant to realize
> That the north has set the Nigger free

sing Randy Newman's Southern Rednecks. Despite their boast that 'we don't know our ass from a hole in the ground', their observation has an ironic acuity that must make any Northern liberal squirm.

For blacks who live in northern cities often feel just as entrapped, though in a different way, as they did in the harshly but openly segregated South. *De jure* has given way to its insidious cousin *de facto*.

The Harlem I first visited in 1965 was a steamy, overcrowded, verminous slum, and after almost 20 years it had scarcely changed. There are patches of improvement, some middle-class corners, a new hospital or two, but the general condition of this sizable section of Manhattan was, if anything, worse than before. Urban blight has hit it with a vengeance. Men with matted hair shuffle around in tatty old coats clutching a bottle of rot-gut hidden from view, as the law requires, in a brown paper bag with just the unstoppered neck protruding. The younger men are more likely to have a joint between their fingers as they crouch on the stoops of derelict buildings. White people don't go to Harlem unless they have business there, which is unlikely. It's not attractive and it certainly isn't safe.

In the 20s and 30s, it had been fashionable for the beau monde to head up to Harlem in the wee hours to listen to Bessie Smith and Leadbelly and Duke Ellington at the Apollo. Those days are long over. The Apollo became a cinema years ago, and now it has closed altogether. If New York as a whole has been let off comparatively lightly by the

228

nationwide recession, the same cannot be said of Harlem or Bedford-Stuyvesant or the South Bronx. In these black slums the unemployment rate has for years been between 30 and 40 per cent, and even higher amongst teenagers. The service industries require data processors and paper-pushers, numeracy and technological savoir faire, and these skills are not easily acquired in ghetto schools, as the despondent comments of the teachers at George Washington High made clear. The pool of unskilled labour is drained off by the Hispanic immigrants, who now compete for the same scarce jobs as the indigenous poor blacks.

It never ceased to astonish me that some of the most luxurious apartments in the world are being constructed in the East and West 80s and 90s, while a few hundred yards away fester the slums of Harlem. New Yorkers blinker themselves against this, unless they travel by the commuter trains that slice through the ghetto at high speed. Drivers leaving the city to the north to reach the Westchester suburbs or New England are more likely to speed up one of the riverside highways than drive through Harlem. As long as the service industries prosper, and the glitter and glamour of the city are constantly refuelled by fresh injections of talent and money, Manhattan will continue to gleam and shine and beckon as the prince of cities, welcoming acolytes who can make their contribution to it. That this prosperity and sophistication sours with every step that you take north of 96th Street doesn't concern affluent New Yorkers. They simply don't see it.

East 96th Street is the Great Divide. It's here that the trains from Grand Central emerge from a long tunnel and thunder north overground. The intrusion scars the street and you enter a world of tenements and public housing projects, variously known as Spanish Harlem, East Harlem, or El Barrio. No more discreet florists or delicatessens for retiring Upper East Siders, but instead PRODUCTOS TROPICALES. Nearby is a modern pharmacy and the sign MEDICAID AND ALL UNION PRESCRIPTIONS FILLED tells one clearly enough that there's a different economic base up here, with many residents on welfare. Over on Lexington a scruffy betting shop displays a sign that could be either a prohibition or a piece of information: POSITIVELY NO POT OR DRUGS OF ANY KIND SOLD ON THESE PREMISES. As in all the other deprived areas of the city, there are burnt-out tenements and semi-derelict buildings that might still be partially inhabited; the broken glass littering empty lots glints in the sun. Not all of the Barrio is shabby and run-down. Third Avenue bustles in a jaunty honky-tonk way, and cut-rate stores sell cheap clothing and discounted electrical appliances. Up on 100th Street a sticker on a door reads CATHOLIC GIRLS HAVE MASS APPEAL, and a local wit has crossed out the M.

Further west, under the railway tracks that wreck this stretch of Park Avenue, is an indoor market that runs from 112th to 115th Street. The butchers stock chicken and beef, but the cheaper cuts dominate: pig ears and snouts, cow feet, beef tripe, pork melts, hog maws. Other stalls offer dozens of herbs and spices, grains and nuts. Produce stalls are piled with root vegetables, sinister beans, and sierras of bananas in every stage of existence, from green to black and rotten. While I made a call from a pay phone near the exit, the stallholder on the phone next to me was explaining to an official that he applied eight months ago for his gun permit and still hasn't heard anything from the Police Department, and would they mind getting a move on.

Further uptown, between Second and Third Avenues, rises a glistening new housing development, Taino Towers. Each of its 30-plus storeys is ringed by balconies, and the stylish white towers exude a sense of luxury far removed from the more typical boxy red-brick clusters that pass for public housing in New York. Yet the gleaming complex seems largely empty; at least two of the towers are unoccupied. From the start, the project has been saddled with still unresolved financial problems. Seen from afar, it appears that East Harlem has given way to Acapulco, but step into the courtyard and you're brought sharply back to the ghetto. Inside is a guarded playground, and a notice tacked to the wire fence lists the rules; one of them forbids taking 'firearms, knives or any weapons' into it. Yet again, it seems, good intentions have foundered on the intractability of the ghetto's social and financial problems. Mustering up my Spanglish, I leave *la yarda* and wander off to *lunchear*.

If more affluent New Yorkers appear indifferent to the

poverty all around them, it may be because there is so little they can do about it; concern without action accomplishes nothing. At the same time, I couldn't help wondering why the city's black population appeared to be so inert in the face of their increasing destitution. Apathy and despair were explanations, to be sure, but they also come to sound like excuses after a while. Was it, I wondered, fair to put all the blame for the deplorable state of Harlem and the other ghettoes on the economy and on white politicians alone?

I raised these issues with Horace Morris, who runs the New York Urban League, a nonprofit organization that operates job assessment and placement programmes, provides services to the elderly, and acts as a pressure group in the fields of education, housing, health and social welfare. Multi-racial, it concerns itself principally with the plight of minorities in the city. Morris nodded as I talked; he'd heard it all before.

He settled his burly form into a chair. 'The reason Harlem is the way it is is a direct result of the city's development policies. Downtown may be booming, but there's very little economic development in central Manhattan and the boroughs. Real estate interests are very powerful in New York and they're not interested in the ghettoes; the land just isn't worth much to them. Black areas in the city also lack political clout. Their residents aren't properly organized. Certain segments of the black community are OK, but in general the range and quality of services — policing, fire, sanitation, you name it — are lower than elsewhere in the city. We've got a lot of people living on welfare. That means low housing allowances, which leads to overcrowding and poor housing.

'All we can do is hold state and local government accountable. One thing we're trying to do right now is put more stress on the voluntary sector. We need to make the voluntary efforts more compatible with the public effort.'

Whatever that means. How could Morris and other black leaders hold politicians accountable when he'd already admitted they had little clout? And wasn't 'voluntary sector' a padded phrase for 'charity'? Was dropping dimes into a collecting box the new solution to the problems of the ghetto?

What could the League do about the shift away from

industrial skills?

'Not much. It's a government job. They've got to retrain people.'

'But they're not going to, are they? The likelihood is that there are simply going to be fewer jobs from now on, and higher levels of unemployment will become regarded as acceptable.'

'I'm not sure that's so. I don't feel there will be fewer jobs in the future, though they will be different kinds of jobs.'

'And in the meantime there's not much you can do.'

'No, we've got to wait for an upturn in the economy.'

'Could be a long wait.'

'It will be. But people need hope, we need to assure the black communities that things will get better.'

'And do you believe they will?'

'Eventually. I'm an optimist.'

'So until the economy improves there's not much the League can do. You're forced to take a passive role.'

'Yes, we are. That's true of white people who've been hurt by the economy too. But our hope is that in 1984 we'll have a new administration in Washington.'

It was too bland a response for comfort. I hoped to whip up some ire by asking Morris about the Mayor.

'Koch? It's fair to say he's written off the black community, though not the black politicians. And vice versa. Koch feels he's doing what's right for the city. He's not going to change his way of doing things much. He's made his political decision, to go with the banks and the real estate people and the insurance companies, and he'll ride it out. But we do have access. We're friends with the Mayor. He listens to us, though he doesn't always do what we want. But we're not too discouraged.'

How gratifying it must be for the black community to know they have access to the Mayor, even though he doesn't pay the slightest attention to their appeals. At least the Urban League isn't discouraged. But I was, and I wanted to hear other black voices. Yet access is so difficult. The few blacks in the city I had contact with were not slum-dwellers; they'd made their escape, or their parents had, and they were indistinguishable in terms of career and aspiration and style of living from their white contemporaries. The only way I was likely to hear a black voice from the ghetto was to go there and hunt down a preacher.

I chose one of the larger Harlem churches, the Abyssinian Baptist Church on West 138th Street. The streets were quiet as I walked briskly — Harlem is no place for a stroll if you're white — the few blocks from the subway to the church. The sunny weather and the tranquillity were mollifying; when I'd been looking at domestic architecture in Harlem a few weeks earlier my exploration took me down some side streets that induced fairly high levels of anxiety in me. On one or two desolate blocks I had a brush with panic as I realized I was quite alone; had any malefactor picked that moment to leap from a doorway and carve his initials on my throat there wouldn't have been much I could have done about it. But that had been a weekday, a day of business, and that includes crime; now it was Sunday, and even the knots of reefer-smoking kids on the stoops I passed paid little attention to me.

I stepped into a fairly large church that was about half full. The congregation had dressed with care — most of the women in hats and cheap furs, the men in jackets and ties. I sat inconspicuously towards the back. Each aisle was patrolled by ushers in uniform: white dress, white shoes, white paper carnation in the hair, and a black corsage. They looked like nurses in a psychiatric ward. The ministers sat on a raised platform in the front of the church; behind them the tiers of a huge choir in cassocks of dusty red and pale grey. After some announcements by the minister, the choir launched into a splendidly operatic *Amazing Grace,* with a coloratura soprano solo and the full choir giving ever louder support.

The preacher that day was Calvin O. Butts. Now there's a name! It was straight out of a nonexistent W. C. Fields film in which that rogue, planning to rush a rich widow to the altar, calls on the minister, none other than Calvin O. Butts. This Dr Butts, however, was in no mood for jesting, for this was Martin Luther King's birthday. He lauded King as one of three great black leaders of the century, the other two being Adam Clayton Powell and Malcolm X. All three had been anointed by God, said Dr Butts, and the reason why no black leader had risen to take their place was that there was no one presently worthy to be so anointed. He spoke acerbically of 'our racist society' and of 'the Koches and the

233

Reagans of this world'. If a national news commentator had linked their names like that, the ex-liberal and the avowed reactionary, there would have been an outcry; yet clearly from a Harlem perspective these men were directly comparable if only because they were both, in the eyes of the black community, pursuing policies that would further obstruct the efforts of that community to haul itself out of its misery and poverty. Certainly no one flinched or stirred when Butts twinned their names. There was, though, a murmur of recognition when he declared: 'The most segregated hour of the week is 11 on a Sunday morning — when white and black go to their separate churches to worship the same God.' Of course he was right: as the only white person there I could witness to that. Dr Butts may not have had the answers to the intractable problems of the ghettoes but at least he had, unlike the amiable Horace Morris, some fire in his belly.

When I went to buy some sausages on Mott Street in Little Italy, I was also given an earful of racism for good measure. Like all the old neighbourhoods of Manhattan, Little Italy is not what it used to be, but it's still heavily Italian despite the swelling Chinese presence, a contesseration of delicatessens, bakers and butchers, restaurants large and small but mostly mediocre, and cafés: opulent Ferrara's on Grand Street, an accurate reproduction of its Milanese or Roman counter-part, and the smaller Roma on Broome Street, the ideal place for cappuccino and macaroons and revolting Italian custard pastries.

It was late afternoon and the shops were closing up. The butcher, as he served me, looked puzzled by my accent.

'Where you from?'

'London.'

'The real London?'

'The one and only.'

'How you like New York.'

'Love it.'

'Yeh.' I could sense him pursuing a still obscured train of thought. He heaved his bulk round the side of the counter and came up to me, signalling a wish to distance himself from the world of meat. 'We're all mixed up here. Know what I mean? Littla this, littla that, people from all over.'

'That's what I like. Walk a block and you hear 10 languages.'

'Know any Italians in London?'

'Some. I like to shop in Soho, our Soho, where there are lots of Italian delicatessens.'

'Lots of people from the south of Italy in London. Naples, Sorrento. Mariners, they tend to live in London.'

'I didn't know that.' Never noticed Italian old salts hanging about on Old Compton Street.

'That's right. Not many from the north. North, south it's like tribes. It *is* tribes. Utterly different. In fact the whole thing's tribunal, know what I mean?'

'Yes.'

'Like the Scots? Right?' He grinned.

'Absolutely. Not English at all. Inferior in every respect.'

'Say, tell me something.' I waited for it. Did he want me to take a package to his cousin in Stoke Newington? Or was he going to offer me a highly paid post in organized crime? 'The blacks give you any problems in England?'

'No.'

'Notice how I phrase that.' He raised a chubby hand to usher down the spirit of pedantry. 'Listen to my phrasing. Do they give *you* problems? Not do you give *them* problems. Here in New York nobody gives them problems, they're the ones making the problems for *us*. Give people their freedom and they don't know what to do with it.'

As I smiled blankly at this plump jovial bigot, I wondered what he put in his sausages. I meandered. 'Well, when people have had a raw deal for centuries —'

'Look. You shouldn't give people things when they're not ready. I love my kids, but do I give my 12-year-old a Cadillac? No.'

I walked a block down Hester to Mulberry and came to Umberto's Clam Bar. This landmark is a favourite spot for Mafia target practice, and friends who warmly recommend the seafood at Umberto's also advised me never to sit with my back to the door. I couldn't stop, I had to get back to the Village, and strolled back up Elizabeth Street as dusk fell. Tatty flags had been strung across the street, probably left over from the San Gennaro Festival of the previous September. Dim unshaded light bulbs shone in the windows of shabby tenements. A chapel brooded on a corner.

Despite a few Chinese signs over some entrances, physically the street can't have changed much over the decades. It was quiet, cosy, atmospheric, undemonstrative, closed in on itself. There was still a community here and in adjoining streets. That I felt myself an outsider here seemed appropriate, even satisfying. So many neighbourhoods in New York are recent inventions, but Little Italy, though shrinking, still has corners that are as private as a convent.

Realizing I was lost I paused on a corner and consulted my map. Looking up I saw a bleary-eyed man standing in front of me. His once fine features had begun to crumble and sag. He jabbed at my map.

'Sir,' he began, 'which is the quickest way to sanity? Can you tell me that?'

CITY HAUL

Victor Gotbaum was in a grumpy mood. He'd been put out of action briefly by a tennis injury that was still troubling him, and his repertory of profanity and charm was being held in check. Gotbaum is the most forceful and visible union boss in New York, leading the 110,000 Municipal Employees. He's a burly man in his mid-60s, and to describe him as brash and irascible — all of which he can be — is to give scant idea of his sophistication and intelligence. Uncompromising yet mercurial, he moves coolly in the highest circle of the city's power brokers without losing touch with his largely working-class membership. His success over the years in delivering the goods to his members has made his position unassailable, and given him the freedom to say what he thinks, a luxury he isn't shy to indulge. During negotiations that began shortly after Koch became mayor, Gotbaum described him as 'a complete disaster', adding that 'his is not a bright mind'. That was praise indeed compared to his assessment of Abe Beame as 'a basket case'. His attitude to Koch had mellowed little when I spoke to him one morning at his offices near the World Trade Center. 'Koch is not the sweetest person to work with, though he's a nice boss to kick in the ass.'

He was no more complimentary about Reaganomics and the widening gap between rich and poor, which he described as 'the unhealthiest manifestation of our economy', though he also believed the trend would reverse itself in time. 'I'm a cautious optimist,' he declared, scowling as he shifted his bruised leg.

Since New York is an overwhelmingly Democratic city, the unions, long a mainstay of the Democratic Party, are intensely political. Their endorsements, and their money, can be crucial to a candidacy, as Koch discovered when he lost the gubernatorial primary to Mario Cuomo, who had built a broader power base that included some of the most influential unions.

Without the aid of the unions, it would have been far harder to sort out the financial mess of 1975. Their pension funds invested $3.5 billion in bonds to help restructure the city's finances. It wasn't just goodness of heart. The unions knew full well that if the city were forced into bankruptcy, the courts would almost certainly scale back precious benefits won from City Hall over the years. The noose that was throttling the city would strangle the unions too, and their generous response was a calculated strategy of self-protection. It was understood when Koch became Mayor that he would have to reward the unions for the 'sacrifices' they'd made. He did so, agreeing to settlements with municipal unions that were far higher than the general level of wage increases during the recession.

Cynics said that the imminent gubernatorial primary encouraged the Mayor to be open-handed, yet Koch had failed to receive their endorsement. Weakened by his electoral defeat, Koch was now under pressure to renegotiate the contracts with the Municipal Employees. Downwards.

Gotbaum conceded this. 'We don't have any new contract negotiations coming up, but there's talk of the Mayor renegotiating what we've already agreed.'

'Are you unhappy about that prospect?'

'I'm not unhappy about that prospect because there is no prospect.'

From Victor Gotbaum's office, it's a five-minute walk to a modest, vaguely Renaissance palazzo that sits demurely in a small park surrounded by the skyscrapers of downtown Manhattan. The city is a trifle larger than it was in 1811, but it is still run from the same City Hall that was built in that year, though squads of departments and offices are housed in other buildings. Nevertheless, the people of New York still come to City Hall to attend the meetings of the City Council and the Board of Estimate, and the Mayor and the President of the City Council have their offices here. In the political zoo, the Council is a lamb: its members represent very local interests, and apart from having to approve the budget and proposed tax increases, most of their discussions deal with minor legislation. The Liberal Party councilman Henry Stern is said to have remarked that the difference between the City Council and a rubber stamp 'is that at least a rubber stamp leaves an impression'.

The Board of Estimate is a more powerful body, far less under the thumb of the Mayor. It has eight members: the Mayor, the Comptroller (the money man), the Council President, and the presidents of the five boroughs. The borough presidents each have one vote, the three more senior officials each have two. It's the Board that votes on such matters as zoning changes; it twiddles the controls of the city, and although the individual cases it decides may seem relatively minor, the overall effect on the city economy can be considerable. The Board's chamber is a curious room: quite grandiose in a debased Robert Adam style with columns and pilasters and plasterwork. The Board members, with a battery of aides behind them, sit up on a dais, while the public sits on white pews in the body of the chamber. It's like a Quaker meeting house deposited in the drawing-room of a Georgian mansion.

After it has raced through routine business, the Board sits patiently while the good citizens of New York come forward to a lectern and petition for favour and mercy. The morning I turned up, some 'senior citizens' had arrived *en masse* to lobby for an old people's home in Yorkville. The scheme was opposed by a community group since a precious small garden would be lost if the home were built. Teams of OAPs in varying stages of decrepitude were wheeled in to testify and of course they won hands down.

Further comic relief was provided by George, an emaciated bearded man with a jutting jaw and mismatched beige clothes; he paced around the chamber, clutching a copy of the calendar of business. At every conceivable opportunity he rushed to the lectern and improvised a point of order. Groans from the dais. 'OK, George, sit down, we've heard you —'

'One moment. Pleece.' He had a German accent. 'Surely, under ze rool zat —'

'George!' The woman sitting in for the Council President (most of the officials on the Board are represented during hearings by surrogates) yelled at him. 'This isn't the time to raise this!'

And George would wander off, only to return a few minutes later when he'd bared another loophole.

The real powerhouse in City Hall, though, is on the ground floor. The west wing houses the Mayor and his staff, and the east contains the offices of Carol Bellamy, President of the City Council. As one of the three top elected officials in the city, the Council President is a powerful figure, though her duties are ill defined. Her power stems from her two votes, matching the Mayor's, on the Board, and she is free to take up whatever issues interest her. As Mayor Koch has moved rightwards in recent years, Carol Bellamy, though fiscally conservative, has been able to stand out as more idealistic, less tied to the moneyed establishment. On the board of the MTA and other committees, she has, she told me, 'a complaints resolution function'; independent of the administration, her office can supply the checks and balances that counter the executive. It seems fitting that Koch and Bellamy sit in opposite wings of City Hall, and there's little love lost between them. Koch once called her 'a horror show' and told a *Playboy* interviewer that she was 'a pain in the ass'.

Although many New Yorkers dislike Ed Koch, even despise him, it's clear that, however crass his persona, he is, in his way, a strong and effective Mayor. After Abe Beame anybody would have looked good, but Koch had energy and flair and a vulgarity that endeared him to many of his citizens. After years as a somewhat retiring liberal congressman in Washington, he'd run for Mayor, and in office had come to embody the chutzpah, the wise-ass style, the brashness, that are the New York stereotypes.

Koch unquestionably has a constituency and is, the pollsters insist, a very popular Mayor, but there's no doubt that his ego was battered by his defeat by Mario Cuomo.

'Everybody thought Koch would be a shoo-in,' observed a lawyer who used to work at City Hall, 'but then he lost to Cuomo and ever since he's been like a broken egg. Still, he seems to be surviving, if only because his awfulness is indulged by the city. He calls fare dodgers "lepers" and everybody claps with delight.'

Another friend offered a more devastating appraisal. 'Ever since Koch became Mayor the city has become perceptibly worse.' (Discount that: New Yorkers have been saying that for 200 years.) 'He's blatantly a mayor for the rich, yet he's rhapsodically popular with the white middle classes, though he does little for them. He insults the poor and the elderly, yet people are still for him in a crazy way. He's a prototypical example of the new breed of Right Democrats. He promises nothing, he delivers nothing, and people call him honest.'

No one doubts that Koch is honest, though municipal politics are notoriously corrupt. Even the left-wing economist Robert Lekachman, no man to mince his words, said, 'I don't think Koch is personally avaricious. He's too busy keeping his head above water politically. In his first term he had an excuse for increasing austerity — everybody was keen to see the city back on its feet — but the excuses are wearing thin. But now he's got little leeway, as he's getting less and less help from the other levels of government. The city is still at the mercy of national and international problems, and there are few resources available to alleviate its sufferings. Even so, Koch continually ratifies his supporters' prejudices and allocates what resources he has to middle-class and commercial interests.

'Koch is probably at a political dead end. Having lost to Cuomo he knows he's unlikely to rise above Mayor. He can go for a third term or pack it in. He's sentenced to three more years in City Hall with no hope of parole.'

I was beginning to feel sorry for him by the time I walked into his comfortable office. With its tall windows and heavy curtains and flags behind the desk, it had the effect, although as an office it is not especially large, of dwarfing us both. I sank into a black couch in the corner. He sat in a chair nearby. He was larger than I expected, with his long bulbous face crowned by baldness, and a body that seemed fairly trim though fleshy. He was unsmiling, but then he has little to smile about. When a few days later I saw Carol Bellamy, her approach was different. She sat at a conference table and placed me directly opposite her, so that we were eyeball to eyeball and could talk back and forth, whereas Koch, it was quite clear, was granting a formal interview. Backchat not encouraged. My best strategy, I decided, was to bumble, to ask embarrassing questions under the guise of naiveté; his strategy, as the interview progressed, was to try to eat me alive.

I asked Hizanna (as New Yorkers refer to His Honor the Mayor) how the city was going to respond to declining levels of federal and state aid: would it mean an inescapable sequence of increased taxes and reduced services?

Koch shrugged it off. 'This problem is hardly unique to New York.' Other cities across the nation were in the same plight, he said, and they would all be getting together to lobby Congress intensely. At the state level, the smaller townships would join New York City in lobbying at Albany. 'We've also got the budget much more under control. New York's been through the wringer before, we're better able to deal with the problem. In Chicago and Boston they've had to close down parts of the city system, such as transportation and education, which we've managed to avoid. The next 18 months to two years will be tough, but after we've weathered that things will improve.'

'So you're an optimist about the future of the city?'

'Yes. But it'll be a good 18 months before we start seeing an upturn.'

Shrewd to keep paradise just around the corner. Of course he hadn't answered the question. Bellamy was more direct. She agreed with the Mayor that the fiscal problem was no longer one of the city's debt but of balancing the budget and she was certain there would have to be further cuts in services. But she found a silver lining: 'For all the hand-wringing about cuts in services, in some areas, such as sanitation, productivity has actually increased.'

Would he agree, I asked the Mayor, that the gulf between rich and poor was widening, and if so, did he have the power to do anything about it.'

'You forget,' said the Mayor with some asperity, 'that New York isn't just Manhattan.'

'I am dimly aware —'

'There are the boroughs too. Manhattan is just Main Street. There have always been plenty of rich people in Manhattan.'

'I know. I'm talking about a gap, not about numbers. Are the middle classes being driven out of Manhattan, leaving the island to the very well off and the very poor?'

'No. It isn't true that the middle classes are leaving in any great numbers. Most Manhattan office workers have always lived in the boroughs or suburbs.'

'So you're saying the gap is no wider than it's ever been.'

'Right. I don't accept your statement that the gap is getting wider.'

Carol Bellamy was good enough to corroborate my own view.

'Yes,' she said briskly, 'the gap is widening and in three ways. The recession makes it harder for those who are struggling anyway. Second, Manhattan is increasingly a city for the young and for the old, rather than for families. And third, the poor have less mobility — the structurally unemployed tend to stay put.'

'Can any city administration, not just this one, have any effect on this?'

'Not much. Local government can only affect the local economy peripherally. The picture isn't entirely gloomy. Remember, there has been a net gain of service jobs to counter the loss of manufacturing jobs. But there are a few things we can do. First, transportation is crucial. Worsening transportation has a more negative impact than high taxes. Second, crime is a factor, even though the perception is worse than the reality. Third, there's education. We need to make it possible for a trained work force to get into the system. Those are things the city can work towards. But there's not much you can do about interest rates, lower business revenues, the withdrawal of the federal government from housing, all that kind of thing.'

Bellamy conceded that the city has two separate and unequal educational systems. 'Remember we can't do anything about private schools, but we can make public school education much more career-oriented. We must develop students' skills to the point where they can enter the system and be more competitive in terms of the market. Standards in public schools have been rising in recent years, but the main problem is discipline and racial tension. On the other hand, the new immigrant groups such as the West Indians and Asians are more disciplined and are having a positive effect on the public schools.'

Koch was unperturbed. 'I believe the schools, like anything else, have to be competitive.' I raised my left eyebrow at this — was Hizanna about to suggest closing them down like exhausted mines? 'There are public schools and there are the private and parochial schools, and I support both kinds. I also support tuition tax credits. I'm for giving people the freedom of choice.'

There'd been a group of bombings on New Year's Eve, and I asked the Mayor whether he felt that New York, as the financial centre of the world, was particularly vulnerable to urban terrorism.

He looked astonished. 'Vulnerable? In England you had 27 people killed by a bomb, blowing up the horses in the park the other day! And in Belfast? More people are killed in Britain than in New York!'

I bowled underarm. 'Is the city better managed since you became Mayor?'

Quick as a flash: 'Yes. It has to be. I'm running it.'

Ah, vintage Koch! That smart-alecky, wise-ass belligerence! Except that he said it straight, without a flicker of humour.

I was saving the big one for last. I asked about tax abatements and exemptions, whether this device to encourage certain kinds of urban development was falling into the wrong hands, namely, rich and powerful property tycoons. It was a sensitive issue; Koch, in many people's eyes, is too closely allied with real estate interests in the city. He gave a long and detailed answer, which I omit for the following rather endearing reason. As I was leaving the Mayor's office, his press officer asked me if I was going to include what Koch had said about property taxes. Possibly, I said. 'Well, if you're gonna get technical with that tax stuff, better call me first. The Mayor got a bit, er, confused between abatements and exemptions. Everyone does, including the Housing Commissioner.'

Aware of the thrust of my question, Koch did insist that although individual judgment on abatements could be criticized or faulted, 'there has never been any suggestion of corruption. In any case, the decision is made by the Board of Estimate, not by the Mayor.' This was curiously defensive, since I had no intention of so much as hinting that the Mayor was corrupt.

When I asked Carol Bellamy whether these abatements and exemptions had been overdone, her reply was crisp and to the point.

'I think that's the right way to put it. Too many people think of abatements as either good or bad, whereas they're just a tool. Real estate is New York's oil industry. In 1975 it was almost dead, and abatements were useful in reviving it, and I think it was right to grant them till about 1978. Then conditions changed. The theory is that abatements encourage investment where it wouldn't otherwise take place. It has been overdone, I suspect, but we don't have enough data to be clear about it. I am opposed to repeal, though, and I still think it's a useful tool, as long as we remember that an abatement is a form of public spending. They should be targeted more, especially to the stronger parts of the boroughs. People need to realize that your arms don't fall off if you move to the boroughs.'

It's no secret that Carol Bellamy would like to be Mayor. Should they clash electorally in a couple of years' time it could be an interesting battle. Bellamy doesn't have the brash gusto of Koch. I colour him turquoise. Bellamy's intensity and seriousness make me colour her grey. Politics seem to fill her life to the brim. We were meeting at 8.30, but her press officer had asked me if I'd be prepared to come in two hours earlier, since she sometimes starts work at 6.30 and doesn't go home till 11.00 at night. She looked desperately tired as she sat opposite me, the bags under her eyes pouchy behind her glasses.

I like a touch of roguishness in my politicians — to sense they're human even to the point of frailty — and there was none of that in Carol Bellamy. Integrity and dedication are written all over her unremarkable features. How tightly, I wondered, does one have to wrap one's righteousness to keep it intact? That she was straight as a die was obvious. But did she sing in the shower, or weep at the movies? She intrigued me precisely because she was wound up so tightly, steeled against giving anything away. She'd won me over by the simple expedient of taking me seriously. Unlike Koch, she hadn't tried to score easy points or gloss over the difficulties. On the other hand, her political fortunes were steadily rising, while Ed Koch is wobbling at the top.

'What,' I asked her, 'is the Mayor's greatest achievement, and where, if anywhere, has he failed — or neglected — to act as you'd wish?'

She thought for a while, no doubt unwilling to allow her usual high-mindedness to slip into an *ad hominem* attack. 'His achievement is that he did give strong leadership. He led the financial renewal of the city and he does balance its budget. But his failing is that he's doing it in an almost inhuman way. One does need some degree of compassion and humanity. Now that the city's finances have been dealt with, we need to deal with its services, and I'm afraid Koch just won't get round to it. He's forgetting there are *people* out there. He's asked the people of New York to do an awful lot for their city, and he mustn't forget that.'

And to Mayor Koch I put the same question more sycophantically: 'At the end of your second term, what would you like to look back on as your greatest achievement?'

'That I gave New York spirit. Until recently, the city had a hangdog spirit. My optimism, my leadership, my ebullience' — he waved his hands in the air as he searched for further terms of self-congratulation — 'have made a difference. It's not just my view. Other people will tell you that too.'

FUZZ

Siren screaming, rooflight flashing, engine roaring, tyres screeching, the blue and white squad car tore up Amsterdam Avenue. A classic chase scene! Officer Mannix at the wheel, with Officer Hetherington at her side, while tensed on the back seat, peering cautiously out of the window as the traffic parted like the Red Sea to make way for us, was none other than myself. Weegee-like, I was prepared for anything, mental flash camera at the ready to record for posterity the doings, brave and iniquitous, of New York's finest, as they patrolled the nocturnal city, prying up its flagstones to reveal the dreadful deeds of its nefarious underworld.

The Police Department had put me in the mood by asking me down to Police Plaza earlier that day, as they were keen for me to see the centralized communications unit. Doing my best to simulate interest in the workings of switchboards I followed big, genial Sergeant Harte around as he explained to me the efficiency with which emergency calls are handled.

As all this was being explained to me, a man came leaping into the offices wearing a Santa suit. A chorus rose from the workers: 'How're you doing, lieutenant . . .'

The festive lieutenant greeted them, then spotted me standing in the middle of the room. He pointed at me. 'You one of my men?'

'No.'

'That's good,' he said, relieved. 'That's good. I'd heard you were incompetent.'

That evening I walked into the headquarters of Precinct 20 on West 82nd Street. A desk officer fetched the precinct captain, who was puzzled by my presence since no one at Police Plaza had informed him that I'd be turning up. He made me fill out forms absolving the Police Department of responsibility should I be injured or wiped out while in the company of police officers.

'Don't know when we'll have a team who can take you along,' said Captain O'Connell grumpily. 'Better sit here for a while until I find someone who can take care of you.'

The main waiting room was drab and cheerless and I sat on an uncomfortable plastic chair set against a wall. For company there was a glass cabinet full of sports trophies and a small Christmas tree. I didn't have to wait for long. A tall policewoman approached me and said: 'OK, you're with me. Let's go.' I followed her out into the parking area. Officer Mannix was in her mid-20s, I guessed, and she chewed gum as steadily as she breathed air. We introduced ourselves and I also shook hands with Officer Hetherington, about the same age, easy-going, friendly.

I climbed into the back of the car and we slowly set off down Broadway. Almost immediately a call ordered us back to the precinct station. Mannix went to see what was up, only to return a few seconds later. To my surprise she opened the back door. 'It's for you. The Captain wants to see you.'

He did more than see me. He told me that I didn't have the proper authorization, that I couldn't go out in a squad car, that we'd have to call the whole thing off. By now a familiar story. But unknown to him, I had a powerful weapon on my side: he was wrong. I did have authorization and two minutes later I was back in the car and we were once again heading down Broadway.

'We're both rookies,' Hetherington informed me. 'Haven't been out of the Academy too long.'

'Why did you join the police?'

'Runs in the family, I guess. My dad and my uncle were both cops, and it's the only thing I ever wanted to be.'

This precinct extends up the West Side from 59th to 86th Street, an area that includes Columbus Avenue, New York's answer to the Boulevard Saint-Germain. North of 80th Street it's more patchy, with pockets of bourgeois infiltration and blocks that are still shabby and badly maintained. Over by the Hudson too, beyond Lincoln Center, are housing projects and desolate stretches devoid of the night life and shopping strips that keep Columbus and Broadway buzzing 24 hours a day. Hetherington explained that the precinct was continuously patrolled by six or seven squad cars. 'We stick to this area, though sometimes we're dispatched to another precinct if they need help. Specially in summer. Then the pickpockets are out and people drink more. They're just more people on the streets. Course, there are a lotta muggings this time of year. People are still shopping for Christmas and they're carrying a lot of money and a wallet full of credit cards. We have some foot posts too, in addition to car patrols.'

'Think we're in for a quiet night?'

'Can't say. Probably. Except every time we say it's awful quiet, 10 minutes later all hell breaks loose. So we don't try to predict.'

'That's right,' chimed in Mannix. She was driving slowly, looking casually from side to side, at pedestrians, at cars, at shopfronts.

It was then that we spotted this white car making a bad turn and we started to follow. When the white car went through a red light, Officer Hetherington opened the box of tricks on the roof and Officer Mannix put her foot down. At last! We were pursuing the personification of crime, a kid in a souped-up car. It didn't take long to catch up and he pulled over. On the loudspeaker Hetherington sounded harsh and peremptory as he told the driver to stay in his car. As the two cops were opening their doors, I said manfully, 'Can I come too?' But Hetherington turned rapidly and said, 'Stay where you are.' I didn't argue.

I watched them checking documents and arguing with the driver, who eventually drove off and the officers returned to the squad car.

'We tell them to stay in the car,' explained Hetherington, 'as you don't want them to come out shooting. They're too many cases of cops getting killed on routine car stops. This kid was no problem, though. Said he was late for class, so we let him off with a warning.'

A few minutes later word came through of an assault further up on Columbus. More automobile hysterics as we raced to the spot and sped down a one-way street the wrong way, with two other squad cars on our tail. But there was nothing there — a false alarm. There was a drunk, though, who took the opportunity to scream at Mannix, 'Hey, Miss Bully! Hey, Miss Bully!' She ignored him. It was brave of him to abuse her, since she's six feet tall and could easily have knocked him over with a flick of her finger or the elastic bounce of her gum-sprung jaw.

'That's the only thing to do with drunks,' said Mannix wearily. 'Ignore them. If we had to get into conversation with every drunk that yells at us, we'd be doing nothing else all night.'

During a quiet patch that followed, Hetherington talked to me about life at Precinct 20. 'I was on switchboard the other night. A woman phoned up and asked me what are our hours. "Mam," I said, "this is a precinct station." "I know that," she snapped back at me, "but I'd still like to know what your hours are." Unbelievable.'

'Yeh,' drawled Mannix, 'I've had three calls like that.'

We were down by Lincoln Center, and the streets were packed with people crossing Columbus and Broadway heading for the Center, and with other people making their way to nearby restaurants. As we dawdled at a red light, I spotted my old friend, and former employer, the publisher David Godine crossing Broadway with a girlfriend in tow.

'Well, well,' I mused aloud. 'There goes a friend of mine.'

'Which one?' Hetherington asked.

'Medium height, tweed coat, dark hair, pretty girl behind him as usual.'

'What's his name?'

'David Godine. Nobody you'd know. Bostonian. Doesn't have much of a record.'

Hetherington leaned forward and switched on the loud-speaker. 'David!' The named boomed out across the street. David turned briefly but then continued on his way. Hetherington tried again, louder this time, and also turned on the red light that began to spin lazily on the roof. 'DAVID!' This time David turned and began walking back across the street to where we were idling. He was shaking his head, clearly puzzled, as who wouldn't be. To compound his embarrassment, Hetherington lowered his window and beckoned him over with a gesture. It wasn't until David was a few feet away that I lowered my window and gave him one of my most fetching smiles.

'Jesus! It's you!' roared David. 'What are you doing there?'

'David,' I said desperately. 'I've been arrested. You've got to help me. Can you lend me the bail money? It's only half a million.'

For some reason he didn't believe me, and with great presence of mind he turned to Hetherington and said, pointing at me: 'Do you know this man? He's dangerous! Do you know that? You're crazy having him in the back of your car!'

'Well, David,' I said, rolling up my window, 'we've got to be on our way. Have some crime to fight, can't hang about chatting all night. See you soon.'

The next thing that happened in our vigilant struggle against the evildoers of New York and Boston publishers was that Officer Mannix handed out two parking tickets on Central Park West. It was dangerous work, but we kept cool and got through unscathed. There was another uptown dash to 82nd Street to investigate a 'suspicious black male', who turned out to be a harmless old bum picking his way through the garbage under the stoops. On Amsterdam we investigated an empty corner which, a radio message had told us, was currently infested with drug-pushing teenagers. We drove on.

'How do you know whether a call is genuine?'

'We don't,' said Mannix. 'We get a lot of hoax calls. But we have to investigate everything that's reported. The switchboard tries to get a callback number, and that helps keep down the number of hoax calls. We also get a lot of calls from EDPs.'

'From what?'

'Emotionally disturbed persons,' chimed in Hetherington, as Mannix swung a U at the top of the precinct and we headed downtown again. 'Years ago we used to call 'em psychos, but you can't do that anymore. There are a lot of people out there leading dull lives, and they know that if they dial 911 and leave a phony message, at least there'll be sirens going and lights flashing and a little action to brighten up their lives for a few minutes.'

I'd asked Hetherington which was the worst precinct in Manhattan, and he said: 'Up between West 100th and 125th. Lotta drugs. On duty up there you see guys with their heads blasted off and think nothing of it.'

So the next morning I phoned the Police Department. 'I had a fine time in the squad car with officers from Precinct 20, but frankly it was a bit dull. Uneventful. So I'm wondering whether you'd be good enough to reschedule another ride for me in a less tranquil neighbourhood further up on the West Side?'

The answer was no, on the grounds that in rougher precincts the patrolmen have far too much on their hands to worry about the safety of passengers.

I was on my way to the Whitney Museum for an opening, rather late in the day for an opening, but this is New York and I knew that even at 10.30 I wouldn't be the last to arrive. I love the Whitney, a brutal pile on a fashionable stretch of Madison, where it's surrounded by private art galleries, Italian shoe boutiques, overpriced food shops, and auction houses. Marcel Breuer built here in 1966 a granite block with a set-back entrance over which loom ponderous and threatening overhangs. Windowless, the Whitney is, it's true, on a scale that intimidates the more genteel architecture around it, yet its primarily sculptural quality strikes me as appropriate to its function, which is to house and display exhibitions of American art.

For two months previously an exhibition of Milton Avery's ravishing landscapes had sent tens of thousands of New Yorkers, and visitors such as myself, into gibbering raptures of delight. Now, though, the Averys had been packed up and dispatched to Pittsburgh, and it was the turn of the more austere Ellsworth Kelly. The floors on which the Kellys were displayed were reached by lift, and this tended to split the party: there were those who were keen to inspect the show for free upstairs, and the rest who were content to pack into the garden level of the museum and guzzle wine. The party was still going strong downstairs, and I tripped lightly down the steps to join the thousand or so revellers. *Black tie,* the invitation had said, but New Yorkers rightly interpret the injunction to mean: Make an effort.

The assembly at Dyansen some weeks before had been more trendy, inviting a stylishness of an eccentric or outrageous kind. Here at the Whitney, which is supported by more patrician benefactors, the style suggested money more than pizzazz. It was here I noticed the aroma and sheen of very rich women, or women with very rich husbands or lovers; they were swathed or sheathed in silk and crepe de chine and other delicate fabrics that don't come off the rack from Gimbel's. These women tend to be tall, with long faces and lacquered hair, a humbug-sized emerald flashing from a tapering finger. From across a room or through a gauze of cigarette smoke, they appear immensely beautiful and it's only close up that one realizes that those flawless complexions are composed of as many layers of underpainting as an Avery landscape, and the marks of age have been temporarily deleted with clever line drawing and tubs of unguent that have filled in the crevices etched by the middle years.

Over by the garden stood a young woman who'd taken pains by viewing her not very attractive body as a kind of living sculpture to be remoulded before each showing. She wore a sailor suit of bright blue velour with white trimming, and a matching hat perched on her curly orange hair. Attached to the front of this hat were little plastic sailboats in red, white and blue. Her plump face was crusted rather than just sprinkled with glitter and drops of dark-coloured paint, especially round her eyes. Her nails were ebony, and on her pudgy fingers were rings laden with more plastic sailboats and other domestic objects. In her arms she cuddled a large toy panda. The nautical prima donna was surrounded by an entourage got up in a similar but more muted style. A few days later I spotted her again, on the subway: her face was still a-glitter but this time she was wearing trousers with each leg a different colour, and above it a jacket with a Warhol-style cartoon in primary colours transferred or painted onto the back.

But where was the army of little old waitresses in tutus carrying trays of champagne? They'd been replaced by a complicated system whereby you queue up to buy drink tickets which you then exchange at the bar for the beverage of your choice. This avoids congestion at the bar, and creates congestion at the sales tables instead. I couldn't be bothered and went back upstairs to look at the exhibition. There I found a patrician lawyer I'd met previously at a dinner party. Though fit and trim, the weight of his ancestry gave his figure a heaviness, as if he'd emerged from the womb with all the burdens of adult responsibility. He was grumbling about the deterioration of the city, a constant theme of those who are thriving within it. He offered an example of what he meant.

'When we would come back from the country on Sunday, we used to swing by the garage on the way home. A driver would hop in for eight blocks, unload our stuff at the apartment, and then drive the car back and garage it for me. But they won't do that any more. The way I see it, Stephen, is that there's been a total breakdown in the social contract.'

After I'd cameo'd at the Whitney, I further enriched the taxi drivers of New York by crossing to a West Side bar, the Dublin House, where my friend Gail had gathered a few friends for what was, in effect, an impromptu party. Gail was busy making the rounds and hastily introduced me to a Scot hunched over the bar. He offered me a drink. I accepted. The Scot motioned to the barman, who brought me a beer and then extracted the appropriate sum from a pile of greens the Scot kept as a sort of bank on the counter in front of him. He turned to me.

'Where you from, then?'

'London.'

He looked aghast. 'My God, I can't believe I just offered a drink to an Englishman.'

Many drinks later Gail suggested we move on, and nine high-octane revellers piled into two cabs and raced down the West Side. Our driver was clearly under the influence of dangerous substances. We bounced and danced over every pothole on the avenue. Rodeo time in New York. I was sitting on the jump seat with my knee in somebody's mouth as we bucked and reared at 60 mph, squashing the flies that ventured between our cab and adjacent cars. I surrendered myself to the prevailing spirit of recklessness. Somehow the maniac in the driver's seat succeeded in depositing us at the Empire Diner far down on Tenth Avenue. Diners are converted railway carriages that over decades have transported the myth of good ole American home cooking. The Empire, though, had been smartened up, its chrome ribbing was polished and gleaming, and its attraction lay both in the lively theatrical crowd it draws and in the modest prices. It never closes.

It was 2.30 when we arrived. The other cabload arrived ten minutes later (their driver, evidently not a walking syringe, had driven at regulation speed). They joined us in the queue. We waited half an hour for a table, and in a diner there isn't much room to wait.

'Mind your backs!' yelled a voice from time to time. 'Angry waiter coming by! Mind your backs!'

As we sat down, eventually, in a cramped booth, Gail murmured to me: 'Trouble with this place is that sitting down is an anti-climax.'

We ordered snacks, just a little something to keep us going till breakfast. Two of our company were in the seventh zone of inebriation and had grown voluble in the droning, incessant way that drunks mistake for repartee. To liven up the proceedings, somebody launched into scurrilous gossip about an acquaintance of ours, and we debated the fascinating issue of whether or not she had herpes, as rumoured, and if so, how far it was likely to travel.

Gail turned to me and smiled sweetly. 'About four or five in the morning our show goes into the act we call character assassination.'

At 4.30 some killjoys announced they were tired and wanted to go home. The two drunks decided to go home together so as to throw up in the same bed. We paid the bill and pried the crowd apart until we reached the door. The uptown contingent had no trouble finding a cab, since no fewer than four yellow taxis were disgorging fresh troops while we loitered on the steps saying our goodbyes. Here, on drab Tenth Avenue, was a definition of an inexhaustible city, a place where even at 4.30 on a winter's morning you have to queue for a table at a restaurant.

I walked over to Ninth, then headed south to the Village. Not the best time or place for a stroll. It was a good 20 minutes' walk during which I could be exposed to ruffianly attack. But I was on a broad avenue, there were other people — one or two — walking about, and a thin but steady trickle of traffic — probably motorized muggers — passing by. So I walked swiftly, nervously, avoiding the doorways, looking constantly about me, watching the demeanour of men approaching me, just as they were scrutinizing me in turn. The frisson kept me nimble and oddly content. I was becoming reacquainted with that defiant unease that rubs shoulders with terror whenever I'm utterly alone, or shadowed by a solitary figure some yards behind who, if ill intention spurred him, could with a swift spring overtake me and add my name to the crime statistics.

The flip side of fear is survival, and there was a charge to be had from recognizing that terror on Ninth Avenue at five in the morning is absolutely reasonable, and then kicking that terror in the teeth. I stepped down hard on the pavement so that the noise of my tread threw up an illusory shield around me until I glimpsed the lights of the all-night greengrocer near my building and knew I was safe.

SOUNDS AND
SWEET AIRS

In Leningrad years ago I rode up an escalator and watched the immobile features of those on the other side travelling down. Unlively eyes gazed from wan sallow faces. It had, I suspected, something to do with the gloom engendered by waking each icy morning and realizing you are in Russia, required to endure indefinitely a foul climate made bearable only by furs and vodka. Standing on Brighton Beach Avenue, between the Zei-Mar Rumanian delicatessen and the Hello Gorgeous Beauty Shop, I looked at the people shopping and exchanging news and realized that Russians look just as stumpy and colourless bathed in the light of freedom as they do under the glare of oppression. Dumpy women of indeterminable age wore the ubiquitous head-scarves, younger women of child-bearing age had grown hefty after 30 and, bundled in blue coats, waddled along pushing prams. Both men and women sported the fashion for bulbous noses, adding a russet blob to their otherwise suety complexions.

Brighton Beach is just down the Brooklyn coast from Coney Island. Near the main Avenue, old women sit in plastic beach chairs in front of small brick apartment blocks to soak in the weak wintry sunshine. I walked down to the shore and stared at the sea in unexpected wonder. Unexpected because for months I'd been living on an island, seeing water every day, without any sense of the marine impinging on my consciousness. Manhattan is surrounded by rivers, not by sea; sea is something else, out there beyond the Statue of Liberty and the harbour. Yet here I was standing on an undeniable beach, complete with waves lapping and ships inching along the horizon while a crisp breeze deposited specks of salt on my lips.

Above the beach runs a splendid boardwalk, broad and weathered; the planks creak without menace beneath each tread. On either side are benches laden with old Russians, talking animatedly in Russian and Yiddish. Over the last 10 years they have come in their thousands as refugees. Many have come from Odessa, and perhaps that is why they have chosen Brighton Beach, this neat but ramshackle seashore community, in which to sink new roots. There are Russian newspapers for sale, and buying a bar of chocolate in a grocery must be transacted in sign language if your Russian is not up to it. Industrious, the immigrants have thrown themselves with zest into the challenge of economic survival. Many of the younger men drive taxis, and one night I struck up conversation with a driver who, true to form, was from Odessa and had been in New York for three years. He was surly and uncommunicative, confirming the reputation of the Russian community in the city as rude and haughty.

These recent arrivals presumably lead lives not too dissimilar from their former lives in Russia. Food, social gatherings, language, celebration, religious ritual — all these could be transported more or less intact. But sooner or later the pressure to assimilate, not just to compromise in order to earn a living, would grow. I doubt that their religious fervour is as great as that of their forefathers who came to America earlier in the century. Those old Russians and Poles, like Marcowitz, had been steeped in traditions of the shtetl and known little else. Those who wished to make their way in American society did just that to the extent of their capability, while those who were content to live on in the old way, a life of trade and prayer and study, were embedded in a sufficiently large community to make that possible.

With assimilation the strict religious practices of Judaism became diluted. A thorough knowledge of the Hebrew liturgy could no longer be taken for granted, yet most Jews were anxious to maintain some ties, however loose, with the rest of their community. In 1845 the first Reform congregation was founded in reaction against traditional orthodoxy, and in 1929 it built Temple Emanu-El, which, with a seating capacity of 2,500, remains the largest synagogue in the world. It's an immense limestone hall facing onto Fifth Avenue; the exterior is a lofty Romanesque, the interior more Byzantine in feel, the whole less a synagogue than a cathedral. Orthodox synagogues place the rabbi and the cantor in the midst of the congregation, facing the ark. Here the rabbi and cantor were placed in matching pulpits on either side of the ark and they faced the congregation, as in a church.

On Saturday morning, prime time, I found no more than 150 people within, sitting isolated in small family groups; they were exceptionally well dressed. The service was conducted almost entirely in English; the singing and chanting so central to Jewish liturgy had been, for the most part, taken from the congregation and handed over to an organist and choir, both hidden from view. The congregation sat there looking bewildered, trying to follow the service and muttering half-hearted responses.

The intention of the Reformers had tripped on the wire of its misconception. By abandoning the Hebrew liturgy, by discarding the *talis,* which makes all men equal in each other's eyes whatever they may be wearing beneath those blue and white shawls, by diluting what had formerly been uncompromising, they had chucked overboard the mystery, the awe, the intensity of traditional Jewish worship. The result was bland and dispiriting. Good works and cultural traditions had been substituted for a world of prayer; their religion had dwindled into a tired, empty performance. By removing the difficulty of worship, they had denuded it of its significance and power. Worship cannot be passive.

I left and continued on my way down Fifth Avenue. Spiritual reflections subsided as I approached the caves of Mammon beyond the Plaza. Late on a Saturday morning, the shoppers were out in full force, stocking up at Tiffany's and Bergdorf's. On the corner of 56th Street was a small band of trumpet players and trombonists, busking away with only moderate skill but with great verve. They were playing *New York, New York.*

We all stood around, hands in pockets, keeping warm on a cold but sunny morning. The light barked against the stone buildings of the Avenue and ricocheted off the glass ones. Horrible children ran laughing between the legs of adults, and impatient drivers honked their horns at cars and buses obstructing a lane. New York was pursuing its business. I looked all around me and up at the sky from my vantage point as a mere dot in the city, and it struck me how all of us, musicians and onlookers, shoppers and tourists, whether we recognized it or not, relished this city. Up Fifth Avenue they were worshipping God and His troubled universe, while down here, a few blocks away, a more mundane but equally fervent act of worship was taking place, unselfconsciously, a song of the city played to the city. It could have been self-congratulatory, but that would have been to mistake the mood, which was one of joy and pride and love.

After my visit to Rikers Island it hadn't occurred to me that I would soon return and least of all for an evening of musical and theatrical entertainment, announced by the Department of Correction as *An Evening of Theater on Rikers Island.* I was in two minds. It sounded too reminiscent of the final scene of Mel Brooks' *The Producers,* in which Zero Mostel and Gene Wilder, imprisoned after the spectacular but fraudulent success of *Springtime for Hitler,* are seen producing the inmates in a new show, *Prisoners of Love.* Alternatively, the evening might turn into a display of radical chic, with East Siders in pressed jeans patronizing the poor, the unfortunate, and the vicious. On reflection, that seemed all the more reason to go.

Once more I made that trek out from the Queensboro Bridge to the island, but this time the almost empty bus stopped at the mainland control post. From there a guard phoned the jail to order the shuttle bus to collect me and the other passenger, and until it arrived we paced up and down trying to keep warm. After five minutes I saw the twinkling bus lights as it loomed over the hump of the causeway. The bus was divided into three sections separated by grilles and doors. We clambered into one of these cages and were noisily shuttled to the prison. Powerful lights beamed down onto the high fences that marked off the compounds. Not a soul was to be seen, and the view was as bleak and chilling as the night.

Security was more feverish than before. A prisoner was missing, had possibly escaped. Asked for identification, I showed them my Visa card, which seemed to satisfy the authorities, though I wondered how flashing a piece of plastic was an efficacious security check. Once inside the lobby there was an electronic frisking, and after buying a ticket I joined the rest of the audience in a queue that shuffled slowly forward as we were admitted in small groups into the decompression chamber I recalled from my previous visit. On emerging into the hall itself, our hands were stamped with invisible ink, which was then read by another guard wielding a blacklight lamp. Finally I signed in and was free to advance to my seat.

The theatre was only a quarter full, so I sat in the front. If I had been expecting a radical chic crowd I was wrong; it was a mixture of city officials, press, and friends and relatives of the performers. TV crews trailed cables down the aisles and got in everybody's way. The show was being presented by The Family, a repertory group founded by Pancho Camillo. Working both in France and America, The Family has performed in prisons and also set up workshops for the inmates. The Rikers project began a few months earlier, when 75 inmates responded to a 'call' from The Family to participate in putting on a show inside the prison. Weekly workshops grew into daily events that culminated in rehearsals for the show itself. The vast majority of Rikers inmates come from the ghettoes, and it seemed improbable that many of them had so much as set foot inside a theatre before, let alone performed in one. I was not encouraged.

The lights dimmed half an hour later, and the chairman of the Board of Correction made a brief speech welcoming us 'to the only uncrowded space on Rikers Island'. He left the stage, out went the lights, and a spot splashed light on a small black figure in the central aisle. He was mumbling and pretending to sweep up, and as he talked more audibly, interspersing his monologue with song, it became clear that he was impersonating a janitor trying to clean a filthy and shitty tenement floor. His act was a mixture of comedy, often scatological, and social protest. It was a clever device to open the show with a vignette rather than a traditional big stage number; it established an immediate rapport with the audience. The prisoner playing this role later told me he had in fact been released from Rikers, but had voluntarily stayed on for a couple of weeks to participate in the show. The oldest member of the company, he was known as Baby.

In the course of his act he moved down the aisle and onto the stage, to be joined by the rest of the company, about 25 in all. They staged a mock fight in the ghetto, with a small

261

band to the side of the stage providing a jagged musical commentary. The cast split up into groups and began to parade slowly down the side of the theatre and up the central aisle. As they climbed the ramp from aisle to stage, they paused one at a time to pose before the audience, flaunting visual and gestural clues as to the kind of person they were portraying. We had a procession of pimps, followed by whores, then homosexuals, then bikers. Of course they were caricaturing them, but at the same time there was ample room for doubt. Too much of the posing had the conviction of a perfect fit; these were not actors playing the part of pimps — these were in many cases pimps being themselves or creating self-parodies. There was menace too, meanness in the air, the actors clearly delighting in the sense of danger they knew they were projecting. Out in the ghetto they were, or had been, mean motherfuckers, and they were rejoicing in their ability to chill our blood as they, hands on hips, eyes invisible behind aggressive shades, looked contemptuously down at us.

There followed a hold-up scene, its violence conveyed by the vigour of the miming. There were no props, no guns of course, nothing but gesture and stance and music. Sheer presence pressed like a weight. The director had grouped the actors cleverly so as to maximize the menace; there was a balletic quality to it, and the rough edges that came scratching through because of the cast's amateurishness didn't matter at all. There followed a parody of a show at the Apollo Theatre, and that lowered the tension as the inmates impersonated the styles of great black performers.

That easing of the mood was to be short-lived, for when the lights went up on the next number, I could hear the pounding of the band and a scuffling sound from the back of the auditorium, where on either side of the theatre an inmate was being dragged slowly by fellow prisoners (impersonating guards) towards the front. The rest of the company was lined up on stage as a chorus, while the two 'prisoners', on opposite sides of the theatre, sang the lines:

> The preacher talked with me, and he smiled,
> Said 'Come and walk with me, come and walk one
>   more mile,
> Now for once in your life you're alone
> But you ain't got a dime, there's no time for the phone'

and then the chorus on stage joined the two singers as they sang the title line *I've got to get a message to you*. This is one of the better Bee Gees songs, sung purportedly by a murderer ('Well, I did it to him, now it's my turn to die') on his walk to the electric chair. The company sang the song over and over, as the two men, resisting, were pulled down the aisle. As one came by just a few yards from me, singing in a soulful and intense voice 'One more hour and my life will be through', I could see the rivers of sweat that ran down his face and left the folds of his white shirt translucent with moisture. He was giving that song every ounce he had. The prisoners performing this song were not too far removed from its subject, and this gave their singing a terrifying immediacy. And the worst was still to come.

'One more hour,' goes the song, and that means one more hour before execution. Here on the stage at Rikers Island, this conclusion was being enacted. As the two singers were painfully dragged towards the stage past the actual guards keeping a vigilant eye on us all, the other performers were bodily transforming themselves into electric chairs, fashioning their limbs and very stances into the arms and seats of those diabolical instruments of execution, in which the chair, a symbol of repose, is grotesquely perverted into a means of extinction. Hands and arms modelled the head clamps and the thongs that both carry the deadly current and hold the body in place as thousands of volts are pumped in. Slowly, the two men, kicking and writhing, were forced into the 'chairs', still singing, frantically, ever more intensely. The human switches were thrown, and the two prisoners twitched spasmodically into the limpness of death.

Other sketches dealing with the criminal life followed, and if they were anticlimactic after what we'd just seen, that was no fault of the material or the performers. Five prisoners were shown making phone calls, one to his ex-wife, another engaging in humorous banter with a girlfriend, another being informed that his mother was dying. The individual conversations were unremarkable but the juxtaposition of five simultaneously was both amusing and unsettling. At a mock trial, an experienced female jailbird was cynically comforting a younger woman dreading prison and the separation from her family that it would entail.

'I never been to jail before,' wailed the younger woman.

'You been to jail before, honey,' remarked the older woman (who, she told me, had five children in 'real life' and knew what separation really meant), 'only this time you get to *stay* there.' She was tough and unsentimental. The emotion was behind the lines, not in them. Feeling could only be indulged when survival and self-protection had been ensured. Later the actors told me that this whole courtroom scene was true to their pooled experience.

When the curtain finally came down on the show, the whole audience rose to its feet, yelling and cheering. We'd been present at a remarkable achievement: these men and women, some of whom had surely committed acts that had scarred the lives of others, had transformed that unacceptable behaviour into a medium that, without a trace of self-pity, did at the very least communicate to those of us sitting free in the auditorium that their lives were more than the sum of their criminality, that in spite of poverty and discrimination and their own brutality or venality, they had a humanity as plain and fundamental as our own.

At the reception afterwards, the audience shared coffee and cake with the performers. My emotional response to them, both as performers and as individuals with whom I was enjoying a talk, was warring with my conventional inability to admit that criminals are just like the rest of us, which they decidedly are not. I couldn't resolve it then, and I can't resolve it now, yet unquestionably my emotions won the day, so much so that it felt truly painful when at 10.30 the party came to a hurried end as the inmates were sent back to their cells and dormitories, leaving the rest of us at liberty to return to the outside world. Many of the performers had told me they hoped to pursue a theatrical career after they were released, and I didn't have the heart to explain that New York is full of would-be actors and that their own chances were remote indeed. I flinched to think how rapidly, and with what consequences, their high hopes would be punctured when they returned to the mainland.

I now had to turn my attention to my own return to the mainland. I'd missed the 10.35 bus and the next departure for the East Side was an hour later. That meant a wait of almost an hour in the cold on the far side of the causeway. On the other hand, the bus to City Hall, which had brought the city workers out to the prison, was about to return. Could I, I asked the orang-utan guarding the exit, catch a ride on that bus?

'You have to return the way you came,' she said expressionlessly.

I remonstrated but she was adamant. 'You ain't got the right pass. You not gonna be able to leave the island without it.'

I went in search of the bus driver.

'No way,' he said firmly. 'No extras.'

A few minutes later the orang-utan opened the heavy doors and city workers began to file out. Soon I would be left alone in the lobby to pray for a shuttle to deliver me to the windtrap on the other side of the causeway. I decided to make a break for it. I had nothing to lose. I joined the rest of the queue, walked straight past the orang-utan and then past the driver, who nodded, murmuring, 'If there's room,' and there was.

I had learnt a belated lesson in how to deal with officials: do, don't ask. They're not devoid of common sense or understanding, despite impressions to the contrary, but if you ask them whether it's permissible to do something that's against the rules, they feel compelled to answer truthfully. It's perfectly logical. They don't care what you do so long as you don't implicate them by asking them to condone the transgression.

The driver dropped me off near Times Square and I began to walk down Broadway. A small group of youths were slowly walking ahead of me. As I overtook, one of them whirled round. 'Man!' he yelled, 'you almost got hit. See that guy' — and he gestured at a shifty, razor-featured youth nearby — 'he was coming up behind me and I was all ready to swing.'

Was I supposed to be grateful to him for not slugging the wrong man? We didn't discuss it. I cantered down the stairs into the subway station and went home.

TOO MUCH OF NOTHING

The Thanksgiving Parade is the starting pistol for Christmas: from that moment on the department stores begin to unveil their Christmas windows and the iconography of the season begins to tiptoe into advertisements — bells, holly, snowflakes. Only half-hearted claims are made for the religious observance of the festive days, usually couched in safe terms of peace and good will, and this is because New York is hardly a nerve centre of Christian belief. Fortunately the two million Jews of New York also have a holiday to celebrate, so the festive joys can be shared more or less equally among the entire population of the city.

Hanukah always manages to sneak in before Christmas, and some time in early December, electric menorahs — the seven-branched candelabrum symbolizing the holiday — begin to appear in shop windows and in apartment building lobbies. In traditional ceremonies Jewish families gather on each evening of the eight-day holiday to celebrate the recapture by Judas Maccabeus of the Temple in Jerusalem in 164 BC, and they mark each day by lighting an additional candle on the menorah. The electric menorahs reproduce the symbolism by being equipped with tear-shaped bulbs that signify candle-light, and as each day passes the doorman or shopkeeper will throw another switch to keep pace with the candle-lighting ceremony. Television newsreaders, too, are mindful of Jewish sensibilities and even the Waspiest weatherman takes care to wish the viewers a Happy Hanukah. In my apartment building a menorah duly made its appearance in the lobby and every afternoon the doorman did his bit by 'lighting' another candle; but on the third day a Christmas tree came to join it, and the symbols of the two creeds enjoyed a bizarre coexistence until after the eighth day of Hanukah, when the menorah was put back in storage. Christmas trees are of course more decorative than menorahs, and children even in overwhelmingly Jewish suburbs feel deprived if their parents don't plant one in the living room. So, with mild embarrassment, many suburban Jews have appropriated the Christmas tree by renaming it the Hanukah bush.

Fifth Avenue is the focus of New York at Christmas time, since it's here that most of the great department stores are based. Each year they mount attractive and ingenious window displays that are one of the more charming manifestations of the season. I dare say the motivation for this annual contest is not artistic pride but to ensure that for a full month the pavements of Fifth Avenue are never less than impassable, with a shoal of shoppers eager to thrust money and plastic into the hands of obsequious shop-keepers. Outside Lord & Taylor's, the store managers have to erect posts and chains to ensure orderly viewing. I often walked past late at night and was able to enjoy the displays at leisure, though at all hours the Avenue was filled with window-gazers, but at midday in the week before Christmas there must have been a hundred or more people queuing just to peek at windows. This year Lord & Taylor had chosen to illustrate 'Christmas in Central Park'. Each window re-created a specific scene, such as the interior of the Metropolitan Museum and a skating evening in the park. The designers used delightful small-scale models, many with moving parts; interiors and costumes were beautifully detailed and the tableaux were especially well lit. It was the delicacy of these tableaux that surprised one, and that was true of some of the other stores' displays too, unexpected in a city where tastefulness doesn't always count for much. New Yorkers seem to feel: If it's worth doing, it's worth overdoing. But here were delightful exceptions.

Bendel's, an elegant little department store on 57th Street just off Fifth, chose to ignore seasonal motifs altogether, but devised a most lovely alternative. The windows, and indeed the entire ground floor, were filled with yellow and gold Japanese lanterns, dozens of them, in clusters and tiers. In the windows were mannequins decked in kimonos beneath the fragile lanterns. What's attractive about Bendel's is its scale. Here are no great spaces, as in Macy's or Saks, but rather a corridor running round three sides of a rectangle, with a row of boutiques on either side. The floors are a parquet of cool white marble. With six floors Bendel's offers the convenience of a department store without the raffishness. Bendel's is selective, which makes it exclusive. Upstairs are the outposts of the big-name designers, such as Ralph Lauren and Zandra Rhodes. On the top floor, worn-out heiresses can repair their surfaces at Skin Care, Tooth Care, and Digits Nail Care.

Tramping through crowded stores at Christmas is not everyone's idea of effortless shopping. The more indolent can stay home with the *Village Voice* and order by phone from a special gift guide section. All religions are catered for: 'Hanukah can be wonderful. Do it with taste. Free consultation. No strings attached. Ask for Jean. Handmade and hand-crafted Judaica and antique ceremonial objects. For sale, strictly for charity. Tax deductible.' What could be better? A tasteful Hanukah and a tax write-off!

You can cater to New Yorkers' obsessions with food by sending a gingergram ('personalized homemade gingerbread sculpture dl'vrd to the door in Mnhttn') or a Salami-o-Grami ('100% Kosher 24" "dressed" salami. Original, hysterical, edible'). For Jewish friends interested in rather different pleasures of the flesh I recommend The Kosher Kondom which 'comes gift wrapped with a prayerbook' for only $4. Perhaps you're overcommitted this year and can't make it to all the parties, so dispatch in your place 'A Singing Santa or Elf' or even 'A Strip-o-Gram Stripping Santa'. Those of more solemn disposition can spend $15 on 'ACCORD — a complete 47 point document designed to keep serious relationships in harmony. Avoid bickering and plan for a loving, responsible future.' After accord has turned to discord, you'll need a Rent-a-Kvetch: 'Our professional complainers will resolve any legit complaint against any product/co./person. Gift certificates $35.' If your teenage child is still unsure about drugs, I'd recommend 'Cocaine Video Tape. State of the art production. Everything you ever wanted to know. How to test cocaine for quality. Beautiful close up photography. Save hundreds of dollars' — by spending 80. I know what I want: the Forget-Me-Not Reminder Service. 'We remind you by mail twice before each of your unforgettable occasions. 10 reminders only $20.'

It was David Letterman, on his late night show shortly before Christmas, who came up with the best selection of Christmas ideas for your kids. He offered Visible Smurfs: 'You can open them up and learn about their digestive system.' Or the Little Pawnbroker set: 'Kids learn that suffering to others can mean a real bonanza to them. With this simple toy they learn how to scavenge off human misery.' Or 'the Mahatma Gandhi Passive Resistance Punchbag, which comes in plain yellow.'

Sometimes New York's grand gestures can be turned to comic effect. Each year there's a ceremony at which a giant Christmas tree is installed and lit up in Rockefeller Plaza. It becomes one more jewel in the bracelet of Fifth Avenue and is rightly admired by an incessant flow of visitors at all hours. But on December 19 no fewer than 400 tuba players descended on Rockefeller Plaza to honk out Christmas carols. Hoffnung himself couldn't have done it better.

Although the Plaza has the grandest tree in the city, more modest and permanent trees that line some residential streets are decorated with fairy lights. It may sound twee, but the effect of hundreds of tiny white lights sparkling like stars in a tropical sky up and down the boughs and branches of city trees can be magical. West 67th Street is charming at any time of the year, especially at the Central Park end. It is lined with artists' studios, built in the early years of this century, though I doubt that many artists still live in these grand and expensive spaces, which more recently housed Isadora Duncan and Noel Coward. Crossing Central Park West into the park itself, one soon comes to the Tavern on the Green. The trees which shelter the restaurant from the street are also hung with fairy lights, so there's a continuous dazzle from Columbus Avenue right into the park.

That's the understated Christmas in New York. For the full blast you must return to Fifth Avenue. On Christmas Eve I wandered into Tiffany's, a lovely shop, lofty and panelled, and even at this late hour in the present-buying calendar full of people, mostly looking but also buying. The crush is even worse at Fortunoff's.

On emerging from Tiffany's, I heard an extraordinary sound coming from the Trump Tower. Although not yet ready for occupation, most of the tower was free from scaffolding and its crisp lines were clearly visible. As this elegant but totally unnecessary addition to midtown's collection of luxurious buildings lifts its black glass arm high into the sky, it pauses for architectural set-backs at various levels. The lowest of these retreats from the corner of Fifth Avenue and there, 50 feet up, an enclosure had been formed, ringed with Christmas lights and spotlit from the other side of the street. At first I couldn't see what was producing the sound; all I could hear was the brilliant bark of a superb brass ensemble, playing, not the tired old carols we'd all heard too much of by Christmas Eve, but what I took for dazzling fanfares by such composers as Gabrieli, who in the early seventeenth century added splendid musical ceremonial to the pomp of the Venetian republic.

As my eyes grew accustomed to the early evening shadowiness, I made out the glint of trombone slides catching the light as they moved. Behind the ensemble the walls rose sheer and black against the rapidly darkening sky. I felt transported. One could, I suppose, draw comparisons between the two sea-girt cities of Venice and New York, two unique manifestations of the urban impulse, both part of a greater cultural power and yet distinct from it — but such comparisons were too studied to spring to mind as I was listening to the glorious music. Instead the music tugged like the moon at the mundane preoccupations of those of us down below on the street, scurrying about doing our last-minute shopping; best of all, it was marvellously gratuitous in the way it was simply ladled onto the bustle below, an offering to the city from the sky. Respond if you wish, ignore it if you wish, but there it was, a blaze of sound travelling up and down the beautiful avenue, bouncing off the solid buildings on either side.

I continued my walk down Fifth Avenue. The street traders were there in force with their usual collection of radios, handbags, cashmere scarves, pirated cassettes, electronic toys. Outside the Public Library the crafts peddlers had set up their stalls, selling jewellery and silver and hand-knitted clothing beneath improvised lanterns. Santa was everywhere: Salvation Army collectors were on the street in their Santa outfits; at the matinee of *The*

Taming of the Shrew which the Joffrey Ballet had mounted that afternoon, no opportunity had been missed to bang the gong of topicality, by such devices as dumping a Christmas tree by Petruchio's fireplace; and later that evening, after dining at the Hungarian restaurant The Red Tulip, I emerged to see a taxi cruising by with the driver wearing a Santa suit and beard.

There were three of us at the Red Tulip that evening: Julie, her friend Jane, and myself. We were plagued by a gypsy violinist, doubtless born in Brooklyn, who went from table to table playing schmaltzy tunes, lilting waltzes and other musical sweetmeats. After a couple of hours I was assuming he'd forgotten us, but no, here he was, violin tucked under arm, obsequious smile on his pudgy lips. What would the ladies and gentleman like to hear him play? Julie simply abdicated, while Jane flippantly suggested *Jingle Bell Rock*. He ignored her. Joining in the spirit of jolly japery, I said satirically 'The theme from *Exodus*', and to my horror the ersatz zigeuner lowered his flabby jaw onto his instrument and his bow brought forth musical bubblegum. Of course the swine was doing it deliberately. My cries of 'Oh no!' on hearing the first gushing notes yowl from the catgut should have alerted him to my discomfort, but he chose to ignore it and compound it. By the time he'd finished there wasn't a wet eye in the place, but he loomed ever closer and as the ladies smiled sweetly at me I dug into my pocket for the obligatory sumptuous tip.

Speaking of tips, Christmas is also the season when honest citizens are systematically stripped of their savings by predatory hints from those who supposedly add to the comforts of our daily lives. I had to fork out modest sums to bribe the doorman and supervisor in my building, but that was peanuts compared to Jane's outlay that year. As she gnawed at her duck, she explained.

'In the building where I live there are four elevatormen, four garage men, and two mailmen. I have to tip them all. In my office there are two mailmen and two receptionists whom I have to tip. But that's my old office. A few weeks ago I moved into a new office and it's still being worked on. That means further tips to the head of the construction crew, the painter, the electrician, the ceiling expert, two doormen and two elevatormen. Then there's my hair stylist, and then the 14 women at the tennis club who arrange my games for me.'

'Too much of nothing,' sings Bob Dylan, 'can make a man feel ill at ease,' and that sounded apposite as I stood at the top of Charlotte Street and stared at the emptiness. Where a decade before there had been blocks of small apartment houses there was now nothing. Except rubble. A few hundred yards away clusters of apartment blocks and tenements were still standing, but most of them were gutted, with black maws for windows.

This is the South Bronx, where often in the last 15 years the sky has been illuminated nightly by the flames of burning buildings, not torched by rioters, but calmly set alight by their very owners and occupants. New Yorkers remark wryly that the South Bronx, once roamed by vicious street gangs and known as Fort Apache for good reason, is now the safest neighbourhood in New York: there's nothing left to steal and nobody left to mug.

Charlotte Street has a special place in the historical geography of the South Bronx, because it was here that President Carter stood in 1977 and swore to initiate federal programmes that would 'turn it around'. Even Ronald Reagan, well-known friend of the poor, has come here and cooed sympathetically. I could find nothing to say as I gazed at the rubble. Just a few miles from the richest real estate in the world is this blighted area that resembles nothing so much as Dresden or Hiroshima after the bombs had done their worst. In Harlem the burnt-out buildings are pockets of blight in a run-down but still active community, whereas in the South Bronx it's the reverse: in some areas inhabited buildings stick out like islets in the ocean of devastation. The South Bronx is hardly a remote outpost of the city: the borough as a whole, if separated from New York, would constitute America's fifth largest city. Since the blight began, the South Bronx has lost a quarter of its population, leaving about half a million inhabitants, though looking about me, I often wondered where even that number actually lived.

The afflicted area is immense, about 20 square miles, easily the size of central London from Chelsea to the City. By the end of the 1970s 2,500 city blocks had been devastated and during that decade 3,000 buildings with about 80,000 apartments were abandoned. This is not an isolated phenomenon in New York City — parts of Brooklyn, such as Bushwick and Bedford-Stuyvesant, are almost as wasted and for similar reasons — but nowhere in the country is the blight as overwhelming as here.

The South Bronx was never a slum, though like all large urban areas it had pockets of poverty. I remember it in 1965 as a clustering of stubby blocks with a substantial lower-middle-class Jewish population. Jews, mostly elderly, still live along the tattered glory of the Grand Concourse. 50 years ago, prospering immigrants moved from the Lower East Side to the fashionable new Art Deco blocks along the Grand Concourse, and some of them are still there; although the Concourse is largely intact, even this triumphal route has been ravaged here and there. The worst affected parts of the South Bronx are, however, to the east and south, where the population is mostly black or Hispanic.

How did it happen? When the neighbourhoods of the South Bronx became less stable during the turbulent 1960s, families began to move to the suburbs; they were replaced by poorer families, a change that in itself provoked further flight from the district. Since many of the new renters were on welfare — 25 per cent of the population is unemployed and about 30 per cent live below the poverty line — apartments became overcrowded and poorly maintained. As a neighbourhood declines, banks become less eager to invest, and difficulty in obtaining mortgages inhibits the development of districts that have been 'redlined' by the banks. Redlining was outlawed in 1974; now instead there's its reverse, greenlining, which encourages loans in up-and-coming areas such as TriBeCa. Stringent rent control regulations and rapidly rising maintenance costs meant that it was no longer profitable for landlords to hang onto deteriorating properties. The consequence was either abandonment or arson — as many as 10 cases a night, during the worst phase — which at least permitted the landlord, if he got away with it, to cut his losses by collecting insurance money on the structure. Once the process began, it made a virulent sweep through the whole South Bronx. Turning it around, despite Jimmy Carter's good intentions, is a task that even Sisyphus might decline.

The spread of the blight has more or less ceased and community groups have organized themselves to prevent further encroachment. Mayor Koch set up the South Bronx Development Organization (SBDO) in 1980, and community leaders and groups have worked to stabilize the area and begin the gargantuan task of rehabilitation. Here and there abandoned buildings, along the Grand Concourse and in the quaintly named Banana Kelly district, have been rehabilitated and are vigilantly maintained by their occupants. When buildings are abandoned the city becomes the landlord, a role it is neither equipped nor eager to fulfil, so it has encouraged tenants to form cooperatives and run their own buildings. The results have been mixed; especially in buildings where residents tend to be transient. Some new single-family houses — which look particularly inappropriate isolated on a few blocks with seas of rubble beyond their back yards — have been built with the trickle of federal housing aid the Reagan Administration has coughed up. An industrial park is being built at Bathgate, with the Port Authority as the first major tenant.

The SBDO official showing me round was understandably anxious to point to the more positive aspects of what the agency had been doing. She took me to the thriving Italian section along Arthur Avenue, the busy shopping area known as the Hub, and to the substantial brownstones of the Longwood Historic District, as well as to rubbish-strewn lots where, eventually, a new hospital or housing complex might be constructed. Near the Bathgate Industrial Park a small agricultural enterprise called Glee Farms trains runaway kids to grow mushrooms and herbs. All very laudable, but a drop in the ocean. The SBDO readily admits that there is no way the South Bronx can or should be entirely rehabilitated. Gutted old apartment blocks without lifts are as a rule not worth saving, but even demolition presents problems, since finding use each year for 300,000 cubic yards of minced building is no easy matter. The good intentions of the politicians hasn't prevented a steady reduction in housing grants and the availability of federal and now state money. The severe social problems, including an appalling lack of services, compounded by the physical destruction of entire neighbourhoods, can't be solved overnight. So the SBDO concentrates its efforts on restoring what it defines as areas of strength, while leaving other sections of the South Bronx to rot. It has little choice. Measurable economic recovery is still a long way off. 'The South Bronx isn't the place to go for a fun night out,' observed a cynical friend. 'No knives and forks from Michelin yet. Well, maybe a few knives . . .'

Standing with my back to deserted Crotona Park, I looked down the emptiness of Charlotte Street.* Turning to face Crotona I saw on my right the public school (threatened with closure, but now 'saved') and to my left one apartment house that was still occupied. There was glass in the windows and the pavement around the isolated building was swept and clean; the structure even had a roof on it, unlike most of the buildings on the horizon. As the blight had spread, the occupants of these apartments had dug their heels in and determined that their building would not suffer the fate of the rest of Charlotte Street. Walking round to the front I read the neatly lettered sign above the entrance:
LAST HOPE TENANTS ASSOCIATION

---

* Later in 1983 some of the rubble was covered over with prefabricated houses and city officials, including Mayor Koch, indulged in an orgy of self-congratulation. The South Bronx remains a copybook slum.

CROSSING THE BAR

Fearful of contamination after my encounters with the New Right, I needed a purificatory dip in the limpid pools of the Left — if I could find the Left. There was always the *New York Review of Books,* but so many of its regular contributors were British. Socialists such as Irving Howe had been admitting recently to their perplexity in the face of radical turbulence during the 1960s and his faith had wobbled. The economist Robert Lekachman struck me as a sounder bet. His book *Reaganomics: Greed Is Not Enough* was a scintillating demolition job.

Like most New York intellectuals, Lekachman considers himself an authority on Chinese food, the staple diet of the Upper West Side. So at 12.30 on New Year's Eve I sat in the Shun Lee West to wait for him. Close to Lincoln Center, it's quite a classy establishment — it has tablecloths and waiters who smile. Lekachman entered, a large shambling man, with that calculated professorial dishevelment originally devised by British dons to conceal the fins and flippers of mental agility. He slung a pile of books and newspapers down on a chair and held out a large hand. Then he removed a layer or two of protective clothing and settled down to his first dry martini.

The Left is a house divided. Lekachman belongs to the Democratic Socialists of America, in company with Howe and Michael Harrington. 'But don't confuse us with the Social Democrats USA. We split off from them during the Vietnam War, which they backed. They now support Reagan.'

'They're socialists?'

'Well, exactly. Their problem is that they're overwhelmed

by their anti-Communism, though my lot is very much anti-Stalinist.'

'How that word keeps cropping up in New York.'

'That's because many people on the New Right, such as Irving Kristol, are ex-Trotskyists or at the very least ex-Communists. That's where I suffer from a serious disability in intellectual circles. During the 1930s I never was a Communist, so it's hard for me to be an ex-Communist now. Why don't we start with some dim sum? Any preferences?'

'You choose.'

'I'd recommend, hmm, the Szechuan wonton — and the Shanghai dumplings the other day were excellent.'

He ordered and we exchanged scurrilous stories about academics we knew.

'Before we go any further, let me ask you if you mind being quoted?'

'Go right ahead. If I speak ill of anyone, chances are that I've also written ill of them, so quote what you like. I think indiscretion is a good thing, to be practiced widely. Anyhow my views are no secret. Everyone knows I find Podhoretz repulsive' — he speared a dumpling, then looked up at me thoughtfully — 'though a strong case could be argued that his wife Midge Decter is even more repulsive than he is.'

I asked him why the Left had been so slow to launch a counter-offensive against Reaganomics. Lekachman mentioned one or two union leaders and politicians who were trying to do just that, and he himself was part of a group attempting to formulate an alternative economic strategy for the Democrats to take to the voters in 1984. But he conceded that there had been no resurgence of the Left in recent years. 'This is a deeply conservative country. My students at Lehman College in the Bronx are mostly working-class kids. They're conservative too. Their principal ambition, and expectation, is to leave their class. They're not interested in greater equality, what they're after is a piece of the action. My, have you tried any of this beef yet?'

I nodded, my mouth full of delicious crisp orange-flavoured beef. We ordered more drinks.

'The intelligentsia,' I resumed, almost tripping over that oddly antique word, 'with a few honourable exceptions, has drifted off to the Right in recent years. Why?'

Lekachman thought briefly as he raised his chopsticks to transport some sliced duckling with young ginger root into his mouth. 'In part self-interest. This country offers great rewards to pliable intellectuals. Foundation money becomes available, academic institutes and think tanks open their doors, businessmen and politicians will gladly listen to well-behaved intellectuals and pay them nicely for their opinions. As they grow older and more prosperous, intellectuals perceive where power lies, and they come to see themselves as enlightened voices counselling the powerful. It's also worth pointing out that a number of so-called liberals, such as our Senator Moynihan, always had conservative instincts but prudently played the liberal game in the sixties. When the political climate changed they weren't slow to revert to their original sympathies. Remember too that Americans don't care for losers, they don't want to be losers. When the Right came to power in 1980, intellectuals too suddenly began to perceive new and unsuspected virtues in the winners.'

When the bill arrived, Professor Lekachman must have felt a sudden prompting from his bladder, since the distinguished economist swiftly disappeared and returned after some little while to find the far from trifling sum had been taken care of. Our meeting over, he gathered his books and papers, smiled benignly and said to me: 'I must say I thoroughly enjoyed our conversation — as I usually do when I do most of the talking.'

Putting politics aside, I concentrated my attention on the imminent New Year celebrations. The first party of the evening was at Katy's loft near the garment district. The broad windows offer a sweeping, if far from inviting, view of Sixth Avenue. Louise — an old friend with cascades of prematurely greying hair and a bohemian temperament — and I walked from the West Village through largely deserted streets, encountering a few early revellers who, like ourselves, were making bottle-laden journeys, but most of the people we passed were sad bums, whose solitariness would in some cases be walled in to the point of suffocation by the festivities that would be intensifying around them as the hours went by.

Since Katy is a designer, her party was full of other

designers and book people. The mice with whom she shares the loft had taken refuge in the bedroom. A man of medium build, with dark curly hair, charged through the door, and when he reached the table where I was sitting with Louise and Maria, who was wearing fawn leather trousers that took my breath away, he stopped in his tracks, pointed at me, and identified me. My astonishment was equally great, since I had no idea who he was. He introduced himself.

'You still don't remember me, do you?'

'I'm afraid not.'

'My name's Dan. We used to meet at Harvard years ago, though I saw more of your wife. I was madly in love with that philosopher she was having an affair with.'

'Oh *him*.'

'Gorgeous,' he said wistfully. 'That beard . . .'

Dan disclosed that he was a convert New Yorker, even more in love with Manhattan than he'd been with the magnetic philosopher. 'There's so much to do! Endless possibilities!'

'I've inspected quite a few, but there's a major gap. Nobody's offered me any cocaine in two months. I'd heard it was dispensed like sugar but I've never so much as observed anybody removing a spoon from a silk-lined case and vanishing into the bathroom.'

'Can't help you there,' said Dan. 'Anyhow, don't bother. It's so middle-class. I tell you, the chic thing to do is to turn coke down with a sneer whenever it's offered to you. People think of it the way they do of money, and they're astonished when you reject it. It's a vulgar drug, like *New York Magazine* turned into white powder.'

'I buy my drugs mail-order from New Jersey,' chimed in Louise, warming to a topic close to her heart, and she and Dan went into an immediate huddle to swop notes on uppers and downers and the rest of the pharmacopeia. I left them to it and pursued Maria into the kitchen.

At 10.30 Louise and I took a taxi up Fifth Avenue to 74th Street. Carol, who'd invited me to this second party, introduced us to the hostess, an investment banker whose dabblings in interior decoration had transformed her bijou apartment into a baroque suite of confusion: the bedroom was lined with black, white and pink Matisse dancers on every wall, with a golden ceiling to crown the mayhem below. There were mirrors and tassels and too much furniture, and awful pictures on the walls that were, we were told, extremely valuable. So were the guests, an assortment of high fliers: balding men with unreticent bellies, and women with Appalachian shoulders maculated with freckles. Jewels hung from lobes, and there was a chocolatey smell of money in the air.

Louise was bemused. She asked me, loudly, a string of forthright questions: who were these people? why were we here? who was that woman with the ridiculous hairstyle? Carol came over and chatted with practised ease. To her polite questions, Louise would reply with answers that became ever more askew until she had reached that state of inconsequentiality that I had long ago learned to interpret: Louise is plastered. She doesn't sway, she doesn't slur, she doesn't giggle, she doesn't shout. Instead she slowly raises the drawbridge that connects her to the rational world and lets the slightest prompting, from whatever inner source, take over.

Shortly before midnight we all piled out onto the small terrace, which had a soaring view over Central Park. Platoons of champagne bottles were at the ready. Two miles away in Times Square, a 200-pound 'apple' would drop at midnight, inducing a roar that billows into the air from a few hundred throats in the streets below. I didn't hear the roar but a firework launched from the Bethesda Fountain announced the end of the year, and a few seconds later a succession of rockets and flaming fiery rolls whammed into the sky.

'Happy *New* Year!' — Americans accent the second word, which sounds wrong to my ear, but makes better logical sense. Bosoms splashed with exotic perfumes pressed against my person as guests squeezed by to greet and embrace friends. Louise was perched in a fetching gamine pose alone at the end of the balcony, oblivious to the jubilation all around her. I kissed her but she was miles away. Bursts of light overlapped with each other, and rocket tracers, each a different colour, chased up into the black sky, which was by now alive with explosions, echoing bangs and the chatter of aerial firecrackers. The normally inky sky fleetingly illuminated the entire city twenty storeys below.

Central Park, as it so often does, lived up to its name and became the focus for the city ranged on all sides around it. From that balcony Manhattan acquired the density and concentration of a village, with only the sweep of the illuminated George Washington Bridge miles to the north-west to remind us that we were on an island. Every balcony with a view must have been crowded, as ours was, while the streets below were being invaded by full-throated men and women in silly hats.

In the meantime Louise was huddled over her pet magnum, but I managed to drag her over to the populated end of the terrace in time to hear Carol cry, 'They're coming! They're coming!' Following the line of her pointing finger down into the heart of the park, I could make out a thin line of swiftly moving figures snaking along the roads and paths from the West Side, a ghostly procession silently infiltrating the darkness. The Midnight Run. Every New Year's Eve about 3000 runners, some in evening dress and running shoes, forgo their champagne and traverse the chilly lanes of Central Park. It's far from my notion of a good time on a winter's night, but I could imagine, just, the satisfaction of crossing the still park in the middle of the night, safely linked into a human chain, while all around are the sounds of a city in jubilation.

At Louise's insistence, we moved on to the Blue Bar at the Algonquin for an hour. When we emerged, Times Square nearby was still packed with drunken grinning people, thousands of them, many of them searching, as were we, for a taxi. What, I asked myself, would a New Yorker do? Answer: walk over to Ninth Avenue. Which we did, crossing Times Square where we crackled gingerly through seas of broken glass and other detritus of celebration. As in a zombie movie, figures kept lurching uncertainly towards us, but we knew that they were radiantly drunk rather than the living dead. My strategy worked, and we flagged down a cab almost as soon as we hit Ninth, and soon, back in the West Village, closed the door on the unresting world.

Dresden Urquhart — yes, that's her name — fashions satin sculptures in a vast loft on Sixth Avenue, not far from Katy's. She'd been away in Florida for two months, working on *Jaws III* so as to finance her work as an artist, but she was briefly back in town and New Year's Day was the only time when we could meet. Dresden and her friend David drove us down to Chelsea, where David was a habitué of a newish restaurant, all brick walls and high ceilings and hanging plants. We ordered a round of Brandy Alexanders, then another, until at six, when the waitress returned to see if we wanted a third, David announced: 'We're moving into deeper and more dangerous waters than that. We're about to order dinner.'

It was a good dinner, but the heavy consumption of brandy and bottle after bottle of very expensive Californian wine had affected Louise's delicate and complex internal wiring. She was mounting her hobby-horses and I could sense her preparing to ride them recklessly down the field. The owner of the restaurant, Jimmy, joined us at our table. Round after round of brandy was on the house. Jimmy explained that he was a former bartender who'd put his savings into a restaurant on Columbus Avenue. One night a film star went there for dinner and became a regular. Jimmy was made: night after night prosperous West Siders queued to get into his suddenly ultra-fashionable restaurant. So Jimmy bought another restaurant here in Chelsea which was not yet mobbed and far more pleasant. He was delighted with his purchase, though he'd had to learn how to deal with armed gangs eager to earn protection money.

Louise, innately suspicious of anybody who owns any-thing, especially a business, started firing questions at Jimmy, and demanded to know how much he paid the waitresses. I caught David's eye and shrugged. Jimmy answered Louise.

'And another thing,' she continued, draining her brandy glass, 'how come you don't go in for profit-sharing?'

'Profit-sharing? Profit-sharing?' gasped Jimmy, then roared with laughter. 'If I instituted profit-sharing, my staff would have to pay *me* $300 a week.'

'You mean your restaurants don't make money?'

'They do, but you should see what I owe in back taxes. That's the bottom line.'

'Bottom line?' retorted Louise. David clutched his head in his hands. 'That's a good question. Where's your bottom line, then?'

'It's where it is, that's where.'

'It's where you *think* it is,' returned Louise, cryptically.

'Exactly.'

'How much time off do you give your staff?'

'Louise —' began David, throatily.

'I'd like to know, I really would.'

'One of my waitresses, if you want to know,' began Jimmy, 'who's an aspiring actress like most of the people who work for me, had two months off and she had a job waiting for her when she came back.'

'And the rest of them?'

'Louise —' David staring straight at her, but she wasn't talking to him.

'So how about the rest of them?'

'Louise' — David looked grim — 'I eat here four times a week and you are rapidly burning my bridges' — discreetly concealing his trump card, which was that he was also paying for her dinner — 'and they're not yours to burn.'

FADING OUT

A few days later I packed my bags. My departure left me dry-eyed. This great city of perpetual change doesn't encourage nostalgia. Much that is precious in the memory will have vanished months or years later, and the returning traveller must rediscover the city each time. The scale of New York scorns the indulgences of personal sentiment. The towers of Manhattan are an embodiment of over-achievement, a defiantly artificial megalopolis in which glass and stone and concrete overwhelm the human element. The lifelong sport of being a New Yorker is to overcome these extraordinary self-created obstacles. The art of doing so, which New Yorkers by definition have had to perfect, is urban living at its most extreme, most rhapsodic. Defying all the laws that sociologists lay down, impossibly overcrowded Manhattan functions as well, if not better, than most cities of the same size. Though individual buildings, even neighbourhoods, decay and disappear, the city as a whole is inextinguishable. It is more than an agglomeration; it is an idea, an assertion. Because it is self-renewing it can never, superpowers permitting, be destroyed.

Almost 80 years ago, Henry James wrote of the tall buildings in his native city: 'Crowned not only with no history, but with no credible possibility of time for history, and consecrated by no uses save the commercial at any cost, they are simply the most piercing notes in that concert of the expensively provisional into which your supreme sense of New York resolves itself.' He was right and he was wrong. The 'expensively provisional', much of it, is still standing, and the city has at last decided that it does, rather to its surprise, have a history.

284

Yet James's 'supreme sense' was accurate. New York is no place for antiquarians. There are no ruins, and never will be, in New York City. They would be too costly. New York is exactingly different because it insists that you live precisely in the present, with all your capacities stretched to the limit. It is a good city to leave, for in your absence it will continue to live and breathe and grow, and, in its altered state, like a body in which most of the cells have been replaced, it will be ready for you when, as you surely will, you return.

INDEX